Researching and Writing a Dissertation for Business Students

We work with leading authors to develop the strongest educational materials in management, bringing cutting-edge thinking and best learning practice to a global market.

Under a range of well-known imprints, including Financial Times Prentice Hall, we craft high-quality print and electronic publications which help readers to understand and apply their content, whether studying or at work.

To find out more about the complete range of our publishing, please visit us on the World Wide Web at:
www.pearsoned.co.uk

Researching and Writing a Dissertation for Business Students

Colin Fisher

with

John Buglear

Diannah Lowry

Alistair Mutch

Carole Tansley

FT Prentice Hall
FINANCIAL TIMES

An imprint of **Pearson Education**
Harlow, England • London • New York • Boston • San Francisco • Toronto • Sydney • Singapore • Hong Kong
Tokyo • Seoul • Taipei • New Delhi • Cape Town • Madrid • Mexico City • Amsterdam • Munich • Paris • Milan

Pearson Education Limited
Edinburgh Gate
Harlow
Essex CM20 2JE
England

and Associated Companies throughout the world

Visit us on the World Wide Web at:
www.pearsoned.co.uk

First published 2004

ISBN 0 273 68334 9

British Library Cataloguing-in-Publication Data
A catalogue record for this book is available from the British Library

10 9 8 7 6 5 4 3 2 1
08 07 06 05 04

Typeset in 10/13pt Sabon by 30
Printed and bound by Ashford Colour Press Ltd, Gosport, Hampshire

The publisher's policy is to use paper manufactured from sustainable forests.

Contents

Acknowledgements

I tried the patience of my friends at Nottingham Business School by constant requests for feedback. They replied with good humour, useful feedback and new material. I wish to thank Jim Stewart, Alistair Mutch, Diannah Lowry, John Buglear, Tony Woodall, Val Caven, Denise Fletcher, Carole Tansley, Sue Kirk and John Leopold. Tony Watson deserves particular thanks. It was only when I was writing the book that I realised what an influence he has been on my thinking in the 20 and more years we have worked together at Nottingham Business School. Nevertheless neither he nor any other colleague is responsible for errors or misunderstandings that might have found their way into this guide.

Where colleagues have contributed complete sections to the guide they are acknowledged in the text. Much of any practical wisdom to be found in this guide comes from the many postgraduate students I have worked with at Nottingham Business School when they were doing their dissertations. Many thanks are due to them.

Publisher's acknowledgements

We are grateful to the following for permission to reproduce copyright material:

Exhibits 1.3, 2.1 3.1 and 3.2 photographs by Raj Shirole; Tables 1.2 and 4.2 reprinted by permission of Sage Publications Ltd from Silverman, D., *Interpreting Qualitative Data: Methods for Analysing Talk, Text and Interaction*, © Sage, 1993; Exhibit 1.8 from Managing, crafting and researching: words, skill and imagination in shaping management research, *British Journal of Management*, Vol. 5 (Special issue), pp. 77–97, Blackwell Publishing (Watson, T. J. 1994); Exhibit 2.4 image of Bentham's Panopticon from Bentham Papers 115/44, University College London; Figures 3.2, 3.2 and 3.8 reproduced with the permission of T.J. Watson; Figure 3.3 from Bad apples in bad barrels: a causal analysis of ethical decision-making behaviour, *Journal of Applied Psychology*, Vol. 75, No. 4, pp. 378–85, American Psychological Association (Trevino, L.K. and Youngblood, S.A. 1990); Figure 3.9 from *Kabbalah: Traditions of Hidden Knowledge*, Thames & Hudson Ltd (Z'ev ben Shimon Halevi 1979); Figure 3.10 from Ethical stances: the perceptions of accountancy and RM specialists of ethical conundrums at work, *Business Ethics: A European*

Review, Vol. 8, Issue 4, p. 241, Blackwell Publishing Ltd (Fisher, C.M. 1999); Table 4.4 from *Research Methods for Business Students*, Financial Times Prentice Hall (Saunders, M., Lewis, P. and Thornhill, A., 2002); Figure 4.8 from *Reason by Numbers*, Pelican Books (Moore, P.G. 1980) copyright © Peter G. Moore, 1980; Table 4.5 from *Statistics without Tears*, Penguin Books (Rowntree, D. 1981), © Derek Rowntree, 1981. Exhibit 5.1 reproduced with the permission of J. De Mey.

The Quality Assurance Agency for the extract 'The QAA's Descriptor for a qualification at Masters (M) level' from *The Framework for higher education qualifications in England, Wales and Northern Ireland,* © The Quality Assurance Agency for Higher Education 2001; and The Times Literary Supplement for the extracts 'Anything Goes' by E. Gellner published in *The Times Literary Supplement* 16th June 1995 and 'Why it's fun to be smart' by Eisaman Maus as published in *The Times Literary Supplement* 25th May 2001, © The Times Literary Supplement. Exercise 2.2 from *Resource Allocation in the Public Sector: Values, Priorities and Markets in the Management of Public Services*, Routledge (Fisher, C.M. 1998); Chapter 3 example of conceptualising and theorising in a study of organisational culture based on *Organisation, Culture and the Management of Change in the National Health Service*, PhD dissertation, the Nottingham Trent University (McNulty, T. 1990) reproduced with permission of T. McNulty; Chapter 3 extract from Transforming former state enterprises in the Czech Republic, *Organisation Studies*, Vol. 16, No. 2, p. 215, Walter de Gruyter (Clark, E. and Soulsby, A. 1995); Exercise 5.6 from *A Handbook of Structured Experiences for Human Relations Training*, Pfeiffer, J.W. and Jones, J.E., ©1975 John Wiley & Sons, Inc. This material is used by permission of John Wiley & Sons, Inc.

In some instances we have been unable to trace the owners of copyright material, and we would appreciate any information that would enable us to do so.

Chapter 0 ● ● ● ●

Introduction

This introduction is Chapter 0. Such a quirky way of beginning the numbering of chapters needs to be explained. The guide is structured around six stages in the process of researching and writing a dissertation. These stages in turn reflect the six criteria that typify the standards that dissertations are marked against. The guide contains a chapter for each of these stages cum criteria. I wanted each of them to have the appropriate number, Chapter 1 for stage 1 and so on. This meant that the introduction that precedes the chapters had to be Chapter 0.

Calling the introduction Chapter 0 does not mean it is empty of content. It is quite important to read this chapter if you are going to get full value from the guide because it will achieve the following:

- identify the assessment targets you need to hit for the dissertation to be passed;
- introduce you to methodological issues that can cause students problems if they are not understood;
- explain the structure of the guide and introduce you to further resources.

Contents

- Who is this guide for?
- What does doing a dissertation involve?
  The process of doing a dissertation
  What does working at Master's level mean?
- The assessment criteria
  The learning outcomes and assessment criteria
- Jargon, 'isms' and 'ologies'
- How to use this guide
- Suggested reading
- Other recommended books
- References

●●●● Who is this guide for?

The first readership for the guide is all those doing an MBA, or an MSc or MA course in a management or business topic, and who have to write a dissertation as part of their studies. That said, many of the topics and and skills the guide covers are relevant to anyone who has to research and write a dissertation or a long, research-based paper as part of their programme of study. The guide will be of use to undergraduates doing final-year dissertations and also to DBA and PhD students.

●●●● What does doing a dissertation involve?

Most MBA and Master's in management programmes include a major project in which the students identify an issue of managerial, organisational or business concern and research it. However, different business schools demand different things in the research component of their MBA and other Master's programmes. Most commonly students will be required to write a **dissertation**, which is a report on a major piece of primary research (normally between 15,000 and 20,000 words long) and that gives an account of a student's investigation into a business or managerial issue, provides an analysis of the research and presents the conclusions that are drawn from it. In addition to, or instead of, the dissertation students may be required to write one or more of the following:

- a **proposal**, which is a document that defines what the project is about, explains why it is important and describes how it is to be carried out;
- a **paper**, which is a short (normally around 4,000 to 6,000 words) document suitable for presentation to an academic conference or journal;
- a **management report**, which is a shorter document (2,000 to 4,000 words) that is suitable for presentation to managers and decision makers and that is designed to persuade them to adopt the recommendations you make.

This guide focuses on the proposal and the dissertation but it also gives some help on writing papers and reports.

Some other key terms are used frequently in the guide and it will be useful to define them before we proceed:

- A **project** means all the activities that go towards completing a dissertation.
- A **thesis** is an argument or a proposition supported by evidence and literature.

A Master's degree in a business or management subject brings together an academic concern for theory and understanding with a managerial concern for analysis, planning and action. A dissertation should be written primarily for an academic audience, and it will be marked by academics. However, it should also contain elements that address the concerns of those in the organisations whose problems were the subject of the dissertation. Getting this balance right is one of the skills needed to write a good dissertation.

The aims of the dissertation, and of the proposal and the conference paper if you are required to do them, will vary from institution to institution and you will need to become very familiar with those that belong to your course. However, the following example would not be untypical.

The objective of the dissertation is to give the student an opportunity:

1. to plan, research and write up a project that improves understanding of a significant managerial, business or organisational matter, and that, if appropriate, provides recommendations or findings upon which action can be determined;
2. to learn how to undertake a major project that requires you to:
   - be focused on a complex and important issue;
   - undertake effective and competent primary research;
   - integrate theory and practice;
   - incorporate understanding taken from a critical review of the appropriate literature;
   - base your dissertation on sound analysis and arguments; and
   - be sensitive to the requirements of the different audiences for the dissertation.

The focus of the project is often a matter for you to decide. It may be on any of the following:

- a part of an organisation, or a comparison between parts of an organisation;
- a single organisation;
- a comparison between two or more organisations;
- a study of an industrial or commercial sector;
- a study of a managerial function or profession.

The process of doing a dissertation

In practice doing a dissertation is not a sequential process in which the completion of one stage leads neatly to the next. There are often false starts and returns to earlier stages of the project to reconsider the focus and the aims. Many of the stages of doing a project will be pursued in parallel. While you are reading for the literature review you may also be setting up contacts for interviews or drafting a questionnaire. However, there is a basic logic to the process and this can be used to explain the contents of this guide. This logic is shown, as a series of stages for convenience, in Figure 0.1. In addition to this introduction, the guide contains six chapters. Each of the chapters deals with one of the stages shown in Figure 0.1. Taken together, the chapters will lead you through the processes of researching and writing your dissertation.

Figure 0.1 has three dimensions. The time dimension runs vertically. The height of the cube represents the length of time you have to complete your project and dissertation. The other two dimensions are as follows:

thinking — finding out
confusion — confidence.

Here is a description of the progress of an average project using these dimensions.

Phase 1 – Choosing a topic and designing the project

At the start students are confused about what they are going to study for the project and how they are going to do it. In the first phase thinking about choice of topic and what approach to research is going to be adopted leads to finding out about possible topics and investigating the range of research methods available. The combination of these activities increases students' confidence, but not hugely. They are still a little fazed

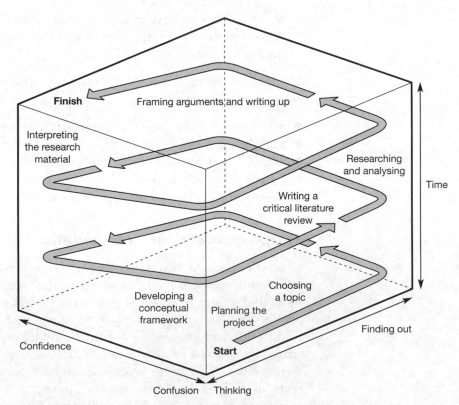

Figure 0.1 The processes of researching and writing a Master's dissertation

at the end of this first phase but they should have a clearer idea of what they want to research, why it is important and how they are going to do it

Phase 2 – Writing a critical literature review

The next phase involves searching for books, academic papers and other materials that are relevant to the project, so quite a lot of energy at the early part of this phase goes into finding out what resources are available. Although finding materials is satisfying there is a tendency to think that the information they contain can be transferred into one's brain by some osmotic process that does not involve actually reading the stuff. This stage of course involves both reading the material and thinking about it. In particular the various theories and frameworks drawn from the literature need to be criticised and evaluated to see which are academically robust enough to be used in your project. The reading and thinking normally mean that students have increased confidence in their project by the end of this phase.

Phase 3 – Developing concepts, conceptual frameworks and theories

As a result of their increasing confidence students feel ready to move into the next phase, which is developing a conceptual framework. This is a 'map' that draws together the concepts that the students will use to guide their research and that suggests how they are related. Conceptual frameworks are normally modifications and developments of models and theories found in the literature. When a conceptual framework is decided upon it gives a great boost to students' confidence. They feel in control of their project because they can see where it is going. However, once it is drafted, and they think about the framework some more, little doubts and worries creep in and the confidence begins to seep away. Then it is time to get into the next stage – of doing the research work.

Phase 4 – Collecting and analysing research material

Some thinking is needed at the start of the research phase of the project. Students have to decide in detail how they are going to conduct the research and organise the practical aspects of conducting interviews or focus groups, identifying people to send questionnaires to and so on. But the bulk of this stage is about finding out. When students start to collect their research results it often boosts their confidence as they conclude that they will have enough material to write their dissertation.

Phase 5 – Interpreting research material and drawing conclusions

After a heap of research material has been collected it then remains to make sense of it – to interpret it. This can be a daunting task and initially there can be an increase in confusion as students think about what the material means. But some hard thinking and interrogation of the research material usually result in students finding out more about their topic.

Phase 6 – Forming arguments and writing up the dissertation

In the final stage the students formulate their arguments arising from all their work and shape them into a written dissertation. The process therefore moves away from 'finding out' towards 'thinking' – although it is interesting to note that students often only find out what they mean when they start writing up the project. If all goes well, by the time they have finished writing up the students will have confidence in their project and their dissertation.

The six chapters in this guide are designed to help you through each of these stages. Their contents are briefly summarised below.

Choosing a topic and designing the project   Chapter 1
- Identifying a topic
- Drafting research objectives
- Planning the research and the project

↓

Writing a critical literature review   Chapter 2
- Searching the literature
- Summarising and précising the literature
- Evaluating key concepts and theories

↓

Concepts, conceptual frameworks and theories   Chapter 3
- Identifying key concepts
- Drafting conceptual frameworks
- Theorising the material

↓

Collecting and analysing research material   Chapter 4
- Choosing and designing research methods
- Conducting the research
- Analysing, sorting and classifying the material

↓

Interpreting the research material   Chapter 5
- Honesty of argument and language
- Interpreting research material
- Drawing safe conclusions

↓

Framing arguments and writing up the dissertation   Chapter 6
- Arguing a thesis as well as writing a dissertation
- Structuring the dissertation
- Producing documents in accordance with the style guide

What does working at Master's level mean?

Studying at Master's level requires an extension of the academic skills you may have used when you were doing diploma-level studies, as well as the development of some new ones. In this section we identify these new skills and abilities and indicate which of the chapters in this guide are intended to help you develop them.

Methodology

Having a general familiarity with some of the philosophical issues and arguments about the process of research. The study of these philosophical aspects is known as methodology. It is not expected that you should become a philosopher. It is expected that you acquire sufficient knowledge of methodology to prevent yourself from making errors such as using inappropriate research methods that will be incapable of answering the research questions you have asked.

See *Jargon, 'isms' and 'ologies'* in this chapter, *Designing your project* in Chapter 1 and *Saying what you mean* in Chapter 5.

Theorising

Attempting theoretical innovation. No one expects Master's students to create new theories (although it is wonderful if they do). On the other hand, neither are they expected simply to take theories from the literature and use them uncritically. You should look for opportunities to develop, modify or adapt the theories you take from the literature. This is often necessary because you may take a theory that was developed in one field of study, or in one context, and try to use it in different circumstances. The theory may need adaptation, or at the least review, before it is relocated. Belbin's (1981) theory of team effectiveness, for example, was derived from studies of managers, yet I have seen many people attempt to use it with production staff without checking the theory's validity on the shop floor.

See Chapter 2 and *Framing conclusions and recommendations* in Chapter 5.

Dealing with complex and ambiguous matters

Developing novel analyses and arguments. At diploma level the task facing students is to understand a management technique or approach so that they can apply it. At Master's level the intention is that complex and intransigent issues and problems should be studied. This implies that existing management techniques will be inadequate for solving such problems.

Therefore, you will have to develop your own ways of thinking through the problem. Techniques will be helpful but in addition you will have to use your own thinking skills to analyse the issues and present arguments as to how the problem should be studied.

See Chapter 5 and *Writing a thesis, not just a dissertation* in Chapter 6.

Learning to learn

Reflecting on your learning. Often this means being willing, as part of doing the dissertation, to challenge the unthought-of assumptions and values that constrain our thoughts and actions. To use the current managerial jargon, you should think 'out of the box'. Another way of learning how to learn is to provide a review and critique of how you tackled the Master's project. It is generally reckoned a good idea to keep quiet about your mistakes when writing up your dissertation. This is itself a mistake. At Master's level errors are for learning from. If you made a mistake in good faith (as opposed to laziness or sloppiness) then report it in the dissertation and show how you have learnt from it. This should gain you extra marks. If, for example, after you have completed a questionnaire survey you decide it would have been better to do in-depth interviews, then explain why in the dissertation and say how you would tackle such issues differently in the future.

See Chapter 5.

● ● ● ● The assessment criteria

In formal terms Master's students have to show, in their proposals, papers and dissertations, that they have achieved a number of learning outcomes in order to pass the module. You should adopt a degree of instrumentality (by assuming the objective of the exercise is to pass the dissertation and gain the Master's degree) and study the learning outcomes and assessment criteria that your business school will use in marking your dissertation.

There is an independent body, the Quality Assurance Agency for Higher Education (QAA), that, amongst other things, sets the qualification descriptors for academic degrees in the United Kingdom. All MBAs and Master's in management programmes may base their learning outcomes for assessing dissertations on the Descriptor, which is shown in Exhibit 0.1.

The learning outcomes and assessment criteria used in the business school where I work are used here to illustrate what the demands of a dissertation are. They are probably not very different from those of your institution, but if they are you should obviously work towards those that will be used to mark your dissertation.

Exhibit 0.1

The QAA's Descriptor for a qualification at Master's (M) level: Master's degree

Master's degrees are awarded to students who have demonstrated:

(i) a systematic understanding of knowledge, and a critical awareness of current problems and/or new insights, much of which is at, or informed by, the forefront of their academic discipline, field of study, or area of professional practice;

(ii) a comprehensive understanding of techniques applicable to their own research or advanced scholarship;

(iii) originality in the application of knowledge, together with a practical understanding of how established techniques of research and enquiry are used to create and interpret knowledge in the discipline;

(iv) conceptual understanding that enables the student:

- to evaluate critically current research and advanced scholarship in the discipline;

and

- to evaluate methodologies and develop critiques of them and, where appropriate, to propose new hypotheses.

Typically, holders of the qualification will be able to:

(a) deal with complex issues both systematically and creatively, make sound judgements in the absence of complete data, and communicate their conclusions clearly to specialist and non-specialist audiences;

(b) demonstrate self-direction and originality in tackling and solving problems, and act autonomously in planning and implementing tasks at a professional or equivalent level;

(c) continue to advance their knowledge and understanding, and to develop new skills to a high level;

and will have:

(d) the qualities and transferable skills necessary for employment requiring:
- the exercise of initiative and personal responsibility;
- decision making in complex and unpredictable situations; and
- the independent learning ability required for continuing professional development.

Source: The framework for higher education qualifications in England, Wales and Northern Ireland. © The Quality Assurance Agency for Higher Education (2001).

The learning outcomes and assessment criteria

These are the learning outcomes for a dissertation module.

At the completion of this module students will be able to:

1. define the objectives of a research project and plan a valid and practicable project to meet the objectives;
2. carry out a critical literature review that provides a structure and focus for the dissertation;
3. define concepts and structure them in ways that give a useful theoretical shape to the dissertation;
4. design and apply appropriate research methods and analyse the research material systematically;
5. frame, and argue for, a clear thesis in the documents and draw safe conclusions;
6. write a clearly structured, adequately expressed and well-presented dissertation.

This guide has been structured so that each of the six chapters deals with one of these learning outcomes.

The learning outcomes set the standard for what students have to achieve. However, they do not define the criteria that markers will use to decide whether a student has reached an appropriate level of achievement against each of the learning outcomes. These criteria can be seen in Table 0.1, called the assessment matrix. A number of points need to be made about this table:

- The matrix is for assessing a complete dissertation. If you also have to submit a written research proposal or an academic paper for assessment, then probably only some of the criteria would apply.
- The matrix identifies a number of levels. Most are self-explanatory. The borderline fail level needs explanation, however. A student who is marked 46–49 per cent is classified, in some institutions, as a borderline fail. This indicates that the dissertation would only need relatively minor changes and improvements to bring it up to pass standard. In some programmes it may be possible to show this improvement at a viva voce examination.

Table 0.1 Assessment criteria for postgraduate dissertations in business, organisational and management studies

	Identify a research question and design a project to answer it	Write a critical literature review	Define working concepts and conceptual frameworks to give structure to the work	Collect and analyse research data efficiently and effectively	Interpret findings sensitively as a basis for making recommendations for action that are practicable and sound	Write reports and dissertations that are persuasive, well structured and well written
80–100% Excellent	An excellent proposal that would be awarded a grant if it were sent to a research funding body	The literature review is itself a significant contribution to the literature	Significant additions to the theoretical and conceptual understanding of the subject	Makes a contribution to the development of methods for collecting and analysing research material and/or methodological debate	Complex and sophisticated interpretation of the material. The conclusions are based on the findings but transcend them. Subtle understanding of action in organisations	A work of art written with style and wit. Strong arguments that refer back to each other
70–79% Very good Distinction level	Clear and specific about research question, project design and research methods. These three elements are shown to be well-coordinated and an appropriate admixture	The literature is cogently described and evaluated from novel or complex perspectives	An attempt, not necessarily wholly successful, is made to theorise beyond the current state of the literature	Modifies and develops methods for collecting and analysing research material in a way that reflects methodological understanding	Interprets the findings in a sophisticated manner. Conclusions are firmly based in findings but show a creative spark. Implementation plans show an awareness of the interaction of understanding and action	Clear and persuasive arguments expressed in good plain English in a well-structured document
60–69% Good	Well-defined research question. Sensible project design and clear plans for conducting the research	The literature is cogently evaluated using positions already available in the literature	A conceptual framework is developed, or an existing one adapted, in context of an evaluated literature	Uses methods for gathering and analysing research material well and shows an understanding of methodological issues	Uses techniques for interpretation but in a mechanical way. Conclusions based well on findings. Practical schemes for action	Either expressed well or technically correct but not both. Clear structure adequately argued
50–59% Competent Pass level	Clear research question. Explicit ideas on design and methods but there are some issues about the fit between question, design and methods	Good description of the appropriate field(s) of literature. Some general criticisms made but no close evaluation of concepts	Concepts are clearly defined and appropriate. They are set in the context of the literature	Methods for gathering and analysing research material are used competently	Treats the findings as straightforward and unproblematic. Conclusions have some connection with the findings. Action plans are general but prescriptive	Adequate expression but a noticeable number of mistakes. Argumentation is sometimes replaced by assumption or assertion
46–49% Borderline fail	Identified an interesting topic but the research question is very broad and the details of the project are hazy	Inadequate or limited description of the appropriate field(s) of literature, and/or no criticism or evaluation	The definition and use of theoretical concepts is confused No attempt at theoretical synthesis or evaluation	Methods for gathering and analysing research material are used in a confused and unsystematic way	The occasional insight takes the place of interpretation. Conclusions have a tenuous link with findings. Action plans are simple exhortations or lacking	Sentences often do not make sense. Uses bullet points to disguise a lack of arguments
≤ 45% Fail	The focus, purpose and method of the project are unclear	The author appears to have read little and understood less	No conceptual or theoretical discussion of any value	No primary research of any value	Provides no evidence that they know what this outcome is about	Scrappy presentation, illogical structure. No arguments or silly ones

● ● ● ● Jargon, 'isms' and 'ologies'

If you are studying for a Master's qualification you have to come to terms with the 'isms' and 'ologies' that are appropriate to your study. This means you will have to read and understand some books and articles that are relevant but difficult. To have a Master's degree in a subject means that you have a mastery of that subject. You cannot have mastery if there are some books and articles that are relevant to it that you declare out of bounds because you consider them too difficult.

Consequently you will have to learn to understand some difficult jargon. Part of the purpose of this guide is to make that task a little easier when it comes to the jargon of doing research. To use a term that was mentioned earlier, an awareness of the methodological issues surrounding research is necessary. There are a number of methodological terms you may come across, and what follows is a brief introductory comment on some of the major ones.

A dissertation is founded on research, which is an effort to find things out. Unfortunately there is a dispute between researchers about what it is possible to discover by research. The argument is not restricted to the business and management field. It is a general one about the nature of knowledge. The proper title for the study of the nature of knowledge is **epistemology**. The epistemological debate has a long history and it is unlikely that the matter will be resolved during your work on the dissertation. It thus remains a dangerous current that threatens to drag you off course as you try to steer your research efforts. This danger is the reason for having a sufficient knowledge of methodological and epistemological issues. An awareness of the currents and tides in this area will help you keep out of danger. The methodological argument affects all aspects of doing a dissertation and its impact can be seen in all six chapters of this guide. In this introduction an attempt is made to provide an understanding of the broad issues in the arguments about methodology so that the more careful arguments in the later chapters can be more easily understood.

A number of different methodological approaches to research are shown in Figure 0.2.

The research approaches are plotted using coordinates from two axes or dimensions. The first dimension concerns the relationship between the knowledge it is possible for us to have about the world external to us and that world itself. At one end it is thought that our knowledge is an exact reflection of the world. At the other end of the dimension the world is thought to be largely unknowable and that what we can know is patchy. There are two intermediate positions plotted between these two extremes.

The terms 'Orthodox' and 'Gnostic' will be used to describe the other dimension in Figure 0.2. These are not terms you will find elsewhere in the literature on research methods. They are taken by analogy from early divi-

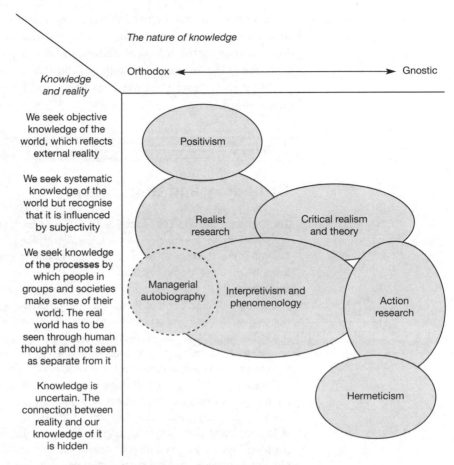

The nature of knowledge

Orthodox ◄──────────────────────► Gnostic

Knowledge and reality

We seek objective knowledge of the world, which reflects external reality

We seek systematic knowledge of the world but recognise that it is influenced by subjectivity

We seek knowledge of the processes by which people in groups and societies make sense of their world. The real world has to be seen through human thought and not seen as separate from it

Knowledge is uncertain. The connection between reality and our knowledge of it is hidden

Positivism

Realist research

Critical realism and theory

Managerial autobiography

Interpretivism and phenomenology

Action research

Hermeticism

Figure 0.2 The main forms of management research

sions in Christianity. The different views of the world taken by the Orthodox and the Gnostics can still be seen in modern perspectives on research. Some idea of the positions taken by the two sides can be gained from Exhibit 0.2.

Exhibit 0.2

The Orthodox and the Gnostic

Orthodox	**Gnostic**
There is an objective truth	Truth is subjective
Truth is simple and transparent	Truth is hidden
Truth is an agreed body of knowledge	Truth is gained through personal struggle
Conformance and obedience	Challenge and diversity
Language is transparent	Language is ambiguous

This distinction will be used to map out some of the major methodological disagreements in research. It is hoped this will give you a starting point for your methodological understanding. If you are not interested in the source of the analogy then skip Exhibit 0.3.

Each of the research approaches shown in Figure 0.2 will be discussed in more detail.

Exhibit 0.3

Orthodoxy and Gnosticism

The Orthodox view of Christianity is to be found in the Bible. Orthodox in this sense refers to the position of all the institutional churches such as the Catholic, the Eastern Orthodox and the Anglican churches. It used to be thought that the books included in the Bible, the canon, were the main Christian texts. It was known that there were various heretical texts in the early years of the Church but that these were marginal. But in 1945 a peasant found pots buried in the Egyptian desert that contained ancient scrolls. These turned out to be early Christian gospels that in most cases had never been heard of before, such as the Gospel of Thomas, the Gospel of Philip, the Gospel of the Egyptians. They were written in the second century AD.

These gospels suggest that there were two versions of Christianity and that each saw the world and the truth in very different ways. The Orthodox gospels see the world as a good place that has a real existence. The task of humankind is to use it well and live according to the rules and values preached in the gospels. Salvation comes from obedience to the rules of the Church; through obedience to rules that are clear and apply to everyone. The Gnostic gospels see the world differently. Gnosis is a word of Greek origin that means knowledge. But it is different to technical knowledge. It is insight into oneself or others gained through intuitive self-examination. The Gnostics cared little about the physical world. They saw it as a snare and an illusion. The important thing was for individuals to develop their own souls through understanding their own subjective processes of thought and understanding. By increasing their inner perfection they could become close to God. Gnostic knowledge was hidden and not easily found. Acquiring this knowledge called for moral worth and intellectual effort.

For Gnostics the world was dominated by chance and irrational forces. Individuals have to learn how to cope with an uncaring world. The Orthodox view was expressed through institutions, through churches, whereas the Gnostics approached religion from an individualist perspective. There were many different forms and sects of Gnosticism. Unsurprisingly, the Orthodox spent most of their time, in the early centuries of Christianity, fighting the Gnostics. The Gnostics spent most of their time squabbling amongst themselves. Historically the Orthodox prevailed over the Gnostics. Pagels (1982) provides a good introduction to Gnosticism.

Positivism

Auguste Comte coined the term 'positivism' in the nineteenth century. It was a statement about the power of science and rational thought to comprehend and manipulate the world. It rejected the metaphysical and subjective ideas and was interested only in the tangible. Positivism holds that an accurate and value-free knowledge of things is possible. It holds out the possibility that human beings and their actions and institutions can be studied as objectively as the natural world. But positivism's emphasis on tangible things is important in this regard. It may be possible to study scientifically the tangible aspects of human activity – behaviours, speech – but not of course the intangible – the internal interpretation or motivation of those externals. Behaviourism was an example of this approach from psychology. Its heyday was in the 1960s and 1970s, and behaviourists held that psychology should be the study of people's observable and quantifiable behaviour and that no regard should be given to their internal processes of consciousness. The intention of positivism is to produce general laws that can be used to predict behaviour, in terms of probability at least, if not with absolute certainty. These general laws would form an open and orthodox body of knowledge, and the positivist method would be the standard approach for all scientific endeavours.

There is no doubt that in some cases, such as mathematical models of crowd behaviour in shops and stadiums and models of market behaviour, a hard scientific approach can be invaluable. However, there are problems with these methods. They can, for example, predict only the average behaviour, not the behaviour of individuals; and in many situations understanding particularities is as important as understanding the norm. Another issue is that many choices and assumptions have been made when developing such models, and these choices open the door for the researchers' values and preferences to enter into the research process. Many researchers argue that research into the social and institutional world cannot be value-free, and that the aspiration for social researchers to become hard scientists such as chemists is not achievable (Robson 2002: 22–23). Probably it would not be possible for MBA students working on their dissertations to adopt an extreme positivist stance, if for no other reason than that they are likely to be researching their own organisations and therefore are not the disinterested observers that scientists are supposed to be. We will not spend too much time on positivist approaches to research in this guide.

Realist research

Realist research is an approach that retains many of the ambitions of positivism but recognises, and comes to terms with, the subjective nature of research and the inevitable role of values in it. Realism still aims to be scientific but makes fewer claims to knowledge that perfectly mirrors the objects of study. Researchers with this stance recognise that things such as 'strategy' and 'job satisfaction' cannot be measured and studied in the same way as can chemical and physical processes. However, they do believe that a worthwhile attempt can be made to fix these subjects and treat them as if they are independent variables.

As an example, let us imagine someone is interested in human resource development (HRD) because they think it is an underrated function of management. They suspect that uncertainty about the values of HRD may contribute to its low status. They wish to rectify the situation by researching the core values of HRD. Taking a realist approach they know that there has been much argument over the definition of HRD but this does not prevent them from believing there is a thing called HRD that can be defined and measured. They send out questionnaires to HRD practitioners and use the responses to identify several core values that define the basis of HRD practice. While they recognise that individual HRD practitioners may have different reactions to these core values they believe that HRD has an existence separate from these individual reactions and that it is possible and sensible to talk about HRD's values. Realist research puts things into categories and labels them, although it is possible to argue about whether the right categories ('should we call it HRD?') have been chosen.

Realist researchers claim to be orthodox. They want to discover the mechanisms that bring about events and they are concerned that their theories should be verifiable and have some generalisability. They are likely, where possible, to try to measure and quantify the things they are studying. However, because the realists recognise the role of subjectivity, all theories have to come with a health warning because different researchers with different values will propose competing theories. The existence of competing, or even of complementary, explanations is one of the features of realist research. The difference between the theories is not so much to do with which is right or which is wrong as concerned with deciding from which point of view you wish to study a topic. Realist researchers often seek to offer generalisable explanations but they are less likely (than positivists) to offer predictions. Many MBA students will take a realist approach when doing their dissertations.

Critical realism

Critical realism, as its name implies, shares the ambitions of realism but it takes a more gnostic than orthodox tack. This is because it adds the notion of layers or stratification into our understanding of knowledge. Critical realists argue that there is a level of reality below the everyday level of events and our experiences of them (see p. 220). It is at this level that the mechanisms that drive events in the world exist. Unfortunately our knowledge of this level is not direct; it can only be inferred. So, as with the Gnostics, there is a claim that there is a level of reality that is not easily accessible because it is hidden from common view. To discover this level of reality requires honest and intelligent people to work hard at the problems and to become adept at discovering these mechanisms. The need for honesty arises because those who do critical realist research into business and management may discover bad things that ought to be made known and have corrective action taken. There is a moral component to the critical realist approach. The implications of this approach to research into management and organisations will be covered in this guide.

Managerial autobiography

This is not really a research approach at all, and so it is marked out with a dotted line in Figure 0.2. However, it is a common body of literature that MBA students are often drawn to. The category is constituted of all those books in which a successful entrepreneur's or chief executive officer's work experience is written down and presented as a clear orthodoxy for those who wish to achieve business success. As this knowledge has not been discovered by an objective type of research, but unashamedly bases its claim to be heard on its very subjectivity, it has been placed at that point on the vertical scale of Figure 0.2 where knowledge is seen through the prism of subjectivity.

My experience of supervising MBA students suggests that this is not a good route for them to take in their dissertation. The student who announces that they wish to use the dissertation as a vehicle for distilling their wisdom, drawn from their experience of a certain industry, often struggles. Their research becomes an apologia or a justification of their actions and a chance to do down those who have opposed them.

Interpretivism and phenomenology

There are many terms for this approach to research. 'Interpretivism' is the one that will be used in this guide, although 'phenomenology' is the preferred term of many textbooks. Other terms used are 'constructionism' and 'naturalistic research'.

This approach is placed near the bottom of the vertical scale because researchers who take this position believe that reality is socially constructed. This means that our understanding of 'reality' is not a simple account of what is; rather, it is something that people in societies and groups form from the following:

- their interpretation of reality, which is influenced by their values and their way of seeing the world;
- other people's interpretation;
- the compromises and agreements that arise out of the negotiations between the first two.

Imagine you work in the procurement division of a large multinational and you are invited to an evening at a casino and dinner at a very expensive restaurant by a senior manager of an overseas company that wants you to give it a large contract. The casino is real and so are the restaurant and the food and wine, although the wine makes the other things seem a little less real. But there is another level of reality, which is – what do you think is really going on? Is the evening's entertainment just a friendly gesture, is it seen as a social obligation because it is what is expected in the senior manager's home country, is it a blatant bribe or is it a mixture of all these things and more? An interpretivist researcher would also be interested in the clues and process by which you decided what the 'reality' of this situation was. Interpretivist researchers are interested in the particularities of a situation, although they will categorise and label the processes for dealing with particulars ('how can we generalise about how people decide what to do in such situations?').

As researchers cannot claim to be studying an objective reality (which exists but is less interesting than the way people make sense of it) they study the following:

- the different accounts people give of issues and topics;
- people's accounts of the process by which they make sense of the world.

Interpretative research has been classified as gnostic in Figure 0.2 because it does not accept the existence of an orthodox or standard interpretation of any particular topic. Rather, it emphasises plurality, relativism and complexity. It is an attempt to understand the processes by which we gain knowledge and so it has affinity with the original gnostic search for one's true self. A feature of interpretative research is that you cannot understand how others may make sense of things unless you have an insightful knowledge of your own values and thinking processes. In research terms, this knowledge is known as reflexivity (see p. 225).

Interpretative research is not as common as realist research in MBA dissertations but it can be the basis of fascinating projects. It will be discussed in some detail in this guide.

Action research

Action research is a further development of interpretative research that goes further towards the gnostic. I have to be careful with this claim, though, because there are different forms of action research and not all would fit my categorisation. Nevertheless one major theme of action research is to seek to understand things by changing them, by experimenting with something new, and then by studying the consequences of the action and using them to reflect on one's values and preconceptions (that is the gnostic bit) before then taking new action. Although there are practical problems in choosing action research as the basis for a project (not least being whether the year that students typically have to complete their dissertation is sufficient to have a few cycles of action and reflection) it can lead to very worthwhile projects and will be discussed in this guide.

Hermeticism

Hermeticism takes its name from Hermes Trismegistus, an apocryphal pre-Christian Egyptian priest whose books were probably actually written in Alexandria in the third century AD. It is often linked with the cabbala (see p. 110) with which it shares a belief that all things in heaven and earth are linked in a harmonious whole but that the knowledge of these connections is secret and esoteric and can only be accessed by a few adepts. Everyday knowledge by contrast is seen as fragmented and confused. You do not often find hermeticism in writing on business and management but Gibson Burrell's (1997) book is an example. Burrell (1997: 101) alludes to his text as a cabbalistic one.

In hermetic thought connections between things are seen as symbolic and spiritual rather than rational and analytical. The idea of overlapping concentric circles replaces the linear form that we associate with rational analysis. The orthodox model of industrial development, for example, sees economic growth as happening in a linear fashion as one stage inevitably leads to a further, and higher, stage. Hermetic thought could see these stages being leapfrogged as, in an actual instance, old cottage-industry forms of work are allied to modern information technology and communication methods to bring products and services to a post-Fordist international market (Burrell 1997: 101–100[1]). This might be small craft producers using the Internet to sell their products globally. In this process the old and the new are intermingled. The modern does not replace the old. Hermeticism focuses on symbolic relationships between things that seem or look alike (see p. 82). This probably is reflected in the liking of many modern management thinkers for metaphor. A metaphor is a judgement that one thing is equivalent to another, which is a symbolic link. It follows that if machines are metaphors for organisations, then organisations should be treated in the same way as machines because, in some non-rational way, a machine is a microcosm of the organisational macrocosm.

However, in this guide we will ignore the two extremes of positivism and hermeticism and focus on the intermediate approaches to research.

Figure 0.2 is something of a caricature, and specialists will take exception to many of its claims. It will be necessary in later chapters to take a more sophisticated view of these matters. But understanding has to start

---

[1] The page numbers are in reverse order because this part of Burrell's book is to be read from back to front.

somewhere, and an overgeneralisation is as good a point as any. This problem is a version of the hermeneutic circle. **Hermeneutics** is the theory of interpretation concerned with the meaning of texts. The hermeneutic circle is a claim that you cannot understand the entirety of a thing until you understand its details; but you cannot understand the details until you understand the entirety. This is certainly true of research methodology. If it is of any comfort, I have been studying this subject for some time but I am still not sure I understand it.

How to use this guide

This guide covers all the main areas relevant to doing a dissertation and associated pieces of work. It is divided into six chapters. They are intended to form a sequence but they can be used in any order. There are many themes that appear in several if not all chapters.

This guide is only a guide, however, and should not be seen as a set of dogmatic rules that you break at your peril. It is also an informal guide, and so its tone is often relaxed. Good guides often reflect their author's prejudices. Whether this guide is good is up to others to decide – but it is certainly opinionated. A certain sceptical or ironical tone also creeps into the text. This is normally at places in the guide where the subject matter is one on which there is no consensus. At these points the irony is a signal to the reader. You, the reader, will be unsure whether my text is to be taken seriously or not. You will have to think through the issue and come to your own conclusion.

The guide offers many examples of how to tackle problems when doing a dissertation. It also provides many 'five easy steps' instructions on how to do things. These illustrations and recipes are mostly designed to stimulate your own thought processes and are not to be followed slavishly. Try to avoid falling into the trap shown in the box.

The role modelling vicious circle

Supervisor: 'You need to develop a conceptual framework.'

Student: 'How do I do that?'

Supervisor: 'Well, a conceptual framework means [etc. …]

Student: 'Uh?! Give me an example…'

Supervisor: 'For example, take this concept and that concept and put them in this 2 × 2 table and …'

Student: 'That's good. Can I use it?'

The guide is also a collection of materials that were to hand. The post-modernists would call such a collage by the French term *bricolage*. This is not a problem. Room is left for you to develop your own approach by following the leads you find in the research literature. To the extent that the guide is a collage, it will resemble your own project, in which you have to make a convincing assemblage – of the pieces of research you have done, the material from the literature, the stuff you learnt on other courses or at school years ago and the ideas and the bees in bonnets collected over the years – as you write your dissertation. It is possible to take the work seriously while also taking a wry sidelong look at its nature. Taking things seriously is often no more than taking oneself too seriously.

For these reasons you need to supplement your study of the guide with reading in the literature on research methods in business, management and organisational studies. In particular it will be necessary for you to read further on the specific research techniques you plan to use in your project.

Suggested reading

Each of the chapters in the guide includes suggestions for further reading in its particular specialist area.

There are a number of general textbooks for people researching in managerial, organisational or business topics. The main ones are listed below.

Easterby-Smith, M., Thorpe, R. and Lowe, A. (2002) *Management Research: An Introduction*, 2nd edn, London: Sage.

Gill, J. and Johnson, P. (2002) *Research Methods for Managers*, 3rd edn, London: Paul Chapman.

Saunders, M., Lewis, P. and Thornhill, A. (2002) *Research Methods for Business Students,* 3rd edn, Harlow: FT Prentice Hall.

Other recommended books

Bell, J. (1999) *Doing Your Research Project: A Guide for First-time Researchers in Education and Social Science*, 3rd edn, Buckingham: Open University Press.

Jankowicz, A. D. (2000) *Business Research Projects*, 3rd edn, London: Paul Chapman.

Remenyi, D., Williams, B., Money, A. and Swartz, E. (1998) *Doing Research in Business and Management: An Introduction to Process and Method*, London: Sage.

References

Belbin, R. M. (1981) *Management Teams: Why They Succeed or Fail*, London: Heinemann.

Burrell, G. (1997) *Pandemonium: Towards a Retro-organizational Theory*, London: Sage.

Pagels, E. (1982) *The Gnostic Gospels*, Harmondsworth: Penguin.

The Quality Assurance Agency for Higher Education (QAA) (2001) *The Framework for Higher Education Qualifications in England, Wales and Northern Ireland: Annexe 1, Qualification Descriptors*. Available online at: http://www.qaa.ac.uk/crntwork/nqf/ewni2001/annex1.htm#4 [accessed 20 July 2003].

Robson, C. (2002) *Real World Research*, 2nd edn, Oxford: Blackwell.

Chapter 1 ●●●●

Choosing a topic and designing the project

Contents

● ● ● ● Introduction

The processes of researching and writing a Master's dissertation

If a man begins with certainties, he shall end in doubts; but if he will be content to begin with doubts, he shall end in certainties.

Francis Bacon (1561–1626), quoted in Schott (2002: 115)

This first chapter is designed to get you started on your Master's research and, if this is needed on your course, to help you write a project proposal. It is divided into three parts:

1. Choosing a topic to research and framing the research questions or objectives.
2. Designing the project. Deciding the style of research you are going to use and making the broad-brush decisions about how the project will be tackled.
3. Writing a proposal document.

> **Learning outcomes for the chapter**
>
> **1** Students will be able to choose and define an appropriate topic for their dissertation.
> **2** Students will be able to frame practicable and feasible research objectives or questions.
> **3** Students will be able to make choices appropriate to their research objectives when designing the broad outline of their project and research methods.
> **4** Students will be able to recognise and respond to ethical issues that may be anticipated in their research project.
> **5** Students will be able to write a research proposal that defines the research topic clearly and specifies the research plan.

Choosing a topic

This is a critical stage in doing a Master's dissertation. If you fail to think about a topic in a systematic manner then you will be frustrated by your indecision and you will risk running out of time to complete the dissertation on schedule. If you make a poor choice then it may be difficult to score well against the marking criteria. The suggestions made in this section are designed to minimise the chance of either of these things happening. As this stage is so critical it is important to discuss your shopping list of possible topics with your tutor and use them as sounding boards to help you formulate your proposal.

Some of you, depending on what course you are doing, will have to make choices of two topics – a topic for your conference paper and a topic for the dissertation.

Criteria for choosing a topic

There are a number of factors you need to take into account when choosing the subject of your Master's project.

Interest and relevance
You should choose a topic that interests and even possibly excites you, otherwise you will have trouble sustaining the motivation and commitment necessary to complete the project. It should also be of interest to some external audience as well. This might be you own department or organisation, it could be a profession or it could be the wider business and management

community. Problems are sometimes met when the student's boss or organisation wants them to research a topic they can raise no enthusiasm for. Should this happen, you need to discuss the situation with your tutor.

Durability

Will the project last the length of the course? Organisations are capable of making very rapid changes in direction and policy. It may be that the topic you choose could become obsolete because of a change in organisational strategy, ownership or other events. Try to choose a subject that will still be relevant in a year's time.

Breadth of research questions

Is there enough substance to your topic? A primary school head teacher, who was doing a Master's in education management, told me the following:

> I have been listening to what you said about choosing a relevant topic. The most important issue in my school, the thing that is limiting the effectiveness of the teaching we do, is the chaos and confusion that is our teaching resources storeroom. Therefore I am going to do the sorting out of the resources room for my dissertation.

Important though it may have been, the issue was simply not broad enough to sustain the work needed for a Master's dissertation.

A more likely problem is that the chosen topic is too broad and you will find yourself flailing around and unable to get a purchase on it. It is important to consider whether the topic is too big for the time and energy available to be spent on the project.

Topic adequacy

Check the assessment criteria used on your course, against which your work will be marked, and ask yourself whether the topic you have in mind will enable you to do well against the criteria.

Access

You may have an excellent topic in mind, but unless you can get access to the people who can answer your research questions, whether by questionnaire, interview or whatever, then the project will be a non-starter. Even if you think the people to whom you need access will agree in principle, the time and effort necessary to secure the access may be too much. If your research is going to take place in the organisation in which you work, the problem may not be too great. But if you need to research third-party organisations, you should assure yourself that you can get the access. Even if you want to send out questionnaires to a general sample of managers you may have trouble getting a list of names and addresses to which you can send the questionnaire. Mailing lists are valuable and you may have to pay for them.

Micro politics

Whenever you research a business issue there is a danger that you may become a partisan in the management debates and politics that surround it. This will be a more important matter if you are studying a topic within your own organisation. You need to be sure that pursuing the project will not get you into political hot water with those in the organisation who can do you harm. Sometimes people choose to do a project that involves organisations other than the one they work for because the political situation in their own organisation (imminent takeover, board room battles and so on) is too dangerous.

Risk and security

Bearing in mind the previous criterion, you cannot avoid all risk. If you choose a topic that is totally safe it will probably be so bland that neither you nor anyone else will be interested in the outcomes. You need to make a balance between risk and safety that you can live with.

Resources

Literature make sure there is enough written about your topic, or about the general academic field in which it is located, for you to be able to do the critical literature review. This should not be a problem. A common difficulty these days is too much literature, not too little.

IT, software and skills Your topic may require access to, and skill in, various software packages. These may include NU-DIST, SPSS, Minitab and Snap for Windows. You may be able to access the software through the computer network of the institution you are studying at. If you do not know how to use the software, make sure you have time to learn. Brief introductions to some of these software packages are given in Chapter 4.

A six-stage process for choosing your topic

What follows is a six-stage process for you to follow when choosing your topic. Even if you have a topic in mind, it will probably be helpful to lay out your idea using these steps.

1. **Identify broad topic and academic discipline(s)**
   The starting point is to decide your broad area of interest. It might be, to give some examples:
   - implementation of mission statements and strategy in multinational companies;
   - the problems caused by a lack of cooperation between GPs and other health professionals in primary care;
   - performance-related pay and flexible benefits.
   It is quite likely that your interest in the topic will be driven by a need to come up with some answers to problems or difficulties that you or

others in the organisation are troubled by. These are strategic questions that concern what ought to be done in a particular situation. An example would be: 'What should we do to improve the company's competitive position in international markets?'

As will be discussed later, under stage 6 of the topic identification process, it is important not to confuse such questions with research questions. Strategic questions are not research questions. They cannot be answered by doing research. Strategic questions can only be answered by an act of judgement and will. A manager faced with a strategic question has to use all they know to help them make a judgement about what it is best to do. No matter how much research has been done, it will not of itself identify the correct answer. Some issues require no research at all; they simply need someone to take action. These issues make poor subjects for dissertations.

Strategic questions concern the future – what should be done? This is why they are not research questions. You cannot research something that has not yet happened. You can only research things that are or have been. There is a general philosophical rule that you cannot drive an *ought* from an *is*. Put in more practical terms, no matter how much analysis of the current situation you do, it cannot logically tell you what ought to be done next. Peters and Waterman (1982) reported that some companies thought analysis could determine right action and fell into the trap of 'paralysis by analysis'.

But at this early stage of the topic-identification process, strategic questions are important because they often provide the managerial motivation for the project. At the end of the project and the dissertation the student should return to these questions and, on the basis of the new knowledge and understanding they have acquired through their research, exercise their judgement and decide what the best way forward would be in relation to the strategic questions they identified at the start.

2. **Determine the scope**
    This is very often a practical matter of where you can get access. You need to decide whether you will be:
    *   studying one part of an organisation;
    *   making a comparison of several parts of an organisation;
    *   studying one organisation;
    *   making a comparison of two or more organisations;
    *   studying a sector.

    Clearly the scope of the study will have an impact on the sorts of research questions you can ask and answer. You will not be able to discover whether performance-related pay generally increases organisations' financial performance if you only study one company. You could, however, explore staff's response to performance-related pay by studying a single organisation.

As a general rule it is sensible to have a comparative element in your study. It makes it easier to find things to write about. Comparing one thing with another trebles the amount of your material. Instead of just discussing one thing, you can describe two things and then discuss their similarities and differences. More importantly, comparison creates contrasts that make it easier to see things clearly.

3. Brainstorm issues, puzzles and questions

Now go into brainstorming mode and list as many different issues, problems and questions that arise from the broad topic area as you possibly can. Do not evaluate them by saying, 'No, that's not impor-tant.' Just make the list as long as possible. For reasons that will become obvious in the next section I recommend that you write the issues on Post-its – one issue per Post-it.

At this stage you will find you should be asking research questions rather than strategic questions. Research questions are those to which it is possible, in theory at least, to go out and find answers. Research questions mostly refer to what is happening or what has happened. They are concerned with describing and explaining what is, not with proposing what should be done. So although you cannot research what should be done to improve international competitiveness (to use the example given earlier), you could research:

- what other companies in similar positions have done to improve their international competitiveness and what the outcomes were; and
- what the company has tried in the past and how well it worked.

However, while you may not be able to research what ought to be done, you could research what people at the present moment *think* should be done. You can research respondents' views about the future.

4. Map and structure the issues

Now you have a pile of issues they need structuring and organising.

Sort and cluster all your research issues and questions in a relevance tree or hierarchical diagram. The relevance tree provides a map of all the issues and questions you could research under your broad area of interest. Note that in Figure 1.1 the question at the top of the tree is a strategic question, whereas all those beneath it are research questions.

You can then decide which of the issues you *are* going to research. The two circled areas in Figure 1.1 represent two of the many possible projects. One would concentrate on how the different regional offices of the organisation (China and the Far East, Central Europe, India and South-East Asia and so on) respond to corporate strategy and research how such differences are handled. The other project would emphasise the different regional management cultures that may exist within the

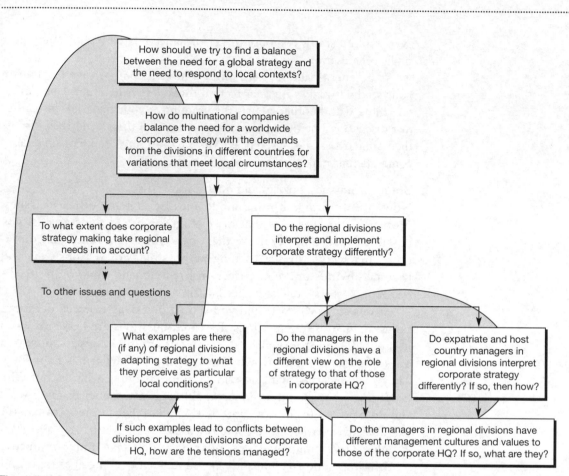

Figure 1.1 A relevance tree for a research project

Doing it with Post-its

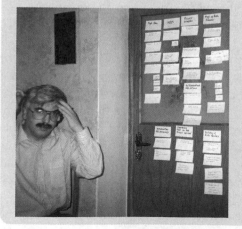

I find using Post-its very helpful for the sorting and sifting stage because they can be easily moved around as you decide how best to cluster them.

Write all your issues and questions on Post-its, making sure to put only one issue or idea on each. Find a flat surface and stick your Post-its on it in random order.

When that is done consider them and begin to move them around so that you can cluster together all those issues that seem similar or related. Then put the clusters in order by showing one cluster as a sub-set of another, for example. You need time and space for this task. In the photograph I was doing the task in a dingy flat in Azerbaijan on a wet weekend while working on a university project. The lack of distraction made thinking easier.

multinational company and study how this can lead to different understandings about what strategy is and what its role is.

This form of analysis is particularly useful if you have to choose a topic for a conference paper as well as a topic for a dissertation. Using the tree diagram you can circle the two topics and use the tree to help you define the connections between the two projects.

5. **Conduct a reconnaissance**

Having arrived at a clear view about what your research topic is going to be, it is sensible to discuss it with others. Discuss it with tutors, colleagues and other managers to see whether they agree that the issue is important and coherent. You should also do an initial trawl of the literature, if you have not already done so, to see what work others have done on the issues that concern you

6. **Frame your research question(s)**

The final stage is to ensure that you are clear in what you are doing by framing your research question in plain English.

The suspicion is that if you cannot ask your research question without using management jargon, then you are probably not clear what you are asking and you need to think about it some more. If your research question resembles this – *I am addressing the issues relevant to leveraging human resource competency to produce turnaround to world-class status and to diagonally integrate professional functionalities* – you probably do not know what you are talking about.

Exhibit 1.2

Framing research questions

- Express them in plain English as a question.
- 'There is clearly a need to investigate how tourists [on escorted cultural tours] develop an understanding of transient destination images.' This is how not to do it!
- They must intrigue and interest you.
- They must be open.
- Avoid assumptions – unless you are researching them.

Once you have found answers to such questions, then you will be in a position to draw conclusions and make recommendations about what should be done in the future. The answers to the research questions cannot dictate what action should be taken but they should provide a firmer basis for judgement and decision making.

Exercise 1.1

Your research question

Identify a topic for your project and dissertation by working through the six stages recommended above. Within the general topic chosen identify:

- a broad 'what should we do about *x*?' strategic type of question that responds to managerial or organisational issues and concerns; and
- one or more research questions that say what you want to find out;

and frame them in language that would be understandable to an interested lay person in a pub who has asked about your research.

If you have tried all of the above but are still having trouble in choosing the topic for your dissertation, then try morphological analysis. Exhibit 1.3 is a series of lists. The first list can be updated or changed to suit your personal preferences. Just enter a series of current business and management topics that interest you. Then step back, shut your eyes and stick a pin at random in each of the lists. You can then read off a description of a project you might do. For example, you could do an ethnographic account of the implementation of BPR in a number of organisations. If you do not like that idea, put the pin in again until you arrive at an acceptable project.

Exhibit 1.3

Morphological analysis

Topic	Aim	Design	Focus
BPR	Classification	Action research	Professional or interest group
Globalisation	Explanation	Ethnographic accounts	Single organisation
Internal markets	Technique development	Mathematical models	Several organisations
Business excellence model	Forcasting	Comparative analysis	Industrail sector
Business ethics	Evaluation	Case study	Single project

● ● ● ● Designing your project

A research proposal is not just a document in which you identify the purpose and focus of your research. It is also a place where you describe the broad nature and style of the project you are going to undertake. You will need to make decisions on the following matters, each of which will be discussed in some detail:

● methodological stance – understanding, action or both;
● your role as researcher;
● breadth or depth – survey or case study;
● main research methods to be used.

Methodological stance

This is a difficult issue because there are many explanatory grids that can be superimposed on methodological matters in an attempt to understand them. The grids share many common features but they also have their own peculiarities. This confusion, which you will discover readily enough in the literature, makes the subject a difficult one – for tutors as well as for students! In this chapter a particular framework will be used to discuss the issues but we will return to the matter in later chapters where other perspectives will be used to clarify the problems of methodology.

Methods and methodology

A brief word of warning is necessary before we go any further. Many tutors, but not all, take exception to the use of the word 'methodology' when the word 'methods' would be quite sufficient. They believe, and they are probably correct, that people merely use the word because it is big and sounds impressive. Mostly, when you are discussing such things as how you used a questionnaire and why this was more suitable than interviews, you are discussing methods. So you do not need to call it methodology. Methodology has a particular meaning. An 'ology' of course is the study of a whole academic field. It is a stepping-back from a subject and a consideration of it at a broader and deeper level. Methodology is the study of methods and it raises all sorts of philosophical questions about what it is possible for researchers to know and how valid their claims to knowledge might be. What we are about to discuss is indubitably methodology. Methods are considered later in this chapter and in Chapter 4.

Understanding and action

Management and business research is different to research in many other subjects because it has both an academic and a practical purpose. Academically such research should contribute to knowledge and understanding about management. Practically it should help managers do their jobs. Management research is about both knowledge and action. The relationship between knowledge and action however is not straightforward. There are at least five ways in which people envisage the relationship, as shown in Table 1.1.

Ivory tower research

This probably has little place in management and business research but it is here for the sake of completeness. From this perspective it is argued that there is no connection between knowledge and action. Knowledge is of value in itself and it does not have to be justified by practical application. It is enough that research adds to the body of knowledge. It can lead to

Table 1.1 Five ways of understanding the relationship between understanding and action in management research

The philosophers have only interpreted the world, in various ways, the point however is to change it.

(Marx 1970: 30)

Type of research	Understanding and action	Characteristics
Ivory tower	Knowledge is valuable in itself; it does not necessarily lead to action	Antiquarianism Intellectual elegance
Realist research	The research identifies and evaluates options for action	Structured variables Reductionism Cause and effect Statistical analysis
Interpretative ethnographic research or fieldwork	Understanding provides a context for thinking about action but does not specify it	Dialogic structures Participant observation Explores meaning Deals with complexity
Action research	Changing our knowledge and understanding constitutes action	Gnosis and reflection Small-scale projects Deals with personal relationships and values
Critical social research	Changing the mass's knowledge of their position to bring about social change	Radical action Raising mass consciousness

antiquarianism, which is a name for what happens when collectors of intriguing facts and trivia build up a cabinet of curiosities that amuses and appalls in turns but that is devoid of practical use. It can also lead to an emphasis on intellectual elegance as an end in itself. I have a susceptibility for this weakness and you may find one or two examples of antiquarianism in this guide.

Typical ivory tower project

Although not many students would do such a project for their MBA or Master's in management dissertation, an example might be *Marketing Strategies in the Airline Industry* 1972–1995. It would probably not do for an MBA dissertation because its focus is entirely historical. Something like *The Use of Rhetorical Figures of Speech in Board Meetings* would be borderline. It could be made appropriate to an MBA or Master's in management dissertation, but it would probably have insufficient practical relevance to be suitable.

Realist research

The case was made in the introductory chapter that realism and positivism, although they are often claimed to be the same, should be treated as separate approaches (Johnson and Duberley 2000: 149). Many textbooks treat the two as the same thing. This is not necessarily a problem. I am not arguing that they are completely different; merely that it is helpful to draw a distinction between the two. The realist researchers into management believe, with the positivists, that the knowledge we gain through research can accurately mirror reality itself, although they think the mirror image may be distorted by the intrusion of subjectivity into the process of knowing.

It has been argued in the introduction that decisions about what ought to be done in any situation cannot be logically derived from what we know about the situation. Only human judgement and determination can make the link between knowledge and action. However, the realists tend to believe that the knowledge we acquire can give good indications of what should be done. This is because such research looks for associations between variables, and where possible tries to establish chains of cause and effect. Typically research in this mode would involve structuring a problem by breaking it into its constituent parts. The relationship between these parts would then be studied, looking for recurrent patterns and associations. These patterns would then be used to establish principles or laws that could be used to select between a series of possible solutions to the problem. If the research indicates, for example, that outsourcing IT operations tends to be associated with reduced costs and improved quality of services, and it is probable that there are no other factors that might explain the changes, then it would be sensible to use this knowledge as a basis for future decision making.

Measurement and statistical methods are often sensible ways of establishing whether there are associations between variables. But it is not the case that all realist research must be statistical. In practice much realist research is based upon a comparison of qualitative case studies, which are analysed to see whether there are any connections between variables. This approach has one advantage over purely statistical approaches. Statistics can show that some variables are associated, and that changes in one are associated with predictable changes in the other. It can even give the probability that the association is a true one and that it is not caused by chance or by the unseen intervention of other variables. But it cannot prove cause and effect. It cannot define the mechanism by which one variable brings about a change in another. Qualitative case studies that provide a broader and deeper understanding of processes may give an opportunity to work out the ways in which one variable is causally linked to others. The disadvantage of a case-based approach is that there is often too small a sample of cases to claim that the links of cause and effect identified apply generally.

The realist approach to research is probably best understood through an illustration. Let us say that the problem to be researched concerns increasing rates of sickness and absenteeism in an organisation. The problem has to be structured by breaking it down into parts. This is often done by identifying variables. The researcher will try to identify dependent variables, which move in regular ways as other, independent, variables change. The statistics on sickness and absenteeism are studied to look for patterns and associations between the many variables involved. It might be that the figures go up at times when the organisation is busy. One possible cause of increasing absenteeism might therefore be stress. There are other possible causes – the tendency to take Fridays off might suggest that people are getting more satisfaction from their social life than they are from their work. Questionnaires might then be sent to staff to measure their levels of stress and job satisfaction. These statistics can then be compared with the absenteeism figures and correlations and associations noted. These statistical models tell the researcher whether the patterns are significant or merely the result of chance. A relationship between the variables can be used to predict whether certain actions will reduce absenteeism and sickness. If there is a stronger relationship between absenteeism and stress levels than between absenteeism and job satisfaction then the obvious answer to the problem is to do things that will decrease stress at work. A number of options will be devised and evaluated to see which ones would work best. Management research, within this understanding of it, leads directly to clear recommendations for action.

This example illustrates one of the worries that researchers have about realist research. It takes complex things such as the experience of stress and reduces it, simplifies it, to an index number. In a similar manner, realist researchers will use questionnaires to 'measure' people's attitudes towards a thing. Whether such measures are valid is a matter of debate. It can be argued that they miss the point, which is to explore the complex and dynamic ways in which people form and modify their opinions within the developing social contexts they find themselves in. In plainer language, people's attitudes may be flexible and change according to whom they are talking. It is for this reason that those who take a purist positivist approach, such as the behaviourists (see p. 15), avoid dealing with internal processes, for example motivation, satisfaction and attitudes.

Realist researchers form and test hypotheses about patterns of association between selected data. Hypotheses are treated as possible explanations rather than as fixed laws, as positivists sometimes claim scientific laws to be. An example of this process can be taken from Northcote Parkinson (1961: 90), who hypothesised, perhaps with his tongue in his cheek, that just before organisations collapse they spend a fortune on upgrading the reception areas of the office block or, in extreme cases, building a palatial new corporate HQ: 'It is now known that a perfection of planned layout is achieved only by organisations on the point of collapse.'

He gives the British Empire in India as one illustration of this particular Parkinson's Law. The British built an entire imperial capital city at New Delhi and completed it just as the campaign for Indian independence was fulfilling its aims. Northcote Parkinson identifies cases in which this association can be seen, and explains why he thinks there is a causal connection between the two sets of observed facts. However, a hypothesis can only ever be tentative because the realist researcher seeks evidence that would disprove the hypothesis. Once this is found, a new hypothesis has to be developed and tested to destruction in its turn. This is the hypothetico-deductive method, as described by Karl Popper (2002a, 2002b). He pointed out in a famous example (Popper 2002a: 27) that if the hypothesis is that all swans are white, then merely counting white swans does not prove the hypothesis, because no matter how many white swans you find there is always the possibility that the very next swan you see will be black. The problem is the common one that you cannot prove a negative, and the hypothesis that all swans are white presupposes that no swans are black. Of course the danger is that if you believe the hypothesis, you might not believe that the black swan you see can really be a swan. The intention of holding tentative explanations only until they are disproved chimes well with the cautiousness of realist research.

The hypothetico-deductive approach is at the heart of realist research and deserves a little more explanation. I will simplify it into a number of steps:

1. Identify your research question. What is it that you are interested in?
2. Generate some ideas. From the literature and/or your own experience, identify the key concepts or variables that are involved in the subject of your research. Begin to speculate about how they relate to each other. Do changes in one variable cause changes in others? Are the variables

Exhibit 1.4

Nullifying a hypothesis

There may be a black swan hiding some-where. The proper research strategy is to hunt for black swans, and until you find one your hypothesis holds.

related by being different points on the same dimension? This stage is closely related to developing a conceptual framework, a process that is discussed in detail in Chapter 3.

3. Develop testable hypotheses. A hypothesis is a speculation about one or more variables that can be tested to see if it holds true. If I am interested in what affects whether managers make ethical or unethical decisions in difficult circumstances, I might develop a series of hypotheses such as:

   - younger managers are more ethical than older managers in their decisions;
   - managers with religious convictions choose ethical options more often than those without such convictions.

   However, these hypotheses will be useless unless I can find a way of testing them. It is also probably a good idea not to have too many hypotheses. Too many often lead to a confused and ill-focused dissertation.

4. You then have to choose some measures for the variables in the hypothesis. If I take the hypothesis mentioned below about the relationship between age and the ethicalness of a person's decisions, then I need to identify a measure for each variable. Age is easy enough but ethicalness of decisions is tricky. I would probably look to see whether anyone has already developed a questionnaire or inventory that assesses a person's propensity to take an ethical decision. There are several such tools mentioned in the literature, although I would have to seek their authors' permission to use them. The persistent question when choosing a measure is whether it actually measures the thing I am interested in. Often we have to choose proxy measures. These do not measure a thing directly but measure a property associated with the thing. We might choose to measure an organisation's tendency to act in a corporately responsible manner by whether it has a published a policy on corporate responsibility and whether it is regarded as respon-

sible by its peers. Neither of these measures is a direct measure of corporate social responsibility, because it is possible to have a policy and yet not abide by it, and the perceptions of the organisation's peers may be wrong. Nevertheless these measures may be acceptable in the absence of anything better.

5. The next stage is to collect data to test the hypothesis. This may by done by taking data from existing databases, by conducting fieldwork, by sending out questionnaires or by preparing some case studies. In principle, data could be collected by longitudinal studies or quasi-experiments. This would normally involve collecting data before and after a significant event in an organisation. This is often difficult for students to do in the timescale of their projects.

6. The next stage is to analyse the data to see whether they support or refute the hypothesis. This may involve the use of some statistical technique. These will be discussed in Chapter 4.

7. If the analysis shows that the hypothesis is not true, then, although negative results are generally less enthralling than positive ones, the finding is still worthwhile. In this case the researcher should return to the beginning and develop a new hypothesis to explain the phenomenon he or she is researching. Of course there may not be time to do this within the typical MBA or Master's project, and the task is simply identified as one to be done at some unspecified future date. If the hypothesis is supported, then it would probably be still worthwhile to see how it compares with other explanations that other researchers have developed.

Sometimes a false negative result can be thrown up. This is technically known as a type 1 error. (Type 2 errors are when a false hypothesis is accepted.) In the management field this can happen because the relationships between variables are more complicated than the statistical techniques being used can cope with. The research into whether there is a relationship between job satisfaction and job performance may be a case in point. Many of the studies into the matter were done in the 1960s and 1970s and they generally showed a lack of a relationship. Iaffaldano and Muchinsky (1985), who conducted a study of studies, found an average correlation coefficient of only 0.17 (see p. 185 for help in interpreting correlation coefficients). Researchers generally concluded that levels of performance were not much affected by job satisfaction. More recent work has indicated that the lack of a linear relationship does not mean there is no relationship between the two variables. Katzell *et al.* (1992: 210–212) argued that both job performance and job satisfaction were determined by a large number of variables and that the lack of a linear relationship between them did not mean that there were not important relationships between them that were moderated by other factors. They tested this proposal using a path analysis technique and argued that intervening factors (such as goal setting and job involvement) create indirect causal links between job satisfaction and performance. Somers *et al.* (2001) used a different technique (neural nets) but also found non-linear relationships between work attitudes and job performance. They concluded that the relationship between satisfaction and performance might be higher than previously claimed but only under optimal conditions, when all the other factors impinging on performance were right.

This discussion suggests that, certainly at the Master's dissertation level, some hypotheses should not be followed up, not because they are uninteresting but because they would involve more statistical firepower than is available to the average Master's student. This may not necessarily be a bad thing because it is at least arguable that if you need excessively fancy statistics to prove your hypothesis, then it many be a little 'iffy' anyway. I was once sitting in the shade of a large striped umbrella on a Welsh lakeside. It was a hot day and there were many flies in the area. I noted casually to my companion, who was a hard-bitten scientist and positivist, 'Have you noticed how all the flies settle on the red stripes in the umbrella and not on any of the other coloured stripes? You don't need higher mathematics to prove that hypothesis.' He replied: 'If you need sophisticated statistics to prove your hypothesis, it probably isn't true anyway.'

Realist research proceeds by elimination, by rejecting hypotheses. If you were applying this approach to decision making, for example selecting a new software system to buy, you would form a list of options. You would then compare the options against your requirements (cost, quality, reliability and so on) and eliminate the options one by one. The last remaining option would be the best one. The realist approach can therefore also be used in that part of your project where you are choosing recommendations. Each possible recommendation becomes a hypothesis, which can be checked out.

Typical realist research projects

A typical project might centre on identifying factors that encouraged or constrained the introduction of teamworking and quality circle methods in a manufacturing plant. The research might be based on case studies of three or four companies that had tried to make these changes. In such a project, much of the research material may be qualitative, based on interviews and participant observation, although some statistical and documentary sources might also be used. Other realist projects might be more determinedly statistical. A questionnaire might be used, for example, to provide data on whether respondents' perceptions of the degree of fairness with which they are treated by their employer is associated with their ethnic origin, their age or their sex. The completed questionnaires would be analysed to see whether people in any of the demographic categories said they were discriminated against more often than the average for all respondents. A number of statistical techniques would be used to decide whether any variations in respondents' answers were significant or were merely random.

Interpretative research

People who take an interpretative approach to research see the link between understanding and action as an indirect one. Improving understanding and knowledge does not reveal the best actions to take. The link between understanding and action is mediated through people's thinking, values and relationships with each other. The role of capricious human understanding and will, in formulating understanding and in constraining the translation of understanding into action, means that knowledge cannot provide clear prescriptions for action. However, understanding a situation should help us to use our judgement to arrive at a better, if not necessarily the best, choice of action.

The link between understanding and action is seen as indirect because the world is complex and options for action are not always clear. The complexity emerges in two particular ways in an interpretative approach to research. The first is a concern for meanings and interpretations. While structure may be just as important to this form of research as it is to realist research approaches, it is of a different kind. The realist forms structures out of variables; the interpretivist forms structures out of interpretations. These are used to explore how people's sense of their world both influences, and is influenced by, that of others. In positivist research the links between variables are cause and effect relationships. In interpretative research the links between interpretations are **dialogic**. That is to say, people develop their ideas through debate and conversation with themselves, in their heads, and with others. The researcher tries to map the range and complexity of views and positions that people take on the topic of the research. If I were researching staff appraisal I would try to explore the range of views that people took. It might be anticipated that managers and staff might have different views. It might also be the case that both groups have conflicting views. Some things about appraisal might fill them with expectation; other things about it would fill them with anxiety. People may have different views according to the context in which the question was being asked. If I asked a manager about their views on appraisal when they were doing the appraising, the answer might be different to the views they might express about appraisal when they were the ones being appraised.

Interpretative research seeks people's accounts of how they make sense of the world and the structures and processes within it. Ernest Gellner was a positivist by temperament but he had a sufficient understanding of interpretative approaches to be able to parody it. The following quotation is taken from a book review he wrote. It focuses on how people might make sense of an everyday object such as a chair.

> Suppose you tell someone to sit down. No problem, no mystery there, nothing is hidden, nothing requires explanation, you might naively suppose. How wrong you are. A man who sits down knows he is sitting down, he possesses the concept of sitting, which he shares with other members of his culture and which as it were guides and inspires his performance. Without the concept, there would be no action, only an inert physical state.
>
> What does sitting mean? Placing one's bum in steady contact with a chair so two further concepts are immediately and inevitably involved. The notion of a chair is associated with rank, there are people in whose presence you may not sit down first and with the cultural boundary between chair-using and rug-using societies. There is an association with authority-conferring chairs, professorial chairs, thrones, ex cathedra authority. All scholarly, religious, political hierarchy and authority is implicitly present.
>
> As for bum, its associations are at least as potent. The boundary between those who may and those who may not bare their bums is the boundary between children who are not full moral persons and adults who are. Between the latter, baring a bum is a very significant sign of either privileged intimacy or membership of a nudist club. Bums are comic, rude, dirty and sexually stimulating, hence dangerous. Their absurdity is a safety valve, releasing some of the tension engendered by their intense desirability. Hence they are intimately linked to the aesthetic, moral, kinship boundaries of an entire culture. So, every time you sit, you ipso facto employ a concept which in turn links you to an entire cultural-moral universe, its values and its tensions and its conflicts.
>
> (Gellner 1995:7)

Interpretative researchers often take a processual perspective. This is the second way in which interpretative research recognises complexity in the subjects of research. It is an attempt to generalise about how meaning is developed through human interactions. The approach has been used to discuss the managerial role (Watson 1994a), the management of change (Dawson 1994) and strategic planning (Mintzberg 1994). I have used it in a study of business ethics (Fisher and Lovell 2000: Ch. 5). From the processual viewpoint the world is seen as an ambiguous place that people have to struggle to make sense of (Watson 1994a: Ch. 1). A processual study of a subject necessarily emphasises uncertainty and complexity. In his description of a processual analysis of the management of change, for example, Dawson (1994: 3) characterised the approach as follows.

- Processes are not linear and sequential; rather they are 'complex and dynamic'.
- There are competing 'histories' or interpretations of events and issues.

Exercise 1.3

The park bench

Source: Photo by Raj Shirole

You can try this for yourself. Focus on the picture of the park bench. What range of images and associations does it conjure up for you? When you have thought of some, consider them and identify the messages park benches give out about the people who sit on them. Do these messages tell us anything about the culture of the society in which the bench is sited?

Suggested answer

Let us think about the park bench. Most people think of contrary images. On the one hand drunks and derelicts dossing on the park bench. On the other hand young mothers with their children in buggies in the park (nannies and prams if you are old-fashioned). Here we have images of endings and beginnings. Here we have the eternal contradiction between the promise of life and its dire reality. From a park bench we can induce the wider dilemmas of being human – well, almost!

- Processes cannot be viewed synoptically because random events 'during the process of change may serve to impede, hasten or redirect the route to change' (Dawson 1994: 170)
- Politics and political processes are integral to an understanding of issues.

A complex understanding of a subject can only be achieved through a close involvement with the subject of research. Interpretative researchers are often participants in the processes they are studying. They sometimes approach their research topics in as open a manner as they can manage and try to let theories emerge from their research material, in what is known as the grounded approach to research, rather than begin the study with a ready prepared set of theories. Others bring a toolkit of theories that they dip into to find frameworks to help them explain what their research has discovered as illustrated in Exercise 1.4 and discussed on p. 98.

Exercise 1.4

Group formation – using theory to explain research material

1 Imagine you are doing research into group behaviour at work.
2 Read up on the theory of group formation. Buchanan and Huczynski (2001: 297–300) is a good text.
3 Next time you are at a group event consciously make yourself alert to the behaviour that the group exhibits.
4 After the event write down your account and impressions of what happened.
5 Use the theory of group formation to explain what was happening at the group event.
6 Does the use of theory enable you to provide a more systematic account of your experience? Did it give you any new insights?

When you read up on these matters in the literature you will find this approach to research, or aspects of it, described by different names. Other names you are most likely to come across are 'phenomenology' and the 'hermeneutic tradition'.

- **Phenomenology** is a particularly difficult term because people give it many different definitions that share some common features but that also express many nuanced differences (Remenyi *et al.* 1998: 95). The term is now used loosely but in its original formulation, by Schütz (1967), it was the study of how things appear to people, how people experience the world. In particular it was the study of how these common-sense intuitions and knowledge of society feed back into social action and so contribute to the moulding of society.
- **Hermeneutics** is a general term for the process of interpreting human actions, utterances, products and institutions.

Sociology has generated many specialist approaches to this type of research. Here are a few:

- *Ethnographers* try to explain cultures, including organisational cultures, by writing accounts of their subjective experiences of living and working in the culture being studied over a considerable period of time.
- *Grounded theorists* suggest that people's subjective understanding of their worlds should be theorised by studying the themes that people use in giving accounts of their lives and world. Researchers look for these themes and categories in the interviews and observations collected during the research. The researcher then develops theories based upon these themes. Academic understanding, they argue, should not be based on theories chosen in advance of the research (see Chapter 3).

- *Ethnomethodologists* are a sub-variety of phenomenologists. They study how, in everyday trivial interactions, people give rational accounts of what are essentially practical actions in their attempts to understand social interactions (Reed 1992: 150–5).
- *Reflective practitioners* are professionals who systematically improve their understanding of their professional worlds through reflection, with the support of their professional peers, on their professional activities (Schön 1983).

Typical interpretivist projects

Many dissertations that focus on an aspect of organisational or occupational culture adopt an interpretivist approach. If a student worked in a transnational company, for example, they might be interested in how local managers, in the different countries in which the company traded, perceived and managed commercial risk taking. In a UK context, in the public sector modernisation is a major item in the government's agenda. An interpretivist might try to explain how different stakeholder groups within a public service might interpret and value the idea of modernisation. The analysis of the research material, which could include both qualitative material from focus groups and interviews as well as statistical data from questionnaires, would focus on the differences in the views of the various groups and the processes by which these issues were debated and views changed. They might draw upon the work of Weick (1996) and his concept of enactment to understand the processes of sense making that surround the issue of modernisation. Enactment is part of the process of making sense from equivocal information by selecting and editing information through discussion and interaction with others.

Action research

Action research is different to the processual, the positivist and, to a lesser extent, the realist approaches to research. It focuses on the individual researcher's understanding and values relating to the research issue. It further proposes that the only way the researcher can improve and challenge their understanding is by taking action and by learning from experience. From this perspective the belief is that action, or behaviour, can only be changed by changing a person's values and beliefs, and that values and beliefs can only be changed by testing them in action. Action and understanding become enmeshed together in a cycle of learning in which there is a constant movement between reflection and action. Action research therefore combines a focus on action and experimentation with a concern for challenging and developing personal values. In action research the cycle might begin with a researcher using their experience (values) to decide on a course of action designed to solve a problem. The action is tried out and the researcher monitors and studies the consequences of the action, particularly the consequences as seen by other people who are affected by the change. They then reflect on their findings and this may cause them to change or develop their values and beliefs. Because they now see things differently when they next use their experience to decide on a course of action, they inevitably decide to act differently.

Action research tends to focus on small-scale but important issues such as the ways in which a team implements a policy or an individual's professional or managerial practice. It becomes risky to apply this approach to large-scale change projects. A major information system could not be implemented using an action research approach because mistakes would be too costly, and action research involves learning from mistakes.

The nature of action research is a matter of debate. Those who write about it from a background in teaching and education often take a different view from those who write about it in the context of management studies. Most educationalists share many points of view with the interpretivists. Reg Revans (1983), however, who initiated action learning in a management context, often proclaimed himself a positivist. The sensible conclusion is, that in terms of action research's view of the relationship between understanding and action, action research is developing its own unique approach to research methodology that has the following characteristics:

- confronting data from different perspectives;
- closely and iteratively linking reflection and action;
- incorporating reflection and development of values;
- involving holistic and inclusive reflection;
- developing the researcher's competency;
- testing of individual findings through critical professional discussion.

Exhibit 1.5

Definitions of action research

The linking of the terms action and research highlights the essential feature of the method: trying out ideas in practice as a means of improvement and as a means of increasing knowledge.

(Kemmis and McTaggart 1982)

Action research is about improving practice rather than about producing knowledge.

(Elliott 1991)

Both of these definitions are quoted in McNiff *et al.* (1996: 9, 10), which is a useful and practical guide to doing action research for management students, despite being set in an educational context.

Exhibit 1.6

The Humanities Curriculum project

This illustration provides a good example of the link between action and challenging personal beliefs.

The Humanities Curriculum project was an approach to teaching secondary school children. It was designed to expose students to controversial issues. The teacher was to be relieved of the task of giving facts and allowed to concentrate on chairing students' discussions on the issues. Short 'provocative' documents would be used as handouts to provide students with the basic facts and materials.

One teacher reported he was having trouble with the project. The students read the materials but no discussion started. The teacher assumed that the students were having problems understanding the materials. So, using his best judgement and having discussed it with the project researcher, he reverted to giving mini-lectures to explain the content of the documents. However, in the spirit of action learning, the researcher (R) decided to talk to the students (S).

R: 'Well, what do you think of this new approach?'
S: 'I don't like it.'
R: 'What don't you like about it?'
S: 'We don't like these documents, these materials, we don't like them.'
R: 'So what don't you like about them? Are they too difficult to read?'
S: 'Oh no! Oh no! We can read them.'
R: 'Can you all?'
S: 'Of course we can read them.'
R: 'So what's the problem then?'
S: 'The problem is we disagree with what they say.'
R: 'Oh! Good. You actually disagree with what they say?'
S: 'Yes.'
R: 'Well, then you can express your disagreement in class.'
S: 'The teacher wouldn't like it.'
R: 'Well, why wouldn't the teacher like it?'
S: 'Because the teacher agrees with what the documents say.'
R: 'How do you know that the teacher agrees with what these documents say?'
S: [Looking very surprised at the stupidity of the question] 'The teacher wouldn't give you the documents in the first place if he didn't agree with them, would he?'

(Altrichter 1993)

The researcher had his assumptions and beliefs challenged by the feedback he received from the students. When he discussed the situation with the teacher, this new perspective would cause the teacher to try a new action in the next cycle of implementation. The teacher's and the researcher's beliefs about the pupils had changed, and so consequently would their actions. Action research is about gnosis – the Greek word for knowing oneself through self-criticism and reflection.

Typical action research projects

Occasionally an action researcher focuses on their own managerial practice. A manager or team leader for instance might develop their leadership practice through action research. They would change their leadership style, perhaps following the precepts of a particular theory, and use the feedback from their staff to adapt and further develop their leadership values and behaviours. More commonly, an action research project would be concerned with wider changes. For example, an organisation may have decided to provide mentors in support of a major new ICT implementation. Action research could be used to develop the method and values that would be appropriate for mentors in that particular context.

Critical social research

Researchers who profess the critical social research approach believe that the purpose of research should be to change society for the better. Central to this approach is the idea of false consciousness. This is a Marxist notion that describes the tendency of the proletariat to fail to recognise the nature of its self-interest. More generally it is any form of ideology or self-imagery that is held to be inappropriate to the real or objective situation of an actor. Crudely expressed it means that in organisations, employees are being exploited but are oblivious to their situation. The task of critical social research therefore is to reveal the deep and hidden structures at work behind the façade of false consciousness. Once the proletariat becomes aware that they are oppressed, that they are not so much being empowered as being exploited by such things as business process re-engineering and just-in-time production methods, for example, then they will rise in revolt. This is not a form of research that would necessarily find favour with people on management courses but, if used in moderation, in a dissertation it adds piquancy to the analysis.

Critical social research can take other radical perspectives, such as feminism, rather then a Marxist one. A more careful review of this approach is provided in Chapter 5.

Critical social researchers object to positivism (but not so much to realist researchs, of which it is a variant), the interpretative approach and action research. From a critical perspective, interpretivism is seen as giving more importance to understanding the world than changing it. Positivism is viewed as a tool for reinforcing oppressive structures and action research is rejected because it ignores the need for big, radical changes and concentrates on small-scale and individual change.

Typical critical research projects

These are fairly rare in MBA and Master's in management programmes but they are by no means precluded. A radical critique approach might be used to study executive pay and remuneration in large public companies.

The possibility could be explored that the differentials in pay between the top managers and others in such companies could arise from deep-seated and structural class conflicts. This would be in opposition to the opinion that such differences are simply the result of competition in the market for scarce entrepreneurial competency. An example of a radical critique approach can be found in Porter (2002).

Methodological pluralism

The FAQ at this stage is: 'Can you mix and match these approaches to research?' It is often easiest if you choose just one. It reduces the complexity of the chapter in your dissertation on methods and methodology. It also keeps you out of the line of sight of academic snipers, from all camps, which are in a state of constant low-level warfare with each other. While tutors and lecturers may take different methodological positions, you may be encouraged to adopt whichever approach you wish as long as you show it to be a sensible approach for answering the research question you have set yourself.

It is possible, however, with care, to combine some of the approaches. It has already been suggested that a dash of social criticism might add some spice to an otherwise standard piece of realist research. The big question is whether it is possible to combine realist research and an interpretative approach. Gill and Johnson's (1997: 135–6) line on this debate is persuasive. They argue that if you take a realist stance, then aspects of an interpretivist approach could be brought in as a useful adjunct to the research. But they also claim that the reverse is not true. If you are doing interpretivist research, then there is no way that an element of realism (or even more seriously an element of positivism) can add to it. This is because taking a positivist perspective would undermine the methodological basis of the interpretivist approach. The realist position – that what is observed is real and can be, more or less, directly studied and measured – flatly contradicts the interpretivists' belief that our knowledge of the world is socially constructed – which means that understanding derives from the social processes of debate and power that take place between people.

How is it possible for realist research to find a place for interpretivist styles of investigation? Gill and Johnson (1997) argue that positivist (and realist) research identifies associations between variables, between antecedent variables and consequences. They might find, for example, that there is a relationship between people's stress levels and their absenteeism levels. But having identified the pattern positivism can say little more. It does not explain why the pattern is there or how the antecedent factor exerts influence on people's actions. This is because the link between the two variables, in this example stress and absenteeism, is the way in which people make the link in their own minds, in their subjective processes. Realism has no way of studying people's accounts of these processes, but interpretative approaches do. Interpretivist approaches can be used to create a quasi-causal account of how the two variables interact. In brief, interpretivist research can convert the pattern of associations found by positivist work into a quasi-causal connection. Realist research shows there is a connection; interpretivism gives a possible description of how the connection may work.

There are at least two ways in which interpretivism may be called in to aid realist research.

1. As described above a researcher may start off with a piece of realist research that identifies an association between two variables, then use an interpretative approach to understand the causal connection, the mechanism, which shows in all complexity how the different aspects interact.
2. The other possibility uses the ease with which interpretivist research generates hypotheses about the associations between variables. In this case interpretivist research is a ground-clearing operation that precedes a piece of realist research. A researcher might start with a piece of interpretative research that, say, creates all sorts of hypotheses about the causes of absenteeism and then do a piece of realist research to see whether these hypotheses hold true in general.

Exercise 1.5

Deciding on your research approach

When you are designing your project you will need to decide which of these approaches to research is going to be the dominant one in your project.

What approach would be the most appropriate one for your chosen project topic, and why?

The remaining decisions you have to make when designing your project all relate to the big decision about methodological approach that has just been considered.

The researcher's role

The roles that a researcher may take in relation to the people and the organisations they are researching will depend on whether they are a member of the organisation they are researching and on the research approach they have adopted. Figure 1.2 identifies four research roles, each of which has its own advantages and disadvantages.

	Visible	*Invisible*
Involved	Previleged observer – judge	Covert participant observer – spy
Non-involved	Academic – a harmless drudge	Fly on the wall

Figure 1.2 Researchers' roles

The judge

This is a researcher who is studying an organisation in which they are involved and they have told those being researched that they are being studied. This role has the advantage of being open and honest and therefore giving those being studied a chance to put their point of view to the researcher if they fear they are being misinterpreted. The disadvantage is that those being studied may become uneasy and modify what they say and how they behave. They may even become annoyed that the researcher appears to be putting themselves in the privileged position of someone who has the right to judge, to express opinions about, their doings.

The academic – a harmless drudge

The academic is a researcher who is studying an organisation in which they have no involvement except as someone who has been kindly allowed access so that they can gather information for their dissertation. The advantage is that the academic is seen as someone with no axe to grind; but there is the danger that those being studied may try to use the researcher to support them and their projects in the organisation's politics. The main disadvantage is that your project may well be low in the organisation's priorities and you may not be given the access and the time you need.

The covert participant observer

This is someone who works in an organisation so that they can study it, but the people they are studying do not know they are being researched. There has been a long line of such ethnographic studies, as nice middle-class researchers get jobs in fish-gutting factories to report on life in the lower depths. The research can be rich and fascinating. The question is whether it is ethical to study people who have not given informed consent. There is a danger that the researcher might foment situations just to increase the 'human interest' quality of their research material.

The fly on the wall

These researchers try to be invisible but are not necessarily secretive. They might, for example, have permission to observe a meeting. Although their physical presence will be unmistakable, by their demeanour and their quietness they hope those at the meeting will forget they are there. As they cannot affect what they are observing, the ethical problem, while still important, is of a lesser degree. The fly on the wall can use secretive methods of course. A researcher studying consumers' behaviour in a supermarket might use video recordings of shoppers taken without their consent by video cameras that also have a security function.

Breadth or depth

The issue is whether the researcher is trying to obtain a broad and representative overview of a situation, in which case a survey approach would be appropriate, or an in-depth understanding of particular situations, in which event case studies would be appropriate.

Random surveys of a suitably large sample allow you to determine what is average and what the variations around the average are to a definable level of statistical confidence. They also allow you to examine the relationships between the things you measure in the survey and to establish whether any associations or correlations are significant or just random effects. But surveys are not efficient means of studying the complexity of things in particular.

Case studies enable you to give a holistic account of the subject of your research. In particular, they focus on the interrelationships between all the people, groups, policies, technology and other factors that make up the case studies. A case study is written up as an account or a narrative. In other words, you are required in a case study to tell the story of what happened from as broad a perspective as is necessary. The case study form is also very adaptable. You could write up case studies of any of the following:

- individual events in a manager's working life (when a case study would more likely be called a critical incident);
- a process, such as the development and launch of a new product;
- an organisation or part of an organisation in relation to some particular issue, such as use of the Internet;
- the making of a decision (sometimes called decision tracing).

There are many other variations and possibilities.

Case studies inevitably lose representativeness. It cannot be claimed that what happened in one case is typical of all cases. In many instances the power of the case study lies in its capacity to provide insights and resonance for the reader. However, it is not true to claim that case studies lack generalisability. Tony Watson (1994b) argues that case studies do enable generalisations to be made about organisational processes. Yin (1994) points out that case studies can be used like experiments to test a theory. If the case study shows the theory to be untrue, then the rejection of the theory can be generalised (Yin 1994).

You need to be as systematic and rigorous when doing case study research as you are for all other types of research. In particular, you should pay attention to the following:

- Do not rely on one particular type of evidence but use a mixture.
- Research the substance of the case study from the different perspectives of the various interested parties or stakeholders.
- Develop a formal procedure or protocol for use in gathering information so that your material is collected in a uniform manner.
- Keep systematic records of your material that could be reviewed by someone wishing to double-check your work.
- Find a way of creating an audit trail that links your findings and conclusions about the case study to your raw research material.
- Allow your thinking about the case study to be influenced and changed by the material you gather and record your changing views.
- Be aware of bias in the information you obtain from interviewees or from documents and questionnaires. Documents can be slanted and interviewees might give you selected titbits in the hope of settling old scores, for example.
- Do not allow the delights of telling a good human-interest story get in the way of telling the truth as you see it.

Choice of research methods

When designing your project you have to make some general decisions about the research methods you are going to use. These are the most commonly used methods:

- interviews
- questionnaires
- panels, including focus groups
- observation, including participant observation
- documents
- databases.

Detailed descriptions and accounts of their advantages and disadvantages are given in Chapter 4.

It is tempting, but wrong, to make an easy connection between research methodology and particular methods. It is often assumed that realist research means using quantitative research methods and materials (questionnaire surveys and databases) and interpretative research uses qualitative material and methods (interviews, documentary exegesis). These assumptions are wrong: first because it is possible to use any of the research methods to produce either quantitative material (numbers) or qualitative material (words), and second because you can use qualitative

Table 1.2 Approaches and methods of research

Method	Positivist	Interpretivist
Observation	Preliminary work	A major component of the research
Documentary	Content analysis	Understanding categories
Interview	Large random samples, fixed-choice questions	Small samples, open-ended and unstructured questions
Questionnaire	Large random samples, fixed-choice questions	Used for initial mapping, open-ended questions

Source: Silverman (1993: 9)

material as part of a realist project and you can certainly use numbers to illuminate interpretative research. In practice you can use any of the research methods in any of the approaches.

This is not to deny that realist researchers and interpetivists may prefer to use the same research methods in different ways. Silverman (1993) has explained some of the possibilities by comparing qualitative and quantitative forms of research (see Table 1.2 above).

Let us take a couple of examples. Someone doing a realist piece of work may well use interviews. But it will be the sort of interview where the interviewer has to read the questions from a pre-prepared script without deviation. The questions will be pre-coded so that the interviewee will be given a number of possible answers to choose between. An interpretative researcher using interviews, however, would begin the interview with only the broadest view about how the conversation might develop and may indeed encourage the interviewee to determine the direction in which the discussion flows. Sometimes realist and interpretatively inclined researchers use the same combinations of research methods but in different sequences. An interpretative researcher writing a case study in an organisation might well use a questionnaire at the start of the project to get an overall 'feel' for the subject they are studying. But the questionnaire would remain a preliminary and a subsidiary method. A realist researcher might well start a study with open-ended interviews that will be useful to them when they design their highly structured questionnaire to be used with a large sample of respondents. When we consider documentary methods, an interpretative researcher might study the use of metaphor in an organisation's documents whereas a positivist might count the relative frequency with which the words 'customer' and 'profit' are used.

Ethical considerations

When you are doing your research you should not treat people unfairly or badly. You should not harm people, or use the information your discover in you research to harm them, or allow it be used to do harm. This may sound alarmist and you should not assume that you will be beset by such

problems when you are doing research. Nevertheless it is sensible to anticipate whether any such difficulties might occur. The following list rehearses
some of the dilemmas you may come across.

- **Negotiating access**
  - Negotiating terms of reference with organisations
    If you are doing the project in a particular organisation, then it is
    often necessary to agree terms of reference for the project.
    Managements tend to have preferred solutions to the problems they
    are asking you to research and you need to ensure that the terms of
    reference give you scope to investigate the issues from a wide range
    of perspectives.
  - Right to privacy
    There is no obligation on anyone to assist you in your research.
    This raises the question of just how much pressure ('Oh! Come on –
    do it to help out an old friend!') it is proper to put on someone to
    cooperate. I once arranged a research interview with a key inform-
    ant as part of a consultancy project I was doing for a large
    company. His first words were:

    > I don't think it's right that they should have brought some outsider
    > academic like you in to do this project. I have already done much of
    > the preliminary work for this project and I should have been
    > allowed to take the project forward. I do not wish to cooperate but
    > I did want you to know how I felt about the situation.

    I admit that I wangled an interview from him, but what would you
    have done in this situation?
  - Access to personnel or case records
    This is a particularly important issue in areas such as health care,
    where it may be necessary to have your proposal vetted by an ethics
    committee before you can proceed. Students working in the NHS
    need to take particular care because the remit of research ethics
    committees has expanded to include projects that involve research-
    ing NHS staff as well as those projects that involve patients. The
    legislation on data protection requires everyone to be careful when
    they propose to deal with personal records of any kind.
  - Informed consent
    Sometimes this is implicit, as when someone takes the trouble to
    complete and return a questionnaire, but in other projects, which
    are ethnographical, or based on participant observation, the issue
    of informed consent may be tricky. In these cases it may be proper
    to obtain consent after the research has been done but before it is
    written up.
- **Data collection stage**
  - Objectivity and disinterestedness

This may be impossible but you have at least to make a pretence of trying – unless of course you are acting as an action researcher or a social critic researcher.

– Confidentiality and anonymity

Anonymity means changing the names and locations (but not sex) of informants. Confidentiality means not revealing you sources. You need to make it clear that confidentiality does not mean that the material will not be used. Normally these issues do not cause problems; but what if, in the course of your research, you unearth unprofessional practice in a social services department, say, or illegality in an international business operation?

– Practitioner/researcher

What precautions or mechanisms may be necessary to prevent you exploiting the privilege that this role gives you?

- **The reporting stage**
  - Misuse of research

    One possibility is that that the research could be used to do harm to those who cooperated with it. A frequent issue is when the managers who gave permission or access to the researchers try to influence the content or tone of the dissertation. A more invidious form of this problem is when researchers write up the research in a way that will please the sponsors because they expect it will be required of them. A less common possibility is that the sponsors may try to use the research to support positions that the researcher thinks may be harmful to others.

Homan (1991) is a useful guide to the ethics of research.

● ● ● ● Writing the research proposal

When you have been through the six-step process and thought about the design of your project, it might be helpful to summarise your research project. The Watson Box can be used for this purpose. It provides a useful framework for structuring your written research proposal.

The assessment criteria, which can be seen in the introductory chapter, identify a number of features that markers will be looking for in a proposal document:

- The 'what' and the 'why' of the proposal are clear and specific.
- The three elements of:
  - the research questions;
  - the research design; and
  - the research methods
  are well integrated.
- The proposals for the research methods are sensible and practicable.

Exhibit 1.7

The Watson Box

What?	Why?
What puzzles and intrigues me? What do I want to know more about or better understand? What are my key research questions?	Why will this be of enough interest to put it on the library shelves or present to my organisation? Is it a guide to practitioners or policy makers? Is it a contribution to knowledge?
How – conceptually?	**How – practically?**
What models, concepts and theories can I draw upon? How can I develop my own research questionsand create a conceptual framework to guide my investigation?	What research methods and techniques shall I use to apply my conceptual framework (to both gather and analyse evidence)? How shall I gain and maintain access to information sources?

Source: Watson (1994b)

The Watson Box helps you ensure that you have met these criteria.

Exercise 1.6

Completing the Watson Box

Use the blank Watson Box provided to write a summary of your research proposal.

What?	Why?
How – conceptually?	**How – practically?**

You have, of course, freedom to structure your research proposal (if you have to write one) as you please, but should you need guidance the following structure covers most of the issues.

- Introduction
- The objectives and purpose of the project (what?):
  - A brief overall description of the project's context.
  - The strategic question that guides the project.
  - The objectives of the project.
- The justification for the project (why?).
- The research questions (what? – again, but in more detail):
  - Identify and discuss the research questions that you will answer in the project.
  - If you are taking a realist research approach you might frame your research question as a hypothesis. A hypothesis is a speculation about an association between two or more variables. It is important that the hypothesis can be tested by research to see whether it can be disproved.
- An overview of the appropriate literature:
  - Mapping the main writers in the field and their arguments
  - Definition of key concepts and outlining of conceptual framework if necessary and possible. (This is the *how – conceptually?* quadrant of the Watson Box.)
- Research design:
  - What methodological approach are you going to adopt?
  - Research methods, samples, methods for analysing research material.
- Practical and ethical issues:
  - Does the research raise any ethical concerns that need to be resolved?
  - Are there any potential problems of research access?
  - Are there any resource issues such as access to specialist databases or particular research software?
  - Are there issues of commercial confidentially or intellectual property rights?
- A plan or timetable:
  - Consider drafting a Gantt chart (as shown in Exhibit 1.9) that plots against a time line when the major elements of the project will be done.

Exhibit 1.8

A Gantt chart for a research project

Task	Sept.	Oct.	Nov.	Dec.	Etc.
Literature search	←——————→				
Read literature		←————————————→			
Draft interview schedule			←————→		
Pilot schedule				←————→	
Etc.					

If your research is going to adopt a grounded approach, then it will not be possible for you to predict what the key concepts and the conceptual framework might be.

Summary

- Use the six-stage process to think through your selection of a dissertation topic.
- Try to express your central research question as a simple and plain sentence without using academic or business jargon.
- Choose a research approach that is appropriate for your research question.
- You can mix and match your research approaches, but it is risky and you need to be sure that you understand the methodological implications of what you are doing.
- Think about how, practically, you will carry out the project so that you can write the dissertation.
- Use the Watson Box to summarise your proposal.
- Use the suggested list of headings to help you structure the research proposal.

Suggested reading

The standard textbooks recommended in the introductory chapter are the best places to start an exploration of research methodology. If you are considering using case studies as a main vehicle for your research then a look at Yin (1994) is recommended.

References

Altrichter, H. (1993) 'The concept of quality in action research: giving the practitioners a voice in educational research', in M. Schratz (ed.) *Qualitative Voices in Educational Research*, London: Falmer Press.

Buchanan, D. and Huczynski, A. (2001) *Organisational Behaviour: An Introductory Text*, 4th edn, Harlow: Prentice Hall.

Dawson, P. (1994) *Organisational Change: A Processual Approach*, London: Paul Chapman.

Fisher, C. and Lovell, A. (2000) *Accountants' Responses to Ethical Issues at Work*, London: Chartered Institute of Management Accountants (CIMA).

Elliott, J. (1991) *Action Research for Educational Change*, Buckingham: Open University Press.

Gellner, E. (1995) 'Anything goes', *Times Literary Supplement*, 16 June, No. 4811, 6–8.

Gill, J. and Johnson, P. (1997) *Research Methods for Managers*, 2nd edn, London: Paul Chapman.

Homan, J. (1991) *The Ethics of Social Research*, Harlow: Longman.

Iaffaldano, M. and Muchinsky, P. (1985) 'Job satisfaction and job performance: a meta-analysis', *Psychological Bulletin*, Vol. 97, 251–273.

Johnson, P. and Duberley, J. (2000) *Understanding Management Research: An Introduction to Epistemology*, London: Sage.

Katzell, R. A., Thompson, D. E. and Guzzo, R. A. (1992) 'How job satisfaction and job performance are and are not linked', in C. J. Cranny, P. C. Smith and E. F. Stone (eds) *Job Satisfaction: How People Feel about Their Jobs and how it Affects Their Performance*, Oxford: Lexington Books.

Kemmis, S. and McTaggart, R. (1982) *The Action Research Planner*, Geelong, Australia: Deakin University Press.

Locke, L. F., Spirduso, W. W. and Wilverman, S. J. (1993) *Proposals that Work: A Guide for Planning Dissertations and Research Proposals*, London: Sage.

McNiff, J., Lomax, P. and Whitehead, J. (1996) *You and Your Action Research Project,* London: Routledge and Hyde Publications.

Marx, K. (1970) 'Theses on Feuerbach', in K. Marx and F. Engels, *Selected Works in One Volume*, London: Lawrence & Wishart.

Mintzberg, H. (1994) *The Rise and Fall of Strategic Planning*, Hemel Hempstead: Prentice Hall.

Northcote Parkinson, C. (1961) *Parkinson's Law or the Pursuit of Progress*, London: John Murray.

Peters, T. J. and Waterman Jr, R. (1982) *In Search of Excellence*, New York: Harper & Row.

Popper, K. (2002a) *Conjectures and Refutations: The Growth of Scientific Knowledge*, London: Routledge.

Popper. K. (2002b) *The Logic of Scientific Discovery*, London: Routledge.

Porter, S. (2002) 'Critical realist ethnography', in T. May (ed.) *Qualitative Research in Action*, London: Sage.

Reed, M. (1992) *The Sociology of Organisations: Themes, Perspectives and Prospects*, London: Harvester Wheatsheaf.

Remenyi, D., Williams, B., Money, A. and Swartz, E. (1998) *Doing Research in Business and Management: An Introduction to Process and Method*, London: Sage.

Revans, R. (1983) *The ABC of Action Learning*, Bromley: Chartwell-Bratt.

Schön, D. (1983) *The Reflective Practitioner: How Professionals Think in Action*, New York: Basic Books.

Schott, B. (2002) *Schott's Original Miscellany*, London: Bloomsbury.

Schütz, A. (1967) *The Phenomenology of the Social World*, trans. G. Walsh and F. Lehnert, Evanston, Ill: North Western University Press.

Silverman, D. (1993) *Interpreting Qualitative Data*, London: Sage.

Somers, M. J., Dormann, C., Janssen, P. P. M., Dollard, M. F., Landeweerd, J. A. and Nijhuis, F. J. N. (2001) 'Thinking differently: assessing non-linearities in the relationship between work attitudes and job performance using a Bayesian neural net', *Journal of Occupational and Organizational Psychology*, Vol. 74, No. 1, 47–62.

Watson, T. J. (1994a) *In Search of Management: Culture, Chaos and Control in Management*, London: Routledge.

Watson, T. J. (1994b) 'Managing, crafting and researching: words, skill and imagination in shaping management research', *British Journal of Management*, Vol. 5 (special issue), 77–87.

Weick, K. E. (1996) *Sensemaking in Organizations*, Newbury Park, CA: Sage.

Yin, R. K. (1994) *Case Study Research and Design and Methods*, 2nd edn, London: Sage.

Chapter 2 ●●●●

Writing a critical literature review

Contents

- Introduction
- The sources
  Searching for literature
- Mapping and describing the literature
  Describing the literature
- Forensic critique
  Soundness of arguments
  Evaluating arguments
- Radical critique
  The critical approach – *Alistair Mutch*
  Developing a radical critique
- Summary
- Suggested reading
- References

● ● ● ● Introduction

The processes of researching and writing a Master's dissertation

Your manuscript is both good and original, but the part that is good is not original and the part that is original is not good.

Attributed to Dr Samuel Johnson[1]

A dissertation should include a chapter in which the literature relevant to the topic is reviewed (see Chapter 6 for a suggested list of chapters for a dissertation). It should be a critical literature review. It is the purpose of this chapter to explain what a critical review is. The criticism of the literature does not have to be as hurtful as that given by Dr Johnson in the quotation above. The purpose of criticism is not to wound but to ensure that the concepts, theories and arguments that you take from the literature to help you with the dissertation are robust. The purpose of the literature review, to take a broader perspective, is to remove the need to rediscover knowledge

---

[1] The quote, although often attributed to him, cannot be found in any of Johnson's published works. See http://www.samueljohnson.com/apocryph.html

that has already been reported. The literature review helps you to build upon the work that has already been done in the field you are researching. To ensure that things have not been missed in the search it is important to show that you have searched the literature thoroughly and have identified most of the material that could be useful in the project. However, having found material in the literature does not mean that it is fit for use. It is necessary to subject the key materials you are going to use to a critical examination to make sure they are strong enough to sustain the use you are going to put them to in the dissertation. If you base the dissertation on invalid and poorly thought-through concepts and theories, then the whole dissertation will be weak. This does not mean that you must take on the most renowned authors and declare their arguments unsound. That might be a little arrogant. However, it may be necessary to identify the weaknesses and limitations of a writer's theories and arguments or identify their inappropriateness to the particular circumstances of your project.

It would be a good idea to look carefully at the marking scheme for dissertations that is provided in the introductory chapter and to review the benchmarks for the 'literature review' criterion. Treat this carefully, however, because the specific criteria used to mark your dissertation may be different. If you are content to be marked in the 50–59 per cent range, then it is only necessary to identify the appropriate literatures and to describe them competently. To achieve a mark in the 60–69 per cent range, a critical review of the literature is necessary. It is sufficient for this level of mark to base your criticism on those made by other writers. Even at this level, however, it would be sensible to try to form your own criticism of the work being considered. In many cases it may be that other authors have not yet written critiques of a work, in which case you will have to rely on your own resources. If the target is to be marked at a distinction level, then it is essential that you make your own evaluation of the core literature that you are using.

This chapter is divided into four parts:

1. Finding material and literature relevant to your project.
2. Guidelines for summarising and describing the literature.
3. Carrying out a forensic critique of the theories and arguments in the chosen literature. A forensic critique is an evaluation of the strength of the arguments proposed in a journal article or book.
4. Critical theory (or radical critique as it is alternatively known). This makes fundamental criticisms of management and business and is another form of evaluation of theories and arguments. It often takes a moral stance and identifies the ways in which business and management can reinforce tendencies in society to exploit and discriminate against sections of the population. The use of radical critiques in management Master's dissertations is not obligatory.

Learning outcomes for the chapter

1 Readers will be able to search library and other information resources to find appropriate literatures for their dissertation.
2 Readers will be able to map out the literatures and identify the key concepts, theories and arguments that are necessary for their project.
3 Readers will be able to carry out a forensic critique of the core theories, concepts and arguments that they have drawn from the literature.
4 Readers will have an awareness of radical critical perspectives and be able to make radical critiques of key themes and topics presented in the literature.

The sources

The first task in doing a literature review is to find some literature. You need a mixture of materials, but the precise combinations will vary from topic to topic. Try to find some material from most of the categories listed below. Students often ask: 'How many books and articles should I cite in my dissertation?' It is impossible to give a number in answer, although it can be tempting to quote a very large number to scare them and to encourage them not to ask silly questions in future. It all depends on what literature is available and how you use the ideas, material and theory it contains. It is possible to suggest that a list of references with less than 20 items is probably too short.

● Books
There are three sorts of management books as far as researchers are concerned:
– textbooks
– academic monographs and
– 'airport bookstall' books.
Textbooks are useful to help you orient yourself in a field of literature and as a source of references that can be followed up. They may be recognised from their characteristic use of learning devices such as learning objectives, summaries, exercises and text boxes containing illustrative material. They should not be relied upon too heavily. Academic monographs are often difficult to read, but they do alert the reader to developments arising from recent research. These books should be used selectively. 'Airport bookstall' books are mostly written in an accessible style and have attractive jackets. When they are not based on the biographies or experiences of successful managers, they

are often distillations of more academic work. They are mostly presented in a 'can do' format, offering practical guidance for business success. Normally they have attention-grabbing titles that appear to offer solutions to all business problems. They can be assimilated within the duration of a transatlantic flight. They can be useful materials, but they should not be used uncritically because they often oversimplify and contain uncorroborated assumptions.

- Journals

Journals fall into two main categories and you should use both. Academic journals contain articles that have been peer-reviewed. This means that two or more expert referees approved the papers before they were accepted for publication. The general information or style pages, often on the inside of the front or back cover of a journal, should say whether it is peer-reviewed. Non-peer-reviewed journals are often professional or trade journals. The articles in these journals are commonly simpler and shorter than those in the peer-reviewed journals. They can be useful for identifying trends, fashions and current concerns within business, but many are derivative and of questionable quality. Non-peer-reviewed journals should not be used exclusively. Managers doing MBAs and other Master's courses in management often look at the more academic papers in horror and declare, 'We are managers, we cannot be expected to cope with this hugely complex academic writing style'. Well, I have some sympathy because many papers do appear to be written in a style designed to fool, impress or confuse. Nevertheless there will be much pertinent and good material in such papers and you will need to make the effort to understand them. There are some journals, such as the *Harvard Business Review*, that are academically prestigious but are designedly accessible to managers as well as to academics.

Journals will most likely be your main source for a research dissertation, probably being more important than books. This is because the most up-to-date research and debates will be found in journals.

- The World Wide Web

The World Wide Web is a very useful source of material. The better search engines can be valuable in tracking down material. The Web has to be used with care, however, because it includes both high-quality material and utter tosh. Distinguishing between the two is not always easy. In preparing for writing this guide, I found a web page on semantic differential questionnaires (see p. 166). The first few pages read very sensibly and then the web page slowly became an obsessive polemic in which semantic differentials were presented as diabolic devices that bureaucrats were using to remove the liberties of the individual.

In the public sector, where much of the material is in the form of official publications and reports, the Web can be the most convenient means of access to material. The open government web site http://www.open.gov.uk is a good starting point. For those of you working in the field of human resource management, the Department of HRM in the Nottingham Business School maintains a 'Human Resource Management Resources on the Internet' web page. It can be accessed by clicking on the external links button on the www.nbs.ntu.ac.uk/DEPTS/HRM/Index.htm web page.

● Dissertations

Business schools keep copies of past Master's dissertations produced by their students. Some are commercially confidential and cannot be consulted without the author's permission. Many students find it comforting to see others' efforts, and it may be worth asking to see some. Try and make sure that they give you ones that passed comfortably, otherwise you may gain a dangerously low impression of the standard you need to reach.

Searching for literature

Looking for literature these days is mostly an electronic activity of searching through a virtual library. Using a library's online catalogue of books and other materials makes searching for books a lot easier. It is possible to access the online catalogues of academic libraries across the country. NISS (National Information Services and Systems) provides a web site of links to online library catalogues at http://www.niss.ac.uk/lis/opacs.html. The advantages of searching for journal articles and papers by using electronic library resources is that it takes much less time, you are more likely to find what you need and, if you are lucky, the papers may be available online and you can download them or print them off.

Exhibit 2.1

An electronic library

Source: Photo by Raj Shirole

You should spend some time becoming familiar with all the services that your university or institutional library can provide by exploring both the physical library and the virtual library. You may need various user names and passwords to access the latter, and the library staff will be able to help you with these. Do not become so carried away with online searching that you forget about bibliographic serendipity, by which I mean wandering around the library shelves and current journal stands, flicking through books and reading the contents lists on the back pages of journals. It is surprising how often you chance upon useful material that you would otherwise have missed. Many academic libraries have joined a cooperative scheme so that students who live or work at a distance from their university can use libraries closer to them. A web site listing the universities in the scheme can be found at http://uklibrariesplus.ac.uk/.

Electronic resources

There is a range of electronic resources that might be of help.

Electronic journals

Most libraries will subscribe to journals that are published and/or are available online. Check out which relevant publications are provided by your library.

Exhibit 2.2

A more traditional library

Full-text databases

These are databases that allow you to make searches for materials using key words. They provide all the bibliographic details such as authors, titles, journal titles, date of publication, volume, issue and page numbers. They will also include abstracts of papers' and articles' contents. In addition, in many but not all cases they give you access to an html or pdf copy of the article itself that you can read on screen, download, print off or email to yourself. The full-text databases that you are mostly likely to use are listed below:

ABI/Inform – a good all-purpose database.
Business Source Premier – another good all-round database.
Emerald – includes all the journals published by MCB Press.
European Business ASAP – covers finance, acquisitions and mergers, new technologies and products, HRM, marketing and management generally.
IngentaJournals – a general database of papers from a number of publishers.

Bibliographic databases

These databases can be searched in the same way as full-text databases and provide you with all the bibliographic information and with abstracts, but they do not provide full copies of the papers and articles. If you want them you will have to find the hard copy of the journal in the library, and if the library does not have a copy you will have to order the item on inter-library loan. Some databases you might want to use are listed below:

Inside – provides bibliographic information on journals held by the British Library.
PsycINFO – covers the field of psychology, but there are many articles that are relevant to management topics.
Econlit – covers the field of economics, and again there are many relevant references especially for people working on finance topics.

If you are interested in management in health care and medicine, then *Medline* may be worth consulting. If you are working in the public sector, especially in the social services, then ASSIA would be worth a look.

CD-ROM *newspapers*

Newspapers are a valuable source of up-to-date information on many management topics. A number of newspapers are available as searchable databases in libraries. Newspapers, including the *Financial Times*, are also available as online editions on the World Wide Web.

Financial and marketing databases

Strictly speaking these are primary resources rather than secondary materials and so would find their place in the 'results and analysis' part of the dissertation, rather than in the literature review. Nevertheless, here is a convenient place to mention them. FAME is the main financial database. It provides updated financial information on 130,000 companies in the United Kingdom and Ireland. Mintel is one of the main marketing databases. These or other databases will be available at your university library.

It might be worthwhile to check up on the Harvard system of referencing (see p. 269) before you start collecting material. Then you can be sure to record all the necessary bibliographic details as you identify the books and papers. This will save you much time. As I have discovered to my cost it can take hours, after you have finished writing the dissertation, to track down the missing details (year of publication, page numbers for quotations) of material you have cited but that you forgot to record properly. This is time you can ill afford when you are struggling to get the dissertation finished by the deadline. It is much easier to be conscientious about the detail from the start.

● ● ● ● Mapping and describing the literature

In most cases the literature research identifies a lot of material – probably more than can be sensibly dealt with in a Master's dissertation. So the next step in conducting a literature review is to map out and identify the key works and material in the literature. This exercise has two purposes. It is necessary for you to show the person who marks your dissertation that you are aware of the breadth of literature relating to your topic. But it is also necessary, for your sanity, as well as to meet the marker's expectations, to show that you can prioritise the literature and identify the key works, theories or concepts that will be of value in the conduct of your project.

Describing the literature

Describing and mapping the literature relevant to your research project is a step-by-step process that moves from the general to the specific. It is an editing process.

1. Prepare a 'map' showing the location of all the appropriate literatures

The first step involves identifying the different fields of literature that may be appropriate to the study without, at this stage, looking at any of it in detail. By literature I mean a collection of books and papers that deal with the same issues and that respond to each other in the developing debates about a topic. It follows from this definition that there will be many literatures rather than one solitary and unified literature. But it is up to you to draw the boundaries between them. This can be done by skimming through textbooks and following up the references they give, and by dipping into the journal literature via the abstracts in the bibliographic databases.

Figure 2.1 shows a 'map' of the literatures that I thought were relevant when I was planning some research into the fates and attitudes of the survivors of downsizing. The main theme of the dissertation is shown in the middle of the map in bold font. There are a number of key researchers who have written research papers specifically on the subject. There is also a large literature, mostly in journals, that focuses on downsizing as a strategy and on its financial consequences for companies. This literature suggests that the demoralisation of survivors may be a contributory factor to the poor performance of organisations post-downsizing. This link makes the downsizing literature relevant to the project. The literature on redundancy concentrates on the managerial processes involved in choosing people for redundancy. The organisational justice literature assesses such processes and evaluates them for fairness. As it is likely that people's judgements about the fairness of redundancy processes will be a factor in their reactions to it, this literature is also relevant. The literature on emotion in organisation is not directly relevant to downsizing; but because downsizing is an emotional issue there may be some insights from the literature that will be helpful in the study. Finally, in psychology there is a well- established literature on people's reactions to trauma. It suggests a sequence of reactions beginning with disbelief, moving through shock and anger and culminating with readjustment. As being a survivor of downsizing may be as much a trauma as being a victim of it, this literature might provide some helpful frameworks.

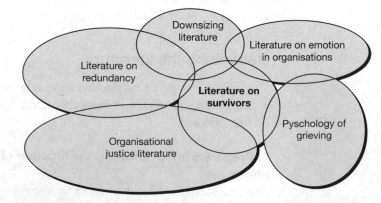

Figure 2.1 Mapping the literature

In the literature review it is important to identify the major literatures relevant to a project, without going into detail, and to explain why they might be significant. The important skill at this stage is to be able to condense or précis large volumes of literature so that the essential views or arguments they contain can be presented in a small number of words.

2. Present an argument about which literatures you are going to concentrate on

Normally the map of the literatures will contain more fields than can be managed in the literature review. It is important to reduce it to two or three. In the first step of the literature review, credit may be scored for showing an awareness of the broad scope of the literature. In this phase credit may gained by choosing the key literatures that will be helpful to the particular study being conducted. In the example of the 'survivors of downsizing study', I chose the literature on survival and the psychology of grieving and emotion in organisation as the key ones for the study I wished to do. The choice of literature will reflect the angle or perspective you wish to take on a topic.

3. Provide an overview of the chosen literature

At this stage it is necessary to give a more detailed description of the literature chosen. When you come to write up this chapter, the overview will provide the bulk of the material. It is important to think carefully about how you will structure it. The way not to structure an account of the literature is to work through a list of works one at a time. Exhibit 2.3, as a caricature, shows how not to do it.

Reading an annotated list such as that shown in Exhibit 2.3 is very boring, especially as the first sentence of each paragraph has exactly the

---

Exhibit 2.3

How not to write a literature review

Wood (1965) wrote an article in the *Journal of Panopticon Studies* that argued that the metaphor of the panopticon was very important. The article is hard to read and uses big words.

Smith (1966) wrote a book called *Jeremy Bentham's Lessons for Modern Managers*. This is a very enjoyable read and contains many practical lessons for managers. He claims that the panopticon would be a good basis for modern office layout planning.

Jones (1967) in an article for the *Bored Accountant* magazine mentions the panopticon.

Etc. ad nauseam (i.e. until you feel sick).

same structure. The citations technically correct but padded out. Do we really need to have the title of the work or the magazine spelt out in the text? The writer telling us whether they enjoyed a work does not constitute a critique, although it may be a criticism. But most importantly, there is no account given of the ideas, theories and material that are presented in the works cited.

Your account of the literature should be structured thematically. You should draw out of the works you are using the main themes, questions or issues that are discussed. These should become the sub-headings within the chapter. Under each sub-heading it is necessary to give an account of the relevant theories and the evidence provided in support of them. The discussion should be comparative, weighing one writer's views and evidence against that presented by others. Similarities and differences should be identified and their significance, if any, explained. One way of thematically structuring an account of a literature is shown below:

1. Identify the main 'camps', 'waves', 'schools', ideological stances or positions.

   There are always arguments and debates within a field of literature. It is necessary to describe the nature of these arguments. Identify the dominant or loudest voices in the debates.

2. Compare and contrast them.

   Decide the depth of the disagreement between the parties and their arguments. Sometimes the differences are great and significant. On other occasions the differences are trivial to all except those involved in the argument.

3. Evaluate their strengths and weaknesses.

   If the differences are significant, decide which side of the argument you believe to be stronger.

Literature reviews can often become detached from the project they are in support of. The discussion of theories and authors may develop its own momentum, and no links are made to the research questions that the dissertation is seeking to answer. The way to overcome this is to state the relevance of each piece of theory to the topic of the dissertation by using sentences similar to the following:

- Mintzberg's theory of structure in fives provides a means of analysing the organisational changes that are the subject of this dissertation.
- … this quotation mirrors the situation that has motivated the research project.
- Hamel and Prahalad's work identifies a number of factors that should be considered when researching ….
- An insight into employees' responses to downsizing in my case study organisations can be gained from Broeckner's work on ….
- Socio-technical theory integrates the two key aspects of this study into …

It is important to follow up these statements with an account of their significance for your project. There is nothing more frustrating to the reader than to be informed that something is 'critical' and then left without an explanation why.

If you cannot think of a way in which a piece of theory or literature aids your thinking and research into your topic, then it is likely you need not include it. A dissertation is not a place to display your encyclopaedic knowledge of a topic, unless it is relevant to your theme.

4. Provide an argument to explain and justify the short list of theories, concepts, frameworks or techniques that you have chosen for use in your project

By this stage a small part of the literature will have been identified that will be useful to the project. It may be down to a handful of concepts, theories and arguments. These will provide basic working materials for the project. At this stage the literature review merges into the process of developing a conceptual framework that will be considered in the next chapter.

5. Provide a critical account of the chosen concepts, theories or arguments

This is a detailed review of particular theories designed to test their fitness of purpose for use in the project.

One student was researching the introduction of teamworking at his place of work. This sentence could be found in his draft literature review chapter:

> Dunphy and Bryant (1996), for example, identify three forms of team, each of which is most suited to the pursuit of a particular aspect of performance. While simple, multi-skilled teams are thus most likely to impact most heavily on an organisation's costs, self-managed teams will have their main effects on value, and self-led teams on innovation.

At face value it appears that this piece of theory might be very helpful in understanding the introduction of teamworking into a particular organisation. It would allow questions to be asked such as whether the organisation had chosen the most appropriate form of teamworking for introduction. However, this sentence was all that was said; and it was inadequate.

A more critical and extensive account needed to be given (assuming that the theory was going to be helpful) by answering some of the following questions:

- How were the three types of teams defined? In particular, what is the difference between self-led and self-managed teams? At first glance these last two seem similar.
- How does this three-fold analysis of team types differ from other writers' classifications?

- Is the claim that each type of team delivers a different strategic outcome (cost reduction, value and innovation) based on sound research?
- How well supported is it by other researchers and writers?
- Are these claims logically and consistently argued for in the work?
- How useful might this theory be to the student's own project?

The best literature reviews are those where themes and ideas are taken from the literature, evaluated, and then woven into a coherent argument about the subject matter of the dissertation.

There are two main forms of criticism: forensic analysis and radical critique. The techniques for doing a forensic critique are described next, and the nature of a radical critique is dealt with in the final part of this chapter.

Forensic critique

The term 'forensic critique' has been invented for this chapter. One of the definitions of forensic is pertaining to public debate. This is relevant to the evaluation of literature because evaluation is a contribution to a public debate on arguments and theories that writers have placed in the public domain. But forensic also has an emerging definition, based on the work of forensic science, which means a minute, detailed and logical examination of evidence. This definition is also relevant to doing a literature review. Once you have identified the key concepts, theories and arguments that you will use in your research, it is important to put them under scrutiny before relying on them. So, in this section, forensic critique means the process of testing academic ideas to assess their usefulness.

There are two ways of tackling a forensic critique. The first is to identify the key arguments in a piece of work and to evaluate the soundness of the logic they utilise. The second is to scour the piece for examples of weak argumentation. Both approaches will be considered in turn.

Soundness of arguments

Books and articles contain many things: accounts, descriptions, summaries, instructions, polemics and so on. The most important item, however, is the arguments they contain. When a book or article is evaluated the main arguments it presents have to be dissected out from the bulk of the text and a judgement made about their soundness and robustness.

All arguments have three components. These can help you recognise when, in a text, an argument and not an assertion or an assumption is being presented:

- **Premises** – these are assumptions or claims that something is true or is a 'fact'. Most arguments are based on several premises, but they can be founded on one only.

- **Inference words** – these are the indicators that the writer is about to draw a logical inference or conclusion from the premises presented. Examples are 'thus', 'therefore', 'because', 'implies', 'hence', 'it follows that', 'so', 'then' and 'consequently'.
- **Conclusions** – a conclusion is an arguable statement. It is either a statement about the relationship between the premises or it is an inference about the likely consequences given the circumstances and the premises.

It should be possible, using this threefold classification and by looking for the inference words, to identify and summarise the main arguments presented in a book or an article. It may even be possible to lay out the arguments as a series of flow charts.

Judging the strength of an argument is a two-pronged activity:

- Assessing the truthfulness of the premises.

  In books and articles, the truthfulness, or validity, of a premise may be supported by research evidence. If this is so, then it is necessary to judge whether the research methods have been sensibly chosen and competently applied.

And:

- Assessing the logical strength of the conclusions drawn from them. When considering the logical strength of an argument, it is likely that conclusions that are drawn deductively will be stronger than those drawn inductively. These terms need definition.

Deduction is when a conclusion is drawn that necessarily follows in logic from the premises that are stated. So a deduction does not depend on observation or experience; it is simply a matter of logic. So, assuming the premises are true, the following is an example of a logically strong piece of deduction.

> Premise 1 – the selection panel thought Jane was a better candidate for the job than John.
> Premise 2 – the selection panel thought John a better candidate for the job than Mark.
> Conclusion, by deduction – Jane must be a better candidate for the job than Mark.

If you are evaluating a piece of theoretical writing, then many of the conclusions drawn will be based on such logic. The question to be asked is whether the logic is true.

'Deduction' is a troublesome word. It has at least two meanings. In the analysis of arguments it has the meaning given here; that is, arriving at a conclusion based on logic and not on experimentation or experience. It follows (an inference phrase) that there can be no doubt about a deduced conclusion. A deduction is certain as long as the premises are true and the world is rational.[2] However, deduction is also defined as making a specific inference from a general law. This definition does not hold in this instance. In arguments, deduction can proceed from the general to the particular, from particular to particular (as in the example above) or from general to general (Hart 1998: 82).

Induction is when a conclusion is drawn from past experience or experimentation. The assumption is made that because things have always been so, then that is how they will be in the future. The strength of inductive arguments is often weaker than that of deductions. However, the more supporting evidence there is, the stronger the probability that the inference is true. Deductions are certainties but inductive conclusions are probabilities. The trick is to make sure that the balance of probabilities is favourable. Consider the following example:

> Premise 1 – Companies that have the ISO 9000 certification have in the past made better supply chain partners than those that have not.
> Premise 2 – Companies that have been selected using the 'selecting a supply chain partner software' prove to be better collaborative partners nine times out of ten.
> Premise 3 – in the past small companies have made better supply chain partners than large ones.
> Premise 4 – Skegmouth Logistics Co. has ISO 9000, has been accepted by the software and is a small company.
> Conclusion, inferred by induction – Skegmouth Logistics Co. would likely make a good supply chain partner.

When inductive arguments have been identified in a piece of writing, it is important to assess whether the conclusion is based more on wishful thinking than on a carefully judged balance of probabilities.

Evaluating arguments

Another way of judging the strength of arguments is to see whether the authors have made any of a number of well-known logical errors. What follows is a list of the most common flaws in argument, based largely on Thouless (1968) and Warburton (1996).

1. The use of emotionally toned words

'The standards of modern examinations have woefully declined. They fail *hopelessly* to prepare students for work in modern organisations. They

---

[2] The world is not always logical. In experiments on people's choices it is not uncommon for people to think, using the example given, that Jane is better than John and that John is better than Mark but also to think that Mark is better than Jane (Wright 1984: 16; Lages *et al.*, 1999).

Exercise 2.1

Reviewing an article

Visit the library or a bibliographic database and choose an article that interests you from a peer-reviewed journal. Read the article and draft a critical review of it. Use the following questions (based on Hughes 1992) as guidelines:

- Identify the main arguments in the paper.
  - What is the main point of the arguments?
  - Identify the 'inference indicators', the words such as 'therefore' that indicate that a conclusion is being drawn from the evidence presented.
  - Assess the context for the argument.
- Identify the premises from which the conclusions are drawn.
  - Locate the premises in the text.
- Check the acceptability of these premises.
  - Are they well supported by evidence?
  - Are they well supported by citations from the literature?
  - Are you convinced they are true?
- Check the logical strength of the conclusions drawn from the premises.
  - Are the conclusions logically based on the premises?
  - How strong are the conclusions?
- Look for counter-arguments.
  - Could the premises support a counter conclusion?

cripple a child's chances of later career success.' Such arguments use a form of emotional blackmail. Who after all would wish to *cripple a child's chances in life*? The argument also rehashes a much used cliché in management: that if things are not modern, then they are bad. It is particularly tempting to use such arguments in the early years of a new millennium – 'preparing ourselves for the challenges of the new millennium' and so on.

2. Making a statement in which all is implied but some is true

In a debate in some parts of Scotland during the early years of the past century, about whether to continue the prohibition of alcohol on Sundays, a poster proclaimed that people should vote against prohibition because any loss of liberty meant slavery (Thouless 1968: 24). This statement is only true if all liberty is lost. The loss of only some liberty (to drink a pint of beer on a Sunday) is not the same as slavery.

3. Proof by selected instances

Where you think someone has chosen only those cases, from all those available to them, that make their point.

4. Challenging an opponent's point by extension or contradiction

In an argument over the relative merits of markets and bureaucracies in delivering public services, a person who believes that there are some services that are best delivered by private sector organisations is drawn into extending their argument into, first, that most services are best delivered so, and, second, that all services are best delivered so. Extended positions are always vulnerable and can be easily demolished with a few well-chosen facts.

5. Proof by inconsequent argument

You make a statement in support of a proposition that is not logically related to it but at first glance looks as if it might be.

> This can often be ensured by making the supporting statement a reference to a learned theory of which one's opponent will be afraid to confess his [sic] ignorance, or at any rate, making the supporting statement in a manner so obscure that one's opponent fears that it would show shameful ignorance if he confessed that he did not see the connection.   (Thouless 1968: 43)

Fairbairn and Winch (1996: 185) refer to this ploy as crafty conflation. The following statement provides an example. 'Organizations that fail to modernize will not survive in the twenty-first century. The acceptance of flexible career patterns and of the loss of careers for life is consequentially essential for organizational survival.' This argument conflates the idea of modernisation and the acceptance of career flexibility. It is not necessarily the case that the latter is necessary to achieve the former. It may or may not be; but the point is worthy of discussion.

6. The argument that we should not make efforts against X, which is admittedly evil, because there is a worse evil, Y, against which our efforts should be directed

In the debate about the extradition of General Pinochet from the United Kingdom in 1998, one of the arguments against extradition was that Pinochet was a lesser tyrant than the Chinese leadership and that he should not be tried for crimes against humanity if the Chinese leadership was not. A failure to deal with one wrong is no reason for not acting against another.

7. The recommendation of a position because it is a mean between two extremes

There may be occasions when the mean is golden, but it rather depends on the choice of the two extremes

8. The use of logically unsound argument

There are many forms of illogicality. Here is just one. The fact of an association between two things does not prove a causal or logical relationship.

It may be that there is a statistical relationship between the number of 'quality stations' in a workplace (with their progress charts, quality awards and photos of successful quality circles) and high output. But the association does not prove that one causes the other or, if it does, which way round the causal chain works. Do the workstations cause the staff to be more highly motivated or does the fact that people are successful lead them to treasure their quality stations?

9. Begging the question

One can prove that all swans are white by refusing to accept that black swans are truly swans.

10. Failing to distinguish factual statements from opinion

The notion of facts is a little difficult to accept if you are of a postmodern persuasion. Nevertheless it should still be possible to separate those things that are generally accepted as if they were true, and for which some research evidence can be presented, and personal opinion. In management research this error occurs when people do not distinguish between what they have discovered about a problem and their beliefs about how it can be solved, as in 'my research shows that the implementation of staff empowerment will enable the organisation to become a world-class business'.

11. Tautology

A tautology is saying the same thing twice. Stylistically it involves redundant words ('LloydsTSB Bank'). By extension a tautological argument is one in which a thing is said twice but in such a way as to make it appear that a logical deduction is being made, as in 'The increased pace of change means that things are moving faster.'

12. Inferring what should be from what the arguer thinks ought to be and assuming that something is right because it is commonly done or is useful

The fact that lots of organisations are doing 360-degree appraisals does not necessarily mean they are a good thing. Equally the author's belief that a proposition will be of practical benefit does not mean that it is right or should be commended.

13. Changing the meaning of a term during the argument

Thouless (1968: 77) gives the following example. Crowds exhibit cruelty, unintelligence and irresponsibility. Democratic government is rule by the crowd. Therefore, democratic government is cruel, unintelligent and irresponsible. This argument involves a subtle change in the definition of the word 'crowd'.

14. The use of the fact of a continuity between two things to throw doubt on the real difference between them

Using the practical difficulty of determining where precisely, in terms of number of staff or amount of turnover, to draw the distinction between large and small organisations to suggest that the distinction is not a useful one.

15. Disguising a lack of clear thought by the extensive use of jargon

Too much use of business and professional jargon, or of obscure and lengthy words, raises suspicions that the author is seeking to disguise their confusion and lack of clear thought.

16. The appeal to mere authority

This false type of argument is that a well-established writer in the field has said x and so it must be true. This should not be seen as a licence not to cite authors in your dissertation. The error is when an author is cited as a lazy substitute for making a case or presenting an argument.

17. Argument by imperfect analogy

'The keen edge of intellect will be blunted by too frequent use.' This might be a tempting maxim for a hard-pressed MBA student. However, most intellects are honed, not blunted, by use. Too frequent a resort to argument by analogy can lead to a hermetic paranoia in which everything is seen as part of a vast and secret conspiracy. Read Umberto Eco's (1989) novel *Foucault's Pendulum* for an insight into the places such thinking can lead.

18. *Ad hominem* arguments

Attacking the arguer and not the arguments. This is normally resorted to when a critic can find no weak points in an argument and so argues that the writer is a bad person and that for this reason their arguments should be discounted. In 2001 and 2002, for example, there was a correspondence in a literary journal about Foucault (see p. 86). The debate was started by Tallis (2001) and continued by Hargreaves (2002) and Sennett (2001) amongst others. Foucault was accused of deliberately infecting his partners with AIDS. It was also alleged that he did not believe in objective truth. This led to an implication that the latter justified the former. In such debates, arguments about a person's theories and arguments become confused with arguments about the morality of the person.

19. The use of persuaders

Fairbairn and Winch (1996: 182) describe these as 'words and phrases that are put into an assertion illicitly to persuade the reader to accept what is said by other than rational means'. For example, 'Surely all accountants must realise that their job is one of the most important in the country' or 'It is the exception that proves the rule.'

There are some criticisms commonly made of books and articles that are not fair. One is 'death by a thousand snips'. This is done by accumulating a large number of petty errors, an author's name misspelt here, a date wrong by one year there and so on. The overall effect is to cast doubt on the author's arguments without actually challenging them. It is a form of *ad hominem* criticism because it is challenging the author's abilities rather than their arguments. Another unfair criticism is to claim that the themes the author has chosen to focus on are the wrong ones. This is tantamount to saying the author should have written a different book or article to the one they chose to write.

Exercise 2.2

Evaluating arguments

Study the argument made in the extract from my book on public sector management (Fisher 1998) shown below, entitled 'On heaps'.

1. Identify the key points in the argument.
2. Write a précis of the piece in less than 200 words. The piece is 1,438 words long.
3. Using the list of flaws in arguments given above, identify as many examples of suspect or improper forms of argument as you can.

Do bear in mind that we all use weak arguments, sometimes out of laziness, sometimes because we have not spotted the flaw and are convinced by the arguments, and sometimes deliberately as a way of ensuring we win, the current round at least, of an argument. This situation ensures that flawed argument spotting is an easy target and it can lead to:

> a cast of mind in the reader such that he looked only for faults, ambiguities and omissions, in order to show the writer to be muddled and incompetent. We recommend that you avoid this approach in your own writing. Scholarship is not, or at least should not be, a form of blood sport. The first business of the reader is to try and understand what is going on in a passage, *then* to subject it to measured evaluation.
>
> (Fairbairn and Winch 1996: 208)

So, approach this exercise as a means of testing your own abilities rather than as a criticism of the passage's author.

ON HEAPS

Academic books can be written in two ways, they are either holes or heaps. When a hole is dug all the earth has to be removed and, in the case of specialised holes such as archaeologists' trenches, the spoil is carefully sieved and the revealed strata minutely surveyed. Similarly when a book of the hole type is written the author sifts and sorts all the material drawn from his or her academic excavations. The literature dug up is finely delineated and the past history of the field of study is revealed. This type of book has a great density of reference and citation to other authorities on the subject as the writers trace through the arguments and counter-arguments that define the academic development of their topic.

Heaps however are made by walking all over the field, picking up objects that look interesting or exotic and throwing them on to a pile. The author of a book of the heap type therefore is constantly on the look out for elegant arguments and exotic and eclectic examples and illustrations. Nennius, the author of a ninth-century *History of the Britons*, which is one of the few sources for the history of the Dark Ages, scoured monastery libraries for old manuscripts. He wrote unapologetically as the first sentence of his collection, '*Coacervarvi omne quod inveni*' (Myres 1986: 16) which loosely translates as 'I have made a heap of everything I have found.' I have studied my chosen subject in a similar manner. Much rummaging through the newspapers, academic and professional journals, and through my own experiences, was necessary in the search for interesting nuggets. Nennius at least had the excuse that, if he had not made his heap, our knowledge of British history in the Dark Ages would have been slighter than it is. Heap making is less excusable in the late twentieth century when we are in danger of suffocating under the mountains of information and data available to us. I justify the use of a heap-making method by claiming that heaps are intrinsically more fascinating than holes because they have a denser concentration of meaning and a wider range of content.

The writer of a heap book is a collector, an antiquarian. A collection is defined by the similarities between its elements. Often the content of the collection is based on little more than the idiosyncratic interests of the collector. If you visit Sir John Soane's Museum in London you will see crammed into a town house a heap of Canaletto and Hogarth pictures, cameos, medals, Etruscan vases, gargoyles, architectural capitals, a skeleton and an ancient Egyptian sarcophagus. The linking theme of the collection is simply that all the objects interested John Soane. Heap books, which also show a diversity of content, can be identified by their eclectic indexes. The subject index to Watson's (1994) book on management contains the following items under 'H': Hawthorne experiments; heaven; hedgehogs; Hill, Benny; human nature; humour and hymn sheets. The book you are now reading includes references, *inter alia*, to potholing, the Hegelian dialectic, the regulation of public utilities, Dante's *Inferno*, school dinners, critical illness insurance, the history of the British Raj in India, public sector policy making and the case of the heart patient who smoked.

Heaps can be fascinating but they are meaningless without a strong linking theme that brings together all the disparate parts. Unfortunately heap makers often get bored when they arrive at this part of collection building. John Aubrey was an antiquarian collector who, in pursuit of his obsession, made a vast heap of biographies of his contemporaries in the seventeenth century. But on his own admission the heap was disorganised and chaotic because he 'wanted the patience to go through [the] Knotty Studies' (Lawson Dick 1972: 18) necessary to put the heap into order. The classical teachers of rhetoric stressed the importance of putting materials and collections into order.

So in speaking however abundant the matter may be, it will merely form a confused heap unless arrangement is employed to reduce it to order and give it connexion and firmness of structure.

(Quintillian 1986: 3)

If care is not taken however the order that is imposed on a heap may be based on similarity rather than on logical connection. Early renaissance thinkers, by way of illustration of the danger, believed that the bulbs of the orchis plant were a remedy for medical complaints of the testes because they looked like a pair of testicles (Eco 1992: 51). The hermetic idea of signatures and correspondences, which proposes that a similarity, of shape for example, between two things must mean that there is a deeper and functional relationship between them, is a very powerful one. It follows, from a hermetic style of argument, that if market principles are right for the economy at large (the macrocosm) then they must also be right for the public sector; and relations, say, between a doctor and patient (the microcosm) should be based on the same economic principles as the relationship between large multinational companies. But other approaches to the doctor:patient relationship emphasise differences rather than similarities. Commentators such as Smith and Morrissy (1994), who see the relationship between patients and doctors as a fiduciary one, in which economic considerations should play no part, objected when market devices such as indicative drugs budgets were introduced into general practice.

Heap makers often assume that, because all the items in their collection share at least one thing in common, there must be some greater significance to the similarities. The bigger the heap becomes the greater is the proof it provides of hermetic links. The assumption of correspondences can be detected in the large heap of organisations that have been privatised since the late 1980s (including British Steel, Amersham International, British Airways, the water companies, The Royal Ordnance factories, international airports and British Rail). They may have been similar in that they all had paying customers; but this disguises the many differences between them that needed to be taken into account when deciding whether and how they ought to have been privatised.

Exercise 2.2 *continued*

There are many other examples of argumentation by hermetic signature, or similarity, in the field of public sector management. The morphological resemblance between a school canteen and a greasy spoon café for example does not necessarily mean that they should be run on the same lines. It is possible to argue that the similarity between them is insignificant and misses the main issue, which is that school canteens are designed to meet school children's *needs* for nutritionally balanced meals whilst greasy spoon cafés are there to meet a *demand* for comforting stodge. I came across another example of this type of thinking when attending a seminar on quality in the provision of care for people with learning difficulties. The technique being discussed was PASS, programme analysis of service systems (Wolfensburger and Glynn 1975). The presenters were explaining a particular method, based on the use of photographs, for alerting care staff to the quality implications of their habitual working methods. They showed a picture of a room and invited the audience to say what it was used for. All agreed that it was a nursery for under five's. It was of course a day room for adults with learning difficulties, but the decoration of the room reflected the staff's unconscious view that their clients behaved as, and should be treated as, kids. In particular there were several posters on the wall showing chimps being naughty, throwing toilet rolls down the toilet pan and suchlike. The staff had put the posters up to 'make the place more cheerful'. The trainers' photographs were used to jolt staff into an awareness of the inappropriateness of their assumptions and behaviours for the task of creating a good environment for the clients. In other words they were pointing out that an apparent metaphorical or morphological similarity between the behaviour of the clients on the one hand and children and chimpanzees on the other was not a sound basis for planning the clients' care.

Unless care is taken the throwing together of materials in a heap can lead to uneconomic and misleading connections and conclusions being drawn. The danger is increased because, in writing this book, I have wandered across many academic fields in which I am not an expert. This book has been put together as a heap and the reader is warned to look out for errors that may have arisen from drawing conclusions from items, which, coincidentally, happen to be found contiguously in the pile. But I hope that the reader will find in this heap enough interesting things to include in their own collection of heuristics, examples and insights concerning public services.

(Fisher 1998: 23–25) Reproduced with the permission of Thomson Publishing Services

Suggested answers

1. The key arguments of the piece can be summarised as follows:
   Premise 1. Academic books are either of the hole or heap type.
   Premise 2. Heap-type books are disorganised and confused collections of materials.
   Inference. Heap-type books need to be organised into structured collections.

   This leads to a further argument:

   Premise 1. Heap-type books are collections of materials.
   Premise 2. Collections are mostly structured and classified according to the similarities between the objects and materials in the collections.
   Premise 3. Similarities can be mistakenly thought to imply logical links of cause and effect.
   Inference. Heap-type books will draw false connections between things that lead to mistakes and misunderstandings.

   That in turn leads to a final argument:

   Premise 1. Heap-type books can be misleading and dangerous.
   Premise 2. Heap-type books contain interesting and insightful materials.
   Inference. Heap-type books may be worthwhile but have to be read with care and caution.

   This is only one of several possible interpretations of the arguments in the piece.

Exercise 2.2 *continued*

2. The following is a précis of the piece. It contains 186 words.

> Academic books are composed of a heap of materials gathered together either from many places or from a careful excavation of a hole into a seam of material. The author of a heap book, such as this one, collects materials that interest him or her from a wide range of sources. This method makes heap books more interesting than books based on holes.
>
> Heaps can be fascinating but they are meaningless without a strong linking theme that brings together all their disparate parts. Heaps, or collections, are often structured according to the similarities between the objects contained in them. Similarities between things can be mistaken for causal links between things. For example, the similarity between public utilities, caused by them all having customers, does not necessarily mean that privatisation, which may work for some of them, would work for all of them.
>
> Unless care is taken, the collecting and classifying of heaps of materials in a book can lead to uneconomic and misleading conclusions being drawn. The insights that may come from a heap book have to be considered carefully lest they lead to dangerous conclusions.

3. Identification of weak arguments used in the piece:

Flaw 2 – making a statement in which all is implied but some is true:
It is implied that because in some cases similarity (particularly similarity of shape) is misleading as an organising principle, then all kinds of similarity are misleading. This is not necessarily so. It is further implied that hermetic similarity is the common organising principle of all heaps. There is no evidence given that this is so and it is admitted by implication that there may be other principles on which heaps can be classified.

Flaw 3 – proof by selected instances:
A number of cases are piled up privatisation, school dinners, services for adults with learning difficulties, to prove that connections of similarity are misleading and dangerous. There may be just as many examples that show argument by similarity to be sound and effective.

Flaw 5 – proof by inconsequent argument:
The orchis and testes example of argument by similarity is intended to raise a chuckle because it is nonsense. This can distract from the fact that this example may not be logically related to the consequent examples of privatisation and school dinners. Just because there is no similarity in the first case does not mean that there is not in the latter cases.

Flaw 8 – logically unsound argument:
It is argued that most heaps are organised according to the similarities of the material in the heap. It is further argued that this type of thinking can be dangerous and misleading. Nevertheless it is argued in the final paragraph that heaps are acceptable because they are interesting. This seems a dangerous inference given the weight of the arguments for the view that heaps are dangerous.

Flaw 16 – the appeal to mere authority:
There is a heavyweight use of authorities here, including ancient Roman ones such as Quintillian. Tony Watson's book is also quoted as an example of a heap book, thereby suggesting that such an approach to writing a book is acceptable. Generally there is a lot of name-dropping in the piece.

Flaw 17 – argument by imperfect analogy:
The key analogy is seeing academic work as being like archaeology. It is implied that those archaeologists who minutely excavate and stratify a trench on a dig are more systematic than those who walk the fields picking up shards of pottery and other finds. The analogy is incorrect because field-walking archaeology is not treasure hunting, since it can be done in a rigorous and systematic manner. The analogy does not fit the case being made about the writing the two types of books.

Exercise 2.2 *continued*

Flaw 19 – the use of persuaders:
In the seventh paragraph of the piece, the phrase 'it was of course a day room for' is intended to draw the reader into an awareness of the unacceptability of the stereotyping that was being reported.

The piece also suffers from a problem, identified in Chapter 6 as a common one amongst historians (one of whom the author of this piece clearly once was), of meandering down obscure byways that interest the author but are uninteresting to most readers.

● ● ● ● Radical critique

There is a managerialist mainstream in business, management and organisational studies that accepts the necessity of the capitalist system and concentrates on making it work effectively. The system, the mainstream writers would argue, is to the benefit of all and it is only necessary to focus on making small improvements. There is an alternative view that challenges the system itself. This critical perspective appears in several of the chapters in this guide. It appears as critical theory in Chapter 1 and as critical realism in Chapter 5. Even if you do not accept the generalised critique of modern society that this approach makes, it can provide an interesting perspective on management issues that can raise difficult questions for mainstream researchers.

The critical approach

Alistair Mutch

What do we mean by the word 'critical'? In one sense we would expect all academic work to be critical; that is, we should always be questioning our assumptions and approaches. This kind of questioning has been discussed in the previous section. However, the word has tended to be appropriated by those who would use it in a broader sense. This sense is of challenging the basic assumptions on which our social world is organised. It is also, to a greater or lesser extent, used to indicate a need for radical change in these basic principles.

The approach originally associated with this sense of the word is Marxism. (Indeed, one current, the 'Frankfurt School', attempted to appropriate not only the word 'critical' but also the word 'theory'. If you see the two together as Critical Theory you will know what is being attempted – and you will see the difference that capitalisation can make!) In this respect, Marxism can be seen as continuing the Enlightenment project. This was the powerful intellectual tradition that emerged in the late eighteenth century. It stressed the importance of Reason and Science (they were fond of capital letters too) over religion and tradition as ways of knowing the world. To this faith in the power of ideas to reveal the truth about the world Marx added a radical political dimension. We have become much more sceptical about notions of truth, and more sophisticated currents in modern Marxism have dropped notions such as 'false consciousness' (the idea that the only reason for the lack of radical change was people holding the 'wrong' ideas – for a discussion see Callinicos (1987) and p. 88 of this book). However, Marxism has lost what was once a dominant position in the 'critical' camp, with other voices now being heard.

Most important of these voices has been that of feminism. Reacting both to material social changes and to the failure of Marxism to address these changes, feminism has brought a new set of challenges, in this case to received gender roles. This has meant shifts in both the topics examined and the way in which they are examined. Again, there are many currents within feminism. Some strive for change within existing arrangements, arguing for the need to change organisations to release the talents of women (and make them better places for men). An example of a writer in this tradition who has had influence within the 'mainstream' is Rosabeth Moss Kanter. Others reject what they see as patriarchy and call for more fundamental change – Pollert (1996) has a useful overview. One impact of feminist writings has been to emphasise the importance of identity in current critical writing.

Identity is central in the intellectual tradition of postmodernism. This spurns what it calls 'grand narratives' such as Marxism (that is, in their terms, theories that purport to have 'all the answers'). Instead, it stresses the fragmentation of current life that is composed of a shifting kaleidoscope of fluid identities. An influential thinker has been the French social theorist Michel Foucault. His emphasis on power as a property of networks and relationships has been a strong influence on thinking in many areas, not least the field of management. It has led to a focus on the micro-politics of local situations and to a divorce between critical analysis and prescriptions for change. This has led to charges (from more traditional critical theorists, such as Marxists) of academic self-indulgence and a loss of relevance. For others, however, this is a realistic adjustment to the contemporary social world and a cause for celebration. What it does seem to produce is complex and difficult language and a tendency to agonised introspection. (For an attempt to reconcile these forms of critical thinking by direct application to management, see Alvesson and Wilmott 1996.) Other social theorists try to steer something of a middle way. Some of these, such as Giddens (lots of work, but see 1990 for a short introduction) and Castells (2000) have important things to say about the nature of the world of work, even if sometimes their detail fails to convince. Finally, the tradition known as Critical Realism (more appropriation! See p. 219) claims to be clearing the way for a more transparent use of concepts – Reed (1997) and Savage *et al.* (1992) provide some applications in the management field, although these are 'works in progress'.

What does all this mean for management researchers? It means that there is a rich body of resources upon which to draw. A little recognised aspect of management history is the way in which ideas that are now mainstream (in change management, for example) had their origins on the left (Cooke 1999). Alternatively, the challenging of basic assumptions can help, even if it ends up by confirming your belief in the soundness of those assumptions. Some of these areas, notably feminism, have had more direct impact on the management field. It is helpful to be aware of the nuances that lie behind the use of this little word 'critical', as you will come across it all the time in the academic literature. This simply reinforces the need for you to be sceptical and challenging in your use of such literature – in a word, to be critical!

Developing a radical critique

To summarise the above discussion: a radical critique is one that challenges assumptions and conventional ways of doing things. It normally does so from a moral stance based on perceptions of injustice; so, for instance, a radical critique could be Marxist (justice to the workers) or feminist (justice to women) or green (justice to Gaia) or based on an anti-globalisation position that would incorporate all of the preceeding. This section looks at how a radical critique of a managerial theme might be constructed using a loose Marxist perspective. Remember, radical critiques are not a necessary part of a literature review.

A (rather caricatured) view of the stages of argumentation followed in the laying out of a radical critique is presented here. The case of computer-isation of administrative and clerical work is used as an example to illustrate the process.

Stage I – identify a conventional position.
Take a conventional and standard argument that is used in the literature and in public debate. Waddington (1977: 16) created the acronym COWDUNG, which stands for 'the conventional wisdom of the dominant group' – OK, it does not quite work as an acronym but it defines the concept well. A few years ago, for example, it was held widely that the increasing use of computers in the fields of clerical and administrative work would make employees' lives more interesting by removing the drudgery from their work.

Stage 2 – problematise it.

Problematising the issue means revealing that the issue is more difficult than commonly thought and probably raises questions of values or ethics. Computerisation may make work more interesting, but management does not want information technology for this reason alone. Management also wants to improve efficiency and profits and this means making staff redundant as computers do more and more of the work. This process causes that which was straightforward to appear morally ambiguous.

Stage 3 – identify contradictions and negations.

Look for contradictions and negations within the process or issue being studied. A negation is a self-destructive feature of a process. Computers are meant to make life more interesting for staff by taking away the boring chores from their work. But computer software not only does sums and clerical chores – it can also make decisions by comparing particular situations against decision-making guidelines. Computers can remove decision making from people and so make their work less interesting and less responsible. Computerisation also disempowers staff by removing their discretion to amend procedures. Staff have to work in the ways required by the software. By enabling management to monitor their work rates, staff are put under an intense scrutiny that prevents them from being flexible in their work methods and rates (i.e. if staff are working on computers, then it is easy for management to see how many transactions they have processed in a shift). So, in summary, computerisation was meant to make employees' lives more interesting and ends up making them less so. This is a form of dialectical analysis that is discussed further on p. 225.

Stage 4 – spot the effects of false consciousness. (This is an optional stage.)

False consciousness may be out of fashion (see p. 86) but it is often a useful element in a radical critique. False consciousness arises when the opposite of what people want is happening but they do not realise it. It is a Marxist concept to describe the tendency of the proletariat to fail to recognise the nature of its interest. More generally it is any form of ideology or self-imagery that is held to be inappropriate to the real or objective situation of an actor. So, for example, imagine you have interviewed a number of clerical staff whose work has been computerised. To your surprise they tell you that they feel the process has made their work more interesting because they have learnt new skills. They have learnt how to use the new software, but they remain oblivious to the fact that the software is insidiously removing responsibility, self-control and higher-level skills from their jobs.

Stage 5 – end with an aporia.

Aporia means being in a state where everything is so complex and ambiguous that you are at a loss about what to do. The critique is ended with a view that something is wrong but that it is difficult to see what can be done about it, short of changing human nature and sensibility. Things, you argue, are so complicated that anyone who believes there can be a quick fix for the issue must be deluded. Here is a typical example taken from a paper that gives a critique of the idea of business ethics:

> The problem I find it impossible to address in the rest of the paper will be what options are left for a project like 'Business Ethics' if all the above are accepted. It would simply be inappropriate for me to tie up a paper like this at the end as if I really did have a magical solution to these problems. (Parker 1998: 35)

However, there is often a final claim that our increasing understanding of the complexity of things will enable humanity to become better. Parker ends his paper in such a way:

> Recognising the paradoxes within 'Ethics' and 'Business Ethics' is one way to stop these words from having so much hold on us. Perhaps we can begin to develop ways of expressing our dreams and nightmares that do not fall back into the *agon* so easily. Parker (1998: 35)

It may not be easy to see quite what this means (the use of the word 'agon' makes it difficult – it means the endless arguments between different and incomparable ways of viewing a topic), but as an ending it sounds upbeat – in an ambiguous sort of a way.

Stage 6 – appropriate references and citations.

Try to make references to Michel Foucault and/or Jürgen Habermas in the text. Surprisingly, references to Jeremy Bentham, the eighteenth-century utilitarian philosopher, and his notion of the panoptican, published in 1791 but more accessible in Božovič (1995), are also well received. The panopticon was a design for a circular prison. The cells were to be set around the circumference of the building and at the centre there was to be a watchtower. This design would allow a warder to observe all the prisoners with ease. An additional element in the design was a series of baffles and blinds. These meant that the warder could see the prisoners but the prisoners could not be sure whether they were being observed. The metaphor of the panopticon works well in the case of information technology in offices. When an employee is working at a computer terminal that is networked to others in the organisation, it is technically possible for the management to monitor the employee's work. The employee knows that they may be being monitored, but they can never be sure whether they are. The metaphor works even better with roadside speed cameras, which reduce average speeds because drivers do not know whether the box really does contain a camera. So they proceed on the basis that it might.

The following citation of Foucault, citing Bentham, achieves a double whammy effect: 'The contemporary popularity of Foucault's version of the panopticon seems to illustrate something rather profound' (Parker 1998: 31).

Exhibit 2.4

Bentham's panopticon

Source: Bentham Papers 115/44, University College London. Image reproduced by courtesy of University College Library, London

The panopticon is discussed in Foucault (1991). An interesting introduction to Habermas is provided by Pusey (1993). Habermas's theory of speech acts is helpful when forming radical critiques.

The six stages of radical critique are simply a teaching aid. No one would follow such a mechanistic process in their writing. Nevertheless these different aspects can be found in academic papers such as Parker (1998). If you have the time and inclination, you might want to locate the six stages in his article.

Radical critique has a jargon and a style of expression of its own. This can be difficult for the novice to penetrate, and it would take much practice to acquire it. Nevertheless a lack of linguistic pretension should not prevent you from trying this type of analysis, especially as it often carries a ring of truth. You may test this out for yourself by doing Exercise 2.3.

If you find it too difficult to write a radical critique there is a web site, http://www.csse.monash.edu.au/other/postmodern.html that produces randomly generated critical essays. Luckily it produces a new essay every time you click on the site, and the reader has no control over the topic of the essay, otherwise you might be tempted to use this facility.

Some people critique critical theory. The most recent cause célèbre was an article written by Alan Sokal (Sokal and Bricmont 1999). In the paper he parodied the writing style of critical thinkers and deliberately introduced scientific misconceptions and mathematical blunders. This did not prevent the paper from being accepted and published in a well-respected academic journal. If you wish to know more about the debate that the publication of the article started, visit http://www.physics.nyu.edu/faculty/sokal/.

Exercise 2.3

Make a radical critique

1. Choose a fashionable concept or package within your field of management, e.g.
   - relationship marketing
   - enterprise resource planning (ERP)
   - Investors in People (IiP)
   - quality assurance.
2. Construct an outline radical critique of it.

Suggested answer

I will use Investors in People as an example. I am not necessarily arguing that the following radical critique is true, but it might be.

1. The conventional view of IiP is that it is a worthwhile attempt to encourage organisations to invest more in the training and development of their staff and to set up performance management systems that focus those skills, and staff's inventive-

Exercise 2.3 *continued*

ness and commitment, towards the achievement of organisational goals. IiP is a set of standards that may be used to assess whether an organisation has achieved these objectives. So important is this purpose that the government set targets for the percentage of organisations that should be accredited against the standard.

2. But this all assumes that employees and the organisation share the same goals. If they do not, then IiP might just be a means of silencing dissenting views in the organisation and, through such devices as appraisal interviews, bring their activities under closer managerial scrutiny. Whether IiP is actually beneficial for employees becomes an issue.

3. There are a number of ways in which the implementation of IiP might contradict its formal aims:

   (a) Organisations were originally assessed for IiP against a list of items in a checklist. This led to a mindset in which gaining IiP became a bureaucratic hurdle in which getting ticks in boxes was more important than delivering better training and development and engaging employees in developing the organisation. To be fair to the IiP programme, an attempt was made to make the assessment process less bureaucratic.

   (b) Government pushed quite hard for organisations, especially public sector organisations, to adopt the standard. There was a possibility that organisations sought it because they felt obliged to fly the IiP flag and put the logo on their letterhead and not because they were committed to investing in their people.

   (c) All the effort put into gaining IiP accreditation may divert an organisation's attention from providing the training and development that investment in people demands. While HRD staff are focused on IiP preparations, they cannot be doing training.

4. However, if you talk to people in organisations they mostly say that IiP is a good thing. This may be because they do not see the threat to their best interests or, in the case of many managers, it may be that they do not think highly of IiP but feel that they must toe the party line that it is a good thing.

5. We might conclude that IiP exhibits the classic dysfunctions of bureaucracy whereby the means – the checklists and the logos – become more important then the ends – developing people and organisations. This syndrome might be thought unavoidable and therefore it is hard to know what to do to prevent the problem.

6. We could certainly use the panopticon as a metaphor for IiP and thereby find an excuse for quoting Bentham and Foucault.

Summary

Do

- identify and discuss key and landmark studies – include as much up-to-date material as possible
- get the details right
- try to be reflexive – examine your own bias and make it known
- critically evaluate the material and show your analyses
- use extracts, illustrations and examples to justify your arguments
- be analytical, critical and evaluative in your review
- make it interesting.

Don't

- omit classic works or discuss core ideas without reference
- discuss outdated or rubbish stuff, or only old material
- use concepts to impress or without definition
- produce a list of items, even if annotated: a list is not a review
- accept anything at face value or believe everything that is written
- only produce a description of the content of what you have read
- drown in information. (Based on Hart 1998: 219.)

Suggested reading

The best book on the topics covered in this chapter is Hart (1998). Fairbairn and Winch (1996) are also useful on the subject of literature and critical evaluation. Warburton (1996) is good on logical traps.

References

Alvesson, M. and Willmott, H. (1996) *Making Sense of Management: A Critical Introduction*, London: Sage.

Božovič, M. (ed.) (1995) *The Panoptican Writings: Jeremy Bentham*, London: Verso.

Callinicos, A. (1987) *Making History*, Cambridge: Polity.

Castells, M. (2000) *The Rise of Network Society*, Oxford: Blackwell.

Cooke, B (1999) 'Writing the left out of management theory: the historiography of the management of change', *Organization*, Vol. 6, No. 1, 81–105.

Eco, U. (1989) *Foucault's Pendulum*, trans. W. Weaver, London: Secker & Warburg.

Eco, U. with Rorty, R., Culler, J., Brooke-Rose, C. and Collini, S. (eds) (1992) *Interpretation and Overinterpretation*, Cambridge: Cambridge University Press.

Fairbairn, G. J. and Winch, C. (1996) *Reading, Writing and Reasoning: A Guide for Students*, 2nd Edn, Buckingham: Open University Press.

Fisher, C. M. (1998) *Resource Allocation in the Public Sector: Values, Priorities and Markets in the Management of Public Services*, London: Routledge.

Foucault, M. (1991) *Discipline and Punish: The Birth of the Prison*, trans. A. Sheridan, London: Penguin.

Giddens, A. (1990) *The Consequences of Modernity*, Cambridge: Polity.

Hargreaves, J. (2002) Letter to the editor, *Times Literary Supplement*, 1 January.

Hart, C. (1998) *Doing a Literature Review: Releasing the Social Science Research Imagination*, London: Sage.

Hughes, W. (1992) *Critical Thinking*, Peterborough, Ontario: Broadview Press.

Lages, M., Gigerenzer, G. and Hoffrage, U. (1999) *Intransitivity of Fast and Frugal Heuristics*, Working Paper in Economics. Available online at: http://netec.mcc.ac.uk/BibEc [accessed 6 July 2001].

Lawson Dick, O. (ed.) (1972) *Aubrey's Brief Lives*, Harmondsworth: Penguin Books.

Myres, J. N. L. (1986) *The English Settlements*, Oxford: Oxford University Press.

Parker, M. (1998) 'Business ethics and social theory: postmodernizing the ethical', *British Journal of Management*, Vol. 9, September, 27–36.

Pollert, A. (1996) 'Gender and class revisited; or, the poverty of "patriarchy"', *Sociology*, Vol. 30, No. 4, 639–659.

Pusey, M. (1993) *Jürgen Habermas*, London: Routledge.

Quintillian (1986) *The Institutes of Oratory*, Vol. 3, trans. H. E. Butler, Cambridge, MA and London: Harvard University Press and William Heinemann.

Reed, M. (1997) 'In praise of duality and dualism: rethinking agency and structure in organizational analysis', *Organization Studies*, Vol. 18, No. 1, 21–42.

Savage, M., Barlow, J., Dickens, P. and Fielding, T. (1992) *Property, Bureaucracy and Culture: Middle-class Formation in Contemporary Britain*, London: Routledge.

Sennett, R. (2001) Letter to the editor, *Times Literary Supplement*, 28 December.

Smith, L. F. P. and Morrissy, J. R. (1994) 'Ethical dilemmas for general practitioners under the UK new contract', *Journal of Medical Ethics*, Vol. 20, No. 3, 175–180.

Sokal, A. and Bricmont, J. (1999) *Fashionable Nonsense: Postmodern Intellectuals' Abuse of Science*, New York: Picador.

Tallis, R. (2001) 'The truth about lying: a review of *The Liar's Tale: A History of Falsehood* by J. Campbell', *Times Literary Supplement*, 21 December.

Thouless, R. H. (1968) *Straight and Crooked Thinking*, London: The English Universities' Press Ltd.

Waddington, C. H. (1977) *Tools for Thought*, St Albans: Paladin.

Warburton, N. (1996) *Thinking from A to Z*, London: Routledge.

Watson, T. J. (1994) *In Search of Management: Culture, Chaos and Control in Managerial Work*, London: Routledge.

Wolfensburger, W. and Glynn, L. (1975) *Program Analysis of Service Systems*, Toronto: NIMR.

Wright, G. (1984) *Behavioural Decision Theory: An Introduction*, Harmondsworth: Penguin.

Chapter 3 ●●●● ●

Concepts, conceptual frameworks and theories

Contents

● ● ● ● Introduction

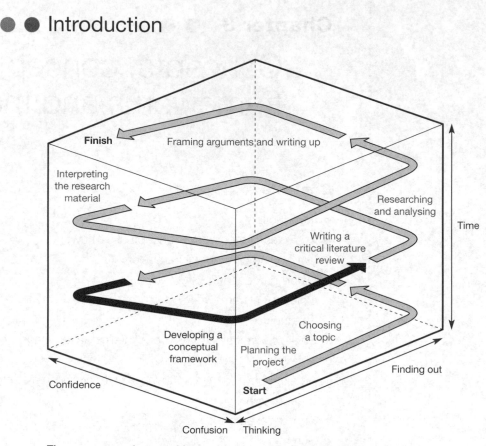

The processes of researching and writing a Master's dissertation

'Here is a lovely face, a Madonna face. What eyes! ... I wish I could make out the story. There is certainly a story. What can this all be?'
     'The fewer theories you form the fewer blunders and dreams you will make.'
     'But we must form theories – we cannot remain awake and not do so.'

Captain Gresley and Mr Ralph on discovering the ancient frescoes in the
Buddhist cave temples at Ajanta, India, in 1836 (Keay 2000: 149)

The purpose of this chapter is to explain what theorising means and to give you some help in defining concepts and formulating a conceptual framework for your dissertation. Theorising is not an added extra in the process of doing research. It will be argued that theorising gives shape and structure to your research. The first stage in theorising is clarifying the terms, or concepts, that you will use to describe the subject of research. The second stage is providing a description of the relationships (i.e. a conceptual framework) between the concepts being used. The third stage is using the conceptual framework to develop theories that explain the patterns and connections that you have found in your research material.

Exhibit 3.1

Ajanta cave painting

Source: Photo by Raj Shirole

The conceptual development phase of doing a dissertation is largely a thinking stage but it does prepare you for undertaking the finding out, the research phase, of the project. Initially it represents a movement from confusion to certainty. When you draft a conceptual framework that seems to work, it gives you a sense of control over the project. You know what you are trying to do. It may take several attempts to arrive at the conceptual framework, and so you may go round the cycle from confusion to confi-

Exhibit 3.2

The Ajanta caves

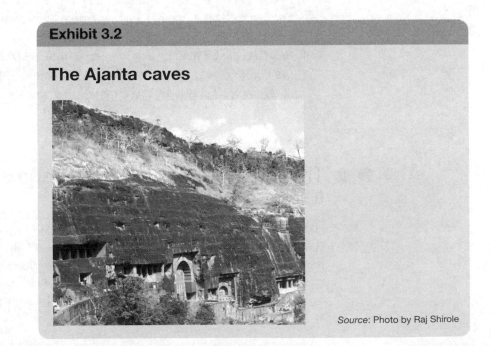

Source: Photo by Raj Shirole

dence and back again several times. However, the first burst of confidence wears off and uncertainty sets in until you can start the next phase and can test the framework out against the findings from your research.

Try not to dodge dealing with theoretical issues by claiming that the topic of your research is intensely practical and that it needs no top dressing of theoretical concerns. Always remember John Maynard Keynes' aphorism:

> Practical men, who believe themselves to be quite exempt from any intellectual influences, are usually the slaves of some defunct economist.
>
> (Gross 1987: 116)

This chapter is divided into three parts:

1. Why developing conceptual frameworks is important.
2. Techniques for developing conceptual frameworks.
3. Some examples of conceptual frameworks.

Learning outcomes for the chapter

1 Readers will understand the importance of concept definitions, conceptual frameworks and theorising in a Master's dissertation.

2 Readers will be able to define their concepts and relate them to the appropriate literature.

3 Readers will have sufficient examples of conceptual frameworks to be able to think imaginatively when developing their own frameworks.

4 Readers will be able to use their conceptual frameworks to guide the primary research phase of their projects and to structure the analysis presented in the dissertation.

● ● ● ● The roles of theory and conceptual frameworks

Defining your concepts and creating a conceptual framework are means of simplifying the research task. These two processes help you clear away all the issues and materials that are not germane to your topic and research question and they also provide a 'map' of your field of study. It helps you to find you way around your research material and it provides structure and coherence to your dissertation.

One of the big practical questions is when in the research process you should define concepts and draft a conceptual framework. There are two main possibilities, at the beginning or at least early on in the process (let us call this the structured approach) or towards the end of the research process (using what is commonly called a grounded approach). In a structured approach you impose a structure on your research based on a preliminary theory, concept or hypothesis; you use the structure to guide your research and in particular your material collection process. In a grounded approach you collect all your material without prejudice, with no preliminary conceptual thoughts about what you may discover. When you have made a big pile of material you study it to see what concepts and frameworks emerge from the heap.

The term 'grounded theory' was coined by Glaser and Strauss (1967). It is a process that allows theory to emerge out of the research material rather than being forced out of it by the use of a predetermined idea or theory. Grounded theory implies that theory is implicit in the material and can be drawn out by an iterative process of coding and comparison (see p. 155).

Exhibit 3.3

How important is the 'emergence of theory' in grounded theory?

In the years following the publication of their seminal work, Glaser and Strauss (1967) appear to have taken different lines on what grounded research is. Strauss, with a new collaborator – Corbin (Strauss and Corbin 1990) – standardised and specified detailed stages, steps and procedures that should be followed by anyone claiming to do grounded research. Glaser published a critique of Strauss and Corbin in 1992. The argument between the two sides was over the degree to which the two approaches could be said to allow theory to emerge from data – which is the central justification of grounded theory.

Glaser argued that Straus and Corbin were neglecting the central tenet and were placing too much importance on prior structures in their procedures for conducting grounded research.

- According to Glaser, the detailed rules and procedures specified by Strauss and Corbin for analysing data, apart from being cumbersome and difficult to recall, represented a prior structure that would force, or even torture, a theory from the material. Glaser, while also recommending stages in the analysis process, preferred a looser style of interpretation that allowed the material to speak for itself.
- Strauss and Corbin allow the research problem to be specified at the start of a project. The problem may be taken from the literature, from personal experience or even from the advice of tutors. Glaser countered that this would pre-empt the emergence of theory and that the research topic, as well as the corresponding theory, should be allowed to emerge from the data.

The arguments between Glaser and Strauss reinforce the importance of the decision about the point in time during a research project at which theory should play a role. It also suggests that there are intermediate positions between that which argues that research should always start from a theoretical proposition and Glaser's view that everything should be done to prevent any prior theorising from distorting the emergence of theory from the research material.

The tale told in Exhibit 3.4 should help to clarify the issues surrounding the problem of when to create a conceptual framework.

There is a moral to this tale. When doing research there is sometimes a trade-off between time and quality. I developed a conceptual framework for my research at a much earlier stage than did the Americans. As a consequence, my search of the archives was much more focused. My structured approach saved me time but diminished the quality of the final product. The Americans' grounded approach took them more time but the outcome was better. This was no doubt because they missed nothing in their search through the material. My focused search, however, probably caused me to miss material that could have generated new insights or theories. There is another price that is paid for taking a grounded approach. It is the frustration of not knowing until near the end of the project whether anything worthwhile will emerge from all your research work. The person who follows a structured approach has the security of knowing what the likely structure and shape of the dissertation will be before they start collecting their research material. The downside of the structured approach is, of course, that having developed an initial framework, people are reluctant to change it even when the research findings absolutely require it to be changed.

Exhibit 3.4

The historian's tale

I was not always a management studies person. History was my first field of study, and in particular Indian history. Many years ago I did my doctoral research on indigo plantations and peasant revolts in Bihar in the nineteenth and twentieth centuries. The research involved delving in the archives of the Secretariat of the Government of Bihar. As chance would have it there were two US history research students working in the archives at the same time. Perhaps because of the different research traditions in the United Kingdom and the United States, we followed different search strategies as we worked through the ancient and dusty cloth bundles of records tied with red tape. The Americans followed a grounded approach. They took notes of anything in the archive that had the least connection with the general field of their research. I, on the other hand, went for a structured approach. I had certain terms, or concepts, that were key to my research, such as plantation, indigo, revolting peasants and so on. I would skim the records and I became adept at spotting my key words if they were in the documents. When I came across a key term I would stop and take notes. At the end of a day in the archives I would have several pages of notes, having gone through many bundles of records, and the Americans would have reams of notes from only a few bundles.

I finished my PhD within four years and it was OK – it passed. The US students took on average eight years to complete their PhDs, but their theses were magnificent.

Exercise 3.1

To structure or to ground?

Consider whether a structured or a grounded approach would be appropriate to the position of someone doing a dissertation on a part-time Master's course.

Suggested answer

In general terms you are free to choose either a grounded or a structured approach to your research. You will certainly not be at a disadvantage if you choose a grounded approach if it is appropriate to your research question and if you have justified its use by reference to the literature on grounded theory. However, on practical grounds alone, it might be sensible to adopt a structured approach. MBA and Master's dissertations are normally done within a tight time schedule of between six months and a year, and there are many other pressures on the student's time during that period (other assignments and projects that have to be done for the course, job demands and family demands). A structured approach increases the student's sense of security that the project can be completed on time and some useful findings obtained.

● ● ● ● Developing conceptual frameworks

This section will give you some helpful hints on defining concepts, drafting conceptual frameworks and theorising. These three activities can be seen as steps to be taken one after the other. To begin with, each of these steps will be defined and the sequence explained. Examples will be given to show how this might all work out in practice.

Defining concepts

Figure 3.1 provides a definition of concepts.

It is important to decide what are the main terms or concepts you will be using in your research and to define them clearly. You are not required to come up with definitions that are absolutely true and will hold for all

Concepts:

- are the building blocks of models and theories;
- are the *working definitions* that are used in particular analyses for which they have been devised or chosen;
- are chosen to be useful, not correct;
- are more than a 'dictionary definition'.

Source: reproduced with the permission of T.J. Watson

Figure 3.1 Concepts

time. You choose a definition that will help you to understand and explain the subject matter of your research. The definitions will largely come from your literature review (see Chapter 2). Definitions taken from the dictionary will be too banal and general for research and theorising. *Collins Pocket English Dictionary* gives eight different definitions of 'culture', and so you still have the problem of choosing the appropriate meaning. Unfortunately you will find that the more you read, the more definitions you will come across. Let us pretend that one of your concepts was personality and that you had found thirteen and a half different definitions of it. If you try to use all the definitions in your dissertation, neither you nor the reader will ever be quite sure what you mean when you use the term. What you have to do is to explain to the reader the range of definitions that are available in the literature (giving the appropriate citations) and then choose one that seems to you the best suited for your research project. Explain to the reader that henceforward in the dissertation the term 'blah blah blah' will mean your preferred definition. Give your reasons for choosing this definition above the others.

Conceptual frameworks

Figure 3.2 provides a definition of frameworks.

In a conceptual framework, you put the concepts together as in a jigsaw puzzle. You work out how all the concepts fit together and relate to one another. The first stage of theorising identifies and clarifies concepts; the second stage concentrates on the connections and relationships between the concepts. A conceptual framework is formed of patterns of concepts and their interconnections. These relationships can be of many types.

Cause and effect

One of the most common relationships described in a conceptual framework is cause and effect. Such frameworks are often shown as 'boxes and arrows' diagrams, such as the one in Figure 3.3. In these diagrams the item at the start of an arrow causes or influences the item at the arrow's head.

Frameworks:

- are analytical schemes;
- simplify reality to make it easier to discuss, analyse or research;
- simplify reality by selecting certain phenomena/variables and suggesting certain relationships between them;
- are judged in terms or utility, not correctness.

Source: reproduced with the permission of T.J. Watson

Figure 3.2 Frameworks

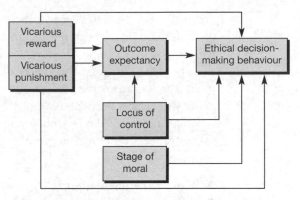

Figure 3.3 A conceptual framework for ethical decision making
Source: Trevino and Youngblood (1990). Reprinted with the permission of L.K. Trevino

The conceptual framework shown in Figure 3.3 identifies the various factors that influence ethical decision making in management. The framework identifies a number of causal factors that influence whether people will act morally. If the jargon is translated, the model is suggesting that:

- seeing other people being rewarded for acting well (vicarious reward)
- and punished for acting badly (vicarious punishment);
- whether people believe they control their own destinies or are at the mercy of forces beyond their control (locus of control)
- and their level of moral development

increases the likelihood that people will make decisions that are ethical rather than pragmatic. Some of the causal factors work indirectly through intermediary factors. Vicarious reward and punishment for example influence people's level of outcome expectancy. This is a concept derived from motivation theory that concerns the extent to which people believe their actions will have consequences. If people believe that, at work, bad actions will not result in bad consequences, then they will not be motivated to behave well.

A conceptual framework does not have to be as complicated as the one shown in Figure 3.3. It might just be a cause-and-effect relationship between two factors that can be shown as a simple graph. Conceptual frameworks based on cause and effect relationships are often the basis of hypothetico-deductive research (see p. 37) because they are the source of the hypotheses that such research seeks to test. The arrows in Figure 3.3 can be converted into a series of hypotheses (for instance, that the higher a person's level of moral development, the more likely they are to take ethical decisions) that can be tested.

Stages in a process
In some conceptual frameworks the concepts are related because they are stages in a process. These relationships are often illustrated by 'boxes and

arrows' diagrams. However, in these cases the relationships are not based on cause and effect but on logic and proper order. The management control loop is an example. It starts, in its simplest form, with planning and then proceeds through the stages of doing, monitoring and revising the plan. This sequence is a logical one because to do the stages in any other order would be a nonsense.

Kolb's theory of the learning cycle (Kolb *et al*. 1995) is an example of a staged process type of conceptual framework. He identified four styles of learning:

● active experimentation
● reflective observation
● abstract conceptualisation
● concrete experience.

These four learning styles were linked in a cyclical process (and so the theory can be shown diagrammatically as a circle, as in Figure 3.4). Effective learning requires going through a complete cycle.

Hierarchical relationships

In many conceptual frameworks, concepts are related because they occupy higher or lower positions on a scale or in a hierarchy. Maslow's (1954) much quoted hierarchy of needs is a good example. The sequence of human needs, going from the lowest to the highest, was as follows:

● physiological needs
● safety needs
● belongingness needs
● esteem needs
● self-actualisation.

If you like presenting your conceptual frameworks in diagrammatic form, then hierarchical relationships can easily be shown as a triangle, with the higher needs at the apex and the lower needs at the base of the triangle, as in Figure 3.5.

Figure 3.4 A cyclical process framework

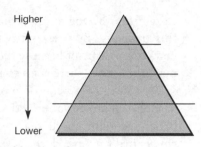

Figure 3.5 A hierarchical framework

Maps and coordinates

Places on maps are found by using coordinates. By reading off the coordinates on the vertical and horizontal scales of the map, you can locate the place you want to find and see how it lies in relation to other places. In a similar fashion you can define the relationships between concepts by plotting them against a series of coordinates. Most commonly, conceptual frameworks use only two scales, as do most maps. In a two-by-two matrix, or table, each scale or axis is divided into two, as in Figure 3.6. These are a very common form of conceptual framework.

Of the many hundreds of these, the most famous is probably the Boston Consulting Group strategic matrix (Stern and Stalk 1998). The matrix is used to assess the levels of investment needed by different strategic business units. It uses two axes:

- rate of market growth
- relative market share.

These axes are each divided into high and low. Business units that have both high market share and a high growth rate are the **Stars** and should be supported. Those with low growth rates but high market shares are **Cash Cows** and can be relied upon to generate income without much investment. If a business unit has a small share of a slow-growing market, it is

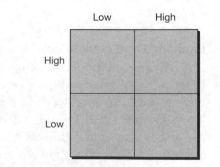

Figure 3.6 A two-by-two matrix

classified as a **Dog** and it would be better if the company withdrew from this business. Business units that have a small share of a fast-growing market are difficult because they represent a gamble, and investing in them may pay off but there is no guarantee.

Of course there can be more than two coordinates. Reddin's (1970) model of managerial effectiveness uses three and so can be drawn as a cube. The figure used at the start of each chapter in this guide is also a conceptual framework that uses three coordinates:

- time
- degree of certainty or confusion
- thinking and finding out.

Even multi-dimensional matrices could be used. However, these are easier to express in databases than they are to draw on sheets of paper.

Pairs of opposites

Concepts may be related by being pairs of opposites. The idea of duality is a very powerful one in academic work. It is the notion that the world can be divided into competing forces that are in continuous tension because neither force is strong enough to abolish the other and because each force is incomplete without its opposite. This sounds very abstract but there are many practical examples of such pairs in studies of management and organisations. Leadership studies are often structured on polar opposites such as transactional and transformational leadership and relationship-oriented and task-oriented leadership behaviour. Leaders have to find a balance between these competing demands because none of the elements in the pairs can be effective on their own in all circumstances.

The force field analysis based on the work of Lewin (1951) uses the idea of competing forces as a tool for thinking about change. The status quo is seen as a point of equilibrium between forces pushing for change and forces resisting change. These forces do not necessarily come in pairs but they are often matched. So staff's fear of the new may be counterbalanced by their enthusiasm for novelty. A force field is shown graphically in Figure 3.7.

Exchange and equilibrium

The idea of equilibrium, which is present in force field analysis, leads to other forms of relationships. Concepts may be related through a mechanism of exchange that leads to a balance or equilibrium between them. Tony Watson (1994: 110–111) developed the idea of 'strategic exchange' as the key conceptual framework for his research on management and strategy. He defined it as follows:

Figure 3.7 A force field diagram

> The main strategic thrust of all organisations is one of strategic exchange to achieve long term survival (with profitability, market share and all the other typical strategic concerns as means towards this).

Every organisation has a number of stakeholders, and it exchanges resources with them in ways that enable both the organisation and its stakeholders to meet their objectives. One particular set of stakeholders are the individuals who work for an organisation, and Watson developed a conceptual framework that shows the process of strategic exchange between individuals and the organisation they work for. The exchange between individuals and organisations is conceptualised as an implicit contract. This is not formalised but it expresses the understanding that each party has of its obligations to, and expectations of, the other party.

The idea of an exchange relationship is a common one in business and management. It is associated with the ideas of equilibrium and trade-offs. This is the basis of much economic analysis. In markets exchange is the process by which a balance or equilibrium is achieved between buyers and sellers. Equilibrium is arrived at by the players deciding the point at which they are willing to trade off one thing for another. The buyer will decide that their wish to have the thing they want to buy now is more important than trying to get additional discount. Their wish to have the product, and their wish for a discount balance, cancel each other out. The idea of trade-offs and balance can be found in many managerial conceptual frameworks. Kaplan and Norton's (1992) idea of the balanced scorecard in performance management is one illustration. The point of the technique is that managers do not achieve one set of targets merely at the expense of a worsened performance against other targets. Rather, the managers have to balance achievements against a number of possibly contradictory areas of performance.

Similarity

Sometimes concepts are related because they are similar. A conceptual framework can consist of groups of like themes that are clustered together. A famous example is the McKinsey '7 S' model. This is a framework for evaluating the effectiveness of an organisation. It incorporates the following seven concepts:

- Strategy ⎫
- Structure ⎬ The cold triangle
- Systems ⎭
- Super-ordinate goals
  (mission and vision) ⎫
- Staff ⎬ The warm square
- Skills
- Style. ⎭

The first three are clustered together and are called the 'cold triangle' and the last four are grouped as the 'warm square'. The cold concepts are all analytical and impersonal, whereas the items in the warm square are all intangible and human. Cold and warm are matters of value and emotion. In other words, the similarities within the two clusters are matters of sensibility rather than of measurement. The relationships between concepts in a framework may, as in this case, be metaphorical or symbolic.

Things to watch out for

Although most of the examples of conceptual frameworks I have given can be shown as diagrams, they do not have to be. A conceptual framework can be expressed adequately in words alone. In fact one common problem is that students show their conceptual framework simply as a diagram. This is normally inadequate. A written explanation of the diagram, and in particular an explanation of the relationships between the concepts, is also required.

There are a number of common mistakes made when creating conceptual frameworks:

- Students' conceptual frameworks are often too complex and busy, and so you need to keep Occam's razor (explained on p. 235) to hand. The razor is the principle that you should keep things as simple as possible. Over-complex frameworks and diagrams are impossible to understand and lead markers to the conclusion that the student has greater facility with the graphics capabilities of word processors than they have with conceptual thinking.
- Sometimes the problem with a conceptual framework is that it does not specify what the relationships between the concepts are. If you have drawn a conceptual framework and the meaning of the arrows in it is ambiguous, or if you have a two-by-two matrix without scales on the vertical and horizontal axes, then you need to do some more work on it.
- Sometime the proposed conceptual framework is too general and is not related to the research question that the project is seeking to answer. This can happen when a student draws a conceptual framework from the literature. It may provide a good map of the literature in the field but it may not be sufficiently specific to help answer the research question.

Theories

Figure 3.8 gives a definition of theories.

Developing theories is the third and final step in the process. This is often an aspiration and it is not always achievable in a Master's dissertation. It is perfectly possible to pass at Master's level with a dissertation that does not extend to developing theory. But, having said that, theorising does not necessarily mean inventing new theory. For most of us, theorising means adapting and developing existing theories. That does not seem such an impossible challenge. In management research, modifying or developing a theory often means adapting a theory developed in one context, say marketing, and applying it in another field.

Theories are an attempt to draw generalisable findings from specific instances. That is what the word 'inductive', in this context, means. Seen from another perspective, theories are attempts to explain research findings. Conceptual frameworks provide generalisations about processes, about the interaction of the concepts, whereas theories provide hypotheses about the outcomes of these processes. A conceptual framework might identify age and sex as factors linked with the propensity to take decisions that are ethical rather than dubious. Theory would show how these factors can explain the behaviours of different groups. It would provide an account of why senior women managers, say, respond, or are likely to respond, to situations in a different manner to, say, younger male managers. Of course at this stage the conceptual framework and any related theories will be based on the literature review, the research having not yet been done. They remain therefore as a hypothesis or as a series of hypotheses.

Theories:

- are, in general terms, ideas about how phenomena relate to each other;
- are, more specifically, ideas about how particular events or actions tend to lead to others or are brought about by them;
- are generalisations;
- are the inductive heart of scientific study.

Source: reproduced with the permission of T.J. Watson

Figure 3.8 Theories

Seeking inspiration: using your 'intellectual baggage'

In general the ideas for your conceptual thinking will come from the business and management literature. However, you can draw ideas from a much wider field. Often ideas and frameworks that you have come across in other academic subjects (and lots of people doing postgraduate studies in management have studied other subjects for their first degrees) can be adapted for use in a business or management dissertation.

An extreme example of borrowing from other fields can be taken from my research into business ethics. I had been browsing in a bookshop and came across a picture book on Cabbala and Jewish mysticism (Halevi 1988). A central aspect of Cabbala is a diagram known as the tree of life. Within this diagram there are ten *sefirot*, a term that can be translated as spheres or stages of consciousness. These *sefirot* link God, the highest universal principle, with the material world. Look at the diagram in Figure 3.9, which represents the 'tree of life', very carefully. It is, at root, a 'boxes and arrows' diagram. There are ten circles (11 if you include *Daat*) that are connected by arrows. It is, in the terms used in this guide, a conceptual framework.

The tree of life also has similarities with force field analysis. The *sefirot* are arranged in three pillars. The left-hand pillar represents restraint, the right-hand pillar growth and expansion and the middle pillar a balance between the two others (Besserman 1997). As in force field analysis it supposes a dynamic between opposing forces that have to be mediated through a series of stages. Cabbalah proposes, in what is known as the lightening flash, a sequence in which the forces of expansion and restraint are triggered and the tensions are resolved.

At the time I was doing research into the responses of financial and human resource management specialists to the ethical dilemmas they experienced at work. As it happens I had identified ten different forms of response and I was trying to see how they all interrelated and connected with each other. As the number of research categories matched the number of *sefirah* I started to wonder whether the one could be mapped on to the other. It should have been possible because, according to the Cabbalists, the tree of life represents the underlying nature of everything. Some of the ethical responses in my analysis were clearly defensive, others were assertive expressions of people's values, and yet others were balancing, compromising positions. After much thinking the conceptual framework shown in Figure 3.10 emerged. You do not need to read the details of the diagram. The purpose of showing it is to give evidence of the transferability of theoretical frameworks.

This was all done with my tongue firmly in my cheek. I am normally sceptical about New Age and mystical ideas. I am not a Cabbalist. However, the conceptual framework of the *sefirot* was intriguing and its dynamics can be applied to many situations. Despite the oddity of the conceptual framework, it was published (Fisher 1999).

An encouragement and a warning

Take heart – you do not need to do anything this complicated. But do keep your mind open to all possibilities. Conceptualisation and theorising are the hardest but also the most satisfying parts of doing a dissertation. The rewards are not purely intellectual. A convincing and elegant conceptual framework is the basis of many profitable pieces of intellectual property and of consultancy solutions to management problems. But developing a

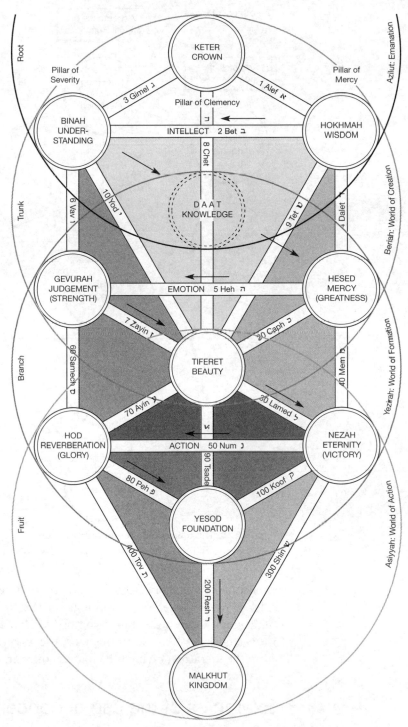

Figure 3.9 The tree of life

From *Kabbalah: Tradition of Hidden Knowledge* by Z'ev ben Shimon Halevi published by Thames & Hudson Ltd, 1979. London. Reproduced with permission

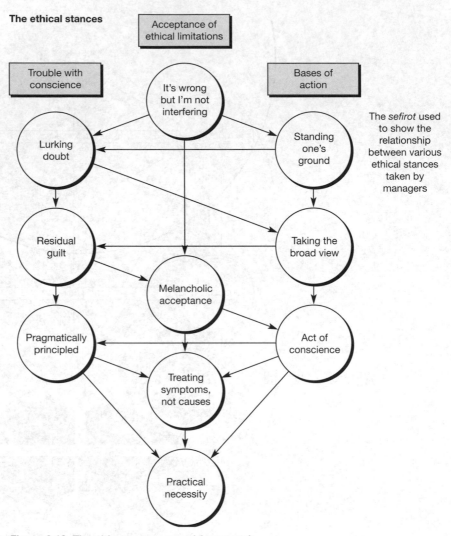

The ethical stances

Figure 3.10 The ultimate conceptual framework

Source: reproduced from Fisher (1999) with the permission of Blackwell Publishing Ltd

conceptual framework is a trial and error process. You will need to create a large pile of rejected scribblings on the floor before everything falls miraculously into place. But if you break through the thinking pain barrier, it does fall into place. If all this fails, use a conceptual framework straight from the literature, giving full citations of course.

● ● ● ● Examples of the use of conceptual frameworks

Two examples will be given of how conceptual frameworks might be developed.

An example of conceptualising and theorising in a study of organisational cultures

This example is based on the doctoral research of Terry McNulty (1990), who received his PhD from the Nottingham Trent University. As it is taken from doctoral-level work it is at a higher level of theoretical sophistication than may be necessary for Master's-level work. However, it does explain the three stages of concept definition, conceptual framework building and theorising very well. The research was into the types of organisational culture found in a number of different hospitals. The concepts needed therefore all related to the idea of organisational culture.

McNulty began by isolating a number of key concepts, some of which are shown in Figure 3.11.

His next task was to give working definitions to all these terms, using the literature on organisational culture as his source. We will not rehearse all these definitions here but simply pick out a few:

- **Official** – sanctioned or published by the top management of an organisation. McClean and Marshall (1991) termed this the 'high profile culture'.
- **Unofficial** – values, beliefs and behaviours chosen by the staff. It is the same as McClean and Marshall's (1991) concept of 'low profile culture'.
- **Structure** – the technologies, procedures, policies and charts that define the 'architecture' of an organisation.
- **Values** – beliefs about what is good and bad and what are proper and improper ways of doing things.
- **Sub-cultures** – organisations do not necessarily have a single, unified culture. Within the organisational culture there are likely to be many sub-cultures that will differ to a greater or lesser extent from the wider corporate culture.
- **Cultural imperialism** – when one sub-culture group in an organisation gains power or hegemony over other groups.

Figure 3.11 Developing a conceptual framework for organisational culture

The next stage was to put the concepts in a framework. Note that not all the concepts available to the researcher were used for this purpose (see Figure 3.12).

The two-by-two matrix is such a commonly used form of conceptual framework that it has become hackneyed. Nevertheless it often works well. This framework has at least two functions. It can be used to define various component parts of organisational culture. It can also be used as an aid to the data-gathering part of the research. The four boxes can be used to store the information gathered during research forays into the organisation as follows:

● Into the official values box go all the things top managers said in inter-views about their values and their vision for the organisation.
● Into the official structure box goes all the documentary evidence, such as mission statements, charts, procedures and computer software that describe how things should be done.
● Into the unofficial structure box goes all the information, from informal observations of the workplace and interviews with staff, which explain how staff actually do their job. This will include information about all the dodges and short cuts that staff use to make their jobs bearable.
● Into the unofficial values box goes the information about the staff's values and beliefs that were probably obtained by interviews and focus groups.

In the chapter of the dissertation in which these results were written up, the four boxes were used as sub-headings for describing the research findings.

The next stage involved developing theories from the conceptual frame-work, as in Figure 3.13.

The theory that Terry McNulty developed related the conceptual frame-work to the idea of organisational effectiveness. He proposed that the effectiveness, or organisational health, of an organisation would be influenced

	Structure	Values
Official	Mission statements, policies, objectives, organisation charts, manuals, job descriptions	Senior managers' ideas, views and visions
Unofficial	The way in which people in the organisation actually do things	The ideas, attitudes, values and opinions of everyone else in the organisation

Figure 3.12 A conceptual framework for organisational culture

Theory

If all the four quadrants complement each other, then you have an effective organisation. If the quadrants are in conflict, then the organisation will, in various ways, be ineffective.

Figure 3.13 Theorising from the framework

by the degree of fit between the four quadrants described in the conceptual framework. Strictly speaking, the theory was a hypothesis because the research findings would be used to test it.

Exercise 3.2

Further theory making

Terry McNulty had used two other concepts in his research – strong glue culture and weak glue culture. Again, the metaphor of culture as a glue had been taken from the literature. In a strong glue culture the culture strongly binds all members of the organisation. In a weak glue culture there are greater tendencies to separation and the organisational culture is not strong enough to hold people together. He used these additional concepts to produce a further two-by-two matrix, as shown in Figure 3.14.

From your own experience and common sense try to identify what the practical outcomes for organisations would be for each of the four blank boxes in Figure 3.14. So, for example, what would happen in an organisation when a strong official (top management) culture meets a strong unofficial culture? What would be the consequence for a coming together of a strong unofficial culture and a weak management culture?

Suggested answer

McNulty's analysis of the outcomes in the four different circumstances is shown in Figure 3.15. You probably will not have come across the terms used in the figure because several are drawn from the historical analysis of colonialism and one comes from sociology. The analysis provides a more practical example than the Cabbalah of how ideas from different disciplines can inform organisational and managerial analysis. So it is unlikely you will have used the same images or headings but check how close your answer, expressed in your own terms, fits with the following descriptions:

Exercise 3.2 *continued*

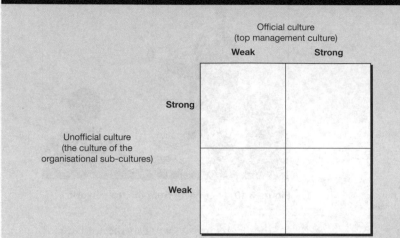

Figure 3.14 Further theorising

- **Balkanisation or informal empire**

  When the top management (official) culture is weak and there are several powerful sub-culture groups, such as doctors and nurses in a hospital, then you would expect constant feuding between the sub-culture groups as they vie for power. The political situation in the Balkans in both the nineteenth and the twentieth centuries provides a metaphor for this process. If one of the groups gains the ascendancy, then the situation will be like that of an informal empire, in which actual power lies with a sub-group, while the official power, the management, maintain control in name only. The term 'informal empire' is an historical one. In the nineteenth century, for example, Britain had an informal empire in South America. Britain was not formally the sovereign body but it controlled the economies and the other important levers of power.

Figure 3.15 Further theorising

Exercise 3.2 continued

- **Dualism and consensus**

  When both the official and unofficial cultures are strong, there are two possibilities. The first is where the two share similar values – the organisation is unified and can aspire to excellence. If the cultures are different, then the two cultures may agree to co-exist and not to interfere with each other. For example, the doctors get on with doing the medicine and the management deals with the other staff and the premises. Dualism is a concept also taken from history. It refers to many colonial countries, in the nineteenth century, in which a modern economy existed alongside, but not interacting with, a peasant subsistence economy.

- **Anomie**

  Anomie is a term from sociology. It means a state where people have lost all sense of purpose and identity. This is likely to be the case when both official and unofficial cultures are weak.

- **Cultural imperialism**

  If the official culture, the top management, is strong but the sub-cultures are weak, then the management will have no difficulty is asserting its control over the organisation. Using another historical metaphor, this is similar to the processes of imperialism.

This second two-by-two matrix suggested another set of theoretical scenarios, which Terry McNulty then investigated by researching what was happening in a number of hospitals and units.

Another example

The following is an extract from an article by Clark and Soulsby (1995) written when they were at Nottingham Business School. The paper is about the ways organisations and managers in the Czech Republic have adapted to the coming of market forces. Study the examples of good practice in the handling of concepts and conceptual frameworks identified in the extract and think about how they might be applied to your work. The extract is presented as a model to aspire to. It was published in a well-considered academic journal and is probably at a higher level than needs to be achieved to pass the dissertation module of a Master's programme.

The study of organisational transformation

The gloss

The key concept of 'organisational form' is defined and related to other similar terms used in the literature. The authors choose a preferred concept from a range of possibilities.

Three other concepts are defined that go to make up the 'organisational form' – sub-systems, structure and culture.

The concept of 'internal coherence' is introduced that links the three components. The relationship between the concepts is one of 'fit' and 'balance'.

The text

Greenwood and Hinings (1988: 296) argue that the notion of a relatively stable organisational state is a prerequisite for the study of organisational change, since it provides the starting point and an end-point of a process of transition which constitutes the focus of such a study. This state of 'relative stablity' has been usefully conceptualised as a 'configuration' (Miller and Friesen, 1984) or a [design] archetype (e.g. Greenwood and Hinings, 1988). We will use the generic concept of an 'organisational form' in order to achieve some consistency in our terminology. Following Laughlin (1991) we conceive of the organisational form as being constituted by three interrelated components. These components vary in their level of abstraction and in their degree of importance for identifying the underlying nature of an organisation and the behaviour of its members (see Figure 3.16). We shall call these components the organisation's 'sub-systems', its 'structure' and its 'culture'.

[A paragraph has been omitted from here that defines the three components in more detail.]

Further, it has been argued that organisations tend towards 'internal coherence' within their organisational form. Under circumstances of successful adaptation to a relatively predictable environment, the organisation's constituent sub-systems, structure and culture will tend to be mutually consistent and supportive, leading to internal resistances to change (Miller and

A boxes and arrows diagram is used to explain and summarise the conceptual framework.

In this diagram the concepts are all linked together in a conceptual framework. Coherence is similar to the idea of balance. Systems, structures and cultures tend towards a state of equilibrium.

Figure 3.16

The gloss

The concept of 'transformation' is introduced and related to the components in the diagram. Once again terms are clarified in relation to similar concepts found in the literature.

Note the wide range of references given.

The conceptual framework is used to mark off the boundaries of this study. The things the study will not do are clearly stated.

Some limitations are reported in the conceptual framework. It is signposted that the framework will be developed by adding to it the concept of human agency. The paper is starting to develop new theory by adapting existing conceptual frameworks.

The limitations of the existing theories and conceptual frameworks are spelt out.

The text

Friesen, 1984; Greenwood and Hinings, 1988: 297–299; Laughlin, 1991: 213). In principle, the components of an organisational form are systematically bound, by virtue of their consistent expression of its underlying values (Greenwood and Hinings, 1987: 2).

The concept of 'transformation' is reserved for complete and significant changes in all three components of the organisational form. This is what Miller and Friesen (1984) call a 'quantum change'; a fundamental shift in the dominant logic or organising principles which underpin the organisational form, effecting a move to another form. Others have used the terms 'reorientation', 'revolutionary', 'radical' or 'second order' change to refer to 'change … in the organisational "core" … [which] is irreversible' (Levy, 1986: 10). Changes within the dominant logic are partial, incremental, piecemeal or superficial, and have attracted terms like 'convergent', 'evolutionary', 'incremental' or 'first order' (cf. Levy, 1986: 8–9; Dunphy and Stace, 1988: 322; Miller and Friesen, 1984: 223–226; see also Child and Smith, 1987; Pettigrew, 1987: 664–665). Such 'reformative' changes do not affect the cultural bedrock of the organisation, and thus leave its essential nature and reality relatively untouched. Such distinctions help to map out conceptual features of organisational change, but the analysis of its ongoing reality requires an approach that recognises the complexity of the simultaneous processes of continuity and discontinuity with the past (cf. Tushman and Romanelli, 1985; Child and Smith, 1987: 569).

Some underdeveloped issues in organisational transformation

By focusing on the internal coherence of system components, and the technical fit between the organisation and its environment, the study of organisational transformation has developed within a discourse that stresses the processes of system integration and crisis. Our research on the management of organisational transformation in the Czech Republic is firmly located within this nexus of concepts, propositions and issues, but we have found certain limits to its usefulness in accounting for our observations. In particular, the current framework virtually disregards institutional processes in the environment, and, by extension, underplays key problems of social integration and legitimation. The role of human agency is especially important in looking at the behaviour of managers who are actively engaged in changing organisational systems, structures and processes.

Transformation and institutional change

As a result of its location within the contingency theory tradition, mainstream research on organisational transformation has tended to focus strongly upon the task (or technical) environment as the source of internal change. For example, 'the trigger for transformation' (Child and Smith, 1987: 575) at Cadbury was

The gloss

The text

primarily identified with changes in the relationship between the firm and its markets; and 'strategic reorientations' at ICI were located in 'economic and business events' and the firm's 'operating environment' (Pettigrew, 1987: 665). While such research recognises the importance of internal culture and its symbolic relationships with external events, it still tends to underplay the role of changes in the organisation's 'institutional' environment.

It is argued that there has been too much attention on internal 'fit' and not enough on the fit between organisational form and the wider institutional environment. Institutions in this context refers to the structures and culture of Soviet society.

Institutionalisation is said to occur when patterns and processes take on a 'rule-like status in social thought and action' (Jepperson, 1991: 145) because they have a 'natural' and unchallengeable appearance. As a consequence of institutionalisation, organisational structures and systems, and the grounds of rational behaviour, become so taken for granted or habitualised that their underlying values and ideologies are not recognised – legitimacy is implicitly accomplished without the active intervention of human choices.

The new concept of 'institutionalisation' is used to begin to extend the conceptual framework. Its implications are drawn out.

In a highly institutionalised setting, where the existing order has become part of the natural attitude, the explanation of organisational transformation requires answers to questions such as:

1. How do the underlying values, rationality and ideologies of an organisational form become revealed so that they can be interrogated?
2. How can the balance of power shift so that the values, once revealed, can be effectively challenged and opposed?

This challenge to legitimacy (in part, a process of demythologising) becomes a threat to the degree of social integration, and allows the possibility of deinstitutionalisation. As Zucker (1991: 105) argues, whereas institutionalisation can occur 'accidentally', deinstitutionalisation needs conscious acts of opposition to overcome the inertia implicit in institutional systems or networks.

Deinstitutionalisation is linked back to the idea of a fit between an organisational form and its environmental circumstances. But it is argued that this process occurs through human agency, i.e. people in the organisation beginning to challenge and question the way the organisation is.

It is evident that institutionalisation and deinstitutionalisation can only be properly understood as social processes at both the macro level or organisation–environment interaction, and the micro level of social accomplishment. At the former level, the process of deinstitutionalisation is related to the changing nature of the organisation's relationship with its socio-institutional environment. Patterns, practice and procedures, as well as their underlying logic, become incongruent with the assumptions of legitimacy, credibility and normality in society. At the micro level, key actors begin to question the way things are done in the organisation, and the existing customs and practices are revealed as inappropriate or non-rational – both in terms of what is required in the institutional environment, and in terms of the organisation's internal, formal coherence.

The new concepts of institutionalisation and human agency are added into the conceptual framework. But this time a diagram is not used.

Managerial action and organisational transformation

We have argued that the dominant systems approach to organisational transformation has neglected the human and social dimensions of

The gloss

The text

organisational change. We have also suggested that a key to understanding transformation from an institutional perspective lies in demonstrating the breakdown of current institutional practices and social processes of institutional reproduction by examining the social accomplishment of change at the micro level. In fact, with one or two exceptions, both the contingency and the institutionalist approaches to organisational analysis have tended to underplay those processes whereby organisational life is socially constructed.

The themes and concepts of human agency and social construction are developed

Managers act as potentially powerful agents in the process of organisational transformation through the contribution of a complex set of cognitive, affective and behavioural influences. The choices that managers make in order to change the organisation result from their perception and understanding of the problems and constraints, their level of education, knowledge and understanding of options available to them (including knowledge of recent fashions and trends in management), and their effective power, social legitimacy and competence to get things done in the organisation. It should also be recognised that managers in any organisation will differ in the values, knowledge, experience, power and competence that they bring to bear on organisational processes.

The two new additions to thinking on the subject – institutional fit and human agency – are highlighted in the summary.

The developments of the conceptual framework are summarised. It is argued that these developments will be useful in improving understanding of organisational transformations.

In summary, this theoretical exploration highlights the complexity of factors which affect the process of organisational transformation. It has argued for consideration of institutional as well as technical factors, and for supplementing the notions of system integration and crisis with those of social integration and crisis. The macro and micro processes of institutional change are highlighted, and it is argued that senior managers perform pivotal roles in transforming the technical and institutional relationships between the organisation and its environment, while all managers are instrumental in the re-establishment of internal coherence in the organisational form. These conceptual frameworks serve to enhance the theoretical framework within which the management of organisational transformation, in a rapidly changing and highly ambiguous societal context, can be more fully analysed.

NB the citations from the abstract have been omitted. If you are interested in the subject, as opposed to the manner in which the conceptual framework has been developed, the full references can be found in the article.

Source: Clark and Soulsby (1995). Reproduced with the authors' permission.

Summary

- Consider carefully the pros and cons of adopting a structured approach rather than a grounded approach in your use of conceptual frameworks.
- Having a conceptual framework is not absolutely necessary to gain a pass mark for a Master's dissertation; but if you do have one it repays you well in marks.
- Work through a three-stage process of defining concepts, formulating conceptual frameworks and theorising.
- You do not necessarily have to invent entirely new conceptual frameworks. You may well be able to adapt frameworks from the literature to fit a new context.
- If all else fails, then use an existing framework from the literature without adaptation.
- Use your imagination to help you in formulating a conceptual framework. Draw inspiration from the breadth of your reading and your 'intellectual baggage'.
- Use your conceptual framework to help you analyse your research material and to structure the analysis you present in the dissertation.

Suggested reading

There is no one book that I can find that focuses mainly on the subject of this chapter. Miles and Huberman (1994) is a wonderful sourcebook for ideas and possibilities for using diagrams to represent conceptual frameworks. Chapter 6 in Hart (1998) is also useful for this purpose.

Hart, C. (1998) *Doing a Literature Review: Releasing the Social Science Research Imagination*, London: Sage.

Miles, M. B. and Huberman, A. M. (1994) *An Expanded Sourcebook: Qualitative Data Analysis*, 2nd edn, London: Sage.

References

Besserman, P. (1997) *The Shambhala Guide to Kabbalah and Jewish Mysticism*, Boston, MA and London: Shambhala.

Clark, E. and Soulsby, A. (1995) 'Transforming former state enterprises in the Czech Republic', *Organisation Studies*, Vol. 16, No. 2, 215.

Fisher, C. M. (1999) 'Ethical stances: the perceptions of accountancy and HR specialists of ethical conundrums at work', *Business Ethics: A European Review*, Vol. 8, No. 4, 236–248.

Glaser, B. G. (1992) *The Basics of Grounded Theory Analysis*, Mill Valley, CA: Sociology Press.

Glaser, B. G. and Strauss, A. L. (1967) *The Discovery of Grounded Theory: Strategies for Qualitative Research*, New York: Aldine.

Gross, J. (1987) *The Oxford Book of Aphorisms*, Oxford: Oxford University Press.

Halevi, Z. S. (1988) *Kabbalah: Tradition of Hidden Knowledge*, London: Thames & Hudson.

Kaplan, R. S. and Norton, D. P (1992) 'The balanced scorecard: measures that drive performance', *Harvard Business Review*, January–February: 75–85.

Keay, J. (2000) *India: A History*, London: HarperCollins.

Kolb, D. A., Rubin, I. M. and Osland, J. S. (1995) *Organisational Behaviour: An Experiential Approach*, 6th edn, Hemel Hempstead: Prentice Hall.

Lewin, K. (1951) *Field Theory in Social Science*, New York: Harper & Row.

Maslow, A. (1954) *Motivation and Personality*, New York: Harper & Row.

McClean, A. and Marshall, J. (1991) *Cultures at Work: How to Identify and Understand Them*, Luton: The Local Government Management Board.

McNulty, T. (1990) *Organisation, Culture and the Management of Change in the National Health Service*, PhD dissertation, Nottingham: The Nottingham Trent University.

Reddin, W. J. (1970) *Managerial Effectiveness*, London: McGraw-Hill.

Stern, C. W. and Stalk Jr, G. (eds) (1998) *Perspectives on Strategy from the Boston Consulting Group*, London: John Wiley.

Strauss, A. L. and Corbin, J. (1990) *The Basics of Qualitative Research: Grounded Theory Procedures and Techniques*, London: Sage.

Trevino, L. K. and Youngblood, S. A. (1990) 'Bad apples in bad barrels: a causal analysis of ethical decision-making behaviour', *Journal of Applied Psychology*, Vol. 75, No. 4, 378–385.

Watson, T. J. (1994) *In Search of Management: Culture, Chaos and Control in Managerial Work*, London: Routledge.

Chapter 4 ● ● ● ●

Collecting and analysing research material

Contents

● ● ● ● Introduction

The great tragedy of science – the slaying of a beautiful hypotheses by an ugly fact.

Thomas H. Huxley (1870)

Research is formalised curiosity. It is poking and prying with a purpose.

Zora Neale Hurston (1942)

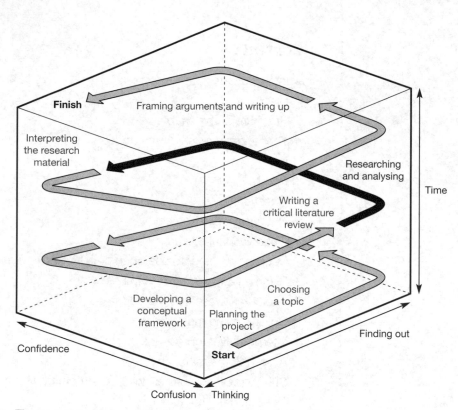

The processes of researching and writing a Master's dissertation

The previous chapters have covered:

- identifying the topic of your dissertation project;
- reviewing the literature; and
- laying down the foundations of research by defining and modelling the necessary concepts.

This chapter is about the primary research phase of the project. It deals with how to find things out by research rather than discovering things by reading the literature. It is more practically focused than some of the other chapters because it is about the technical problems of carrying out research. This phase of a project often begins with a little uncertainty as the student thinks about and plans how the research material is to be gathered. Once these decisions have been made, then the processes of finding things out leads to an increased sense of confidence in the project.

This is the longest chapter in the guide. However, it should not take you any more time than the others because, in normal circumstances, you will only need to read a portion of it. The chapter identifies two broad approaches to collecting research material. It is probable that you will use only one of these styles of research, so you need to read only those sections that deal with your chosen approach. It might just be that you are going to use both approaches, using one in a major role and one in a minor role. In that case, I am afraid, you have twice as much reading to do.

Discoverers

This chapter is about discovery, which theme leads naturally to the metaphor of geographical discovery. The analogy will help to explain two broad approaches to finding out new things. If we think of the great ages of exploration, then the images of two kinds of discoverer come to mind: explorers and surveyors.

Explorers travel into unknown (at least to them if not to the indigenous inhabitants) territory. Their mission is to make the unknown known and to make the strange familiar to those who read their books of adventure and derring-do. In the sense that they are travelling into the unknown, explorers can have no preconception about what they will find. Exploration requires an open approach. Explorers cannot, or should not, anticipate what they will find. Of course they will have preconceptions – or conceptual frameworks – that will lead them to explore one place rather than another; but they should not second guess what they might find on the basis of these preconceptions. Explorers present their discoveries in narratives, they write books and give lectures, or in modern times present television documentaries.

The surveyor often arrives at a later stage of discovery. By this time, the broad configuration of the new land and its peoples will be known. The role of the surveyor is to pin that knowledge down in a precise and reproducible form. Surveyors measure things. They produce maps, coordinates and benchmarks. Often, by the time the surveyors begin their work, it is known where the mountains are, where the rivers flow and what the customs of the inhabitants are. The surveyor finds out how high the mountains are and where precisely they are located, plots the courses of the rivers and conducts censuses of the population. It is difficult to carry out a survey if the broad contours of the subject of the survey are not seek to remain detached from what they are measuring. It is not necessary to become involved with the people in an organisation in order to measure its sales turnover, its profitability, its customer churn rates and its staff turnover. It is important, however, to define very precisely the things that are to measured or counted. It is pointless, for example, to measure profitability of companies without being very precise about the accountancy rules and conventions that are to be used to calculate profit. Otherwise, when the information is to be used, it will be found that like was not compared with like. Survey research is presented as an accurate and generalised representation of the field of study.

Students taking a survey approach to their research ought to adopt a structured approach. That is to say, they should be able to define the characteristics and properties of the subjects of their study before they conduct the research so that they can accurately measure and categorise them. They should ask, mostly, closed questions.

In surveying research, what is to be researched has to be pre-planned in some detail and the measuring instruments to be used have to be well calibrated. These requirements are also the basis of the dangers inherent in this form of research. We can return to the great Victorian age of discovery to explain some of these. The British Raj in India in the nineteenth century was obsessed with surveys; every aspect of its dominion was captured in surveys and censuses. Unfortunately much of the data collected were of suspect accuracy, their collection was influenced by the political agendas of those organising the gathering and in many cases the things they measured were not useful. As one commentator pointed out, all the surveys and censuses in the early nineteenth century gave no premonition of the state of Indian popular feeling before the great Indian mutiny or rebellion in 1857 (Bayly 1996: 221). A more insidious problem was that the mindset of the colonial administrators led them to give heightened importance to things, by measuring them, that had not previously been important. It was a Victorian assumption that some races and classes of people were inferior to others. Consequently there appeared a type of researcher, known as anthropometricians, who surveyed the peoples in India by measuring their skulls. The nasal index was a particularly important measure. These surveys allocated people to categories on a status scale according to, amongst other things, anthropometrical indices. Indian society had always been structured around kinship and clan. However, the formalisation of the status differences between them gave caste greater significance. Once a league table of caste status had been published in censuses, groups would organise themselves and lobby to have their position on the league table improved (Padmanabha 1978: 4). Caste became a more dominant feature in Indian social and political life than it had been before it was formalised by censuses.

Such problems resulting from statistical measurement were not reserved for the nineteenth century. The current debate about the impact of performance measurement in the National Health Service raises the same issues, about the accuracy, the objectivity and the distorting impacts of the measurements, as NHS trusts seek to secure themselves a good position in the performance league tables (BBC 2003). The good surveyor then always questions the usefulness and the accuracy of their measurements.

Structure of the chapter

You may choose to be an explorer or a surveyor, or perhaps both. The choice should depend upon which form of research will best answer your research questions.

The chapter is divided into four parts:

1. Choosing between open and exploratory research methods on the one hand or pre-structured survey research on the other. Everyone should read this part, which describes the two broad choices of approach and gives guidelines and examples to help you make your choice.
2. Collecting and analysing research material using open and exploratory research methods. This part of the guide explains the use of open and semi-structured methods. You need read it only if this is the approach you have chosen to take.
3. Collecting and analysing research material using the pre-structured, pre-coded, survey approach. You need read this part of the chapter only if this is the kind of research method you have chosen to use.
4. Introduction to software for research. This part of the chapter provides brief introductions to the major software products designed for each approach. None of this part may be relevant to you. It might not be necessary for you to use software – and many students do not. If you do decide to use a package, you will need only one of the three described.

This chapter deals with both the collection of research material and its analysis. In the guide a distinction is made between analysis and interpretation. Analysis refers to putting the material in order by summarising, précising it and putting it into categories. Interpretation is the process of drawing the implications and significance from the material and using them as the basis for recommendations or action. Interpretation is the subject of Chapter 5.

Learning outcomes of the chapter

1 Readers will be able to choose the degree of openness or pre-coding appropriate to their research task.

2 Readers will be able to design and use open and semi-structured research techniques in a competent manner; and/or

3 Readers will be able to design and use pre-coded and structured research techniques in a competent manner.

4 Readers will be able to analyse quantitative and survey-based material; and/or

5 Readers will be able to analyse qualitative and case-based material.

6 Readers will be able to make well-judged decisions about the appropriateness or otherwise of using software packages for analysing quantitative and qualitative material and be able to identify appropriate software packages.

The range of research methods

There is a great variety of means at your disposal to carry out the primary research phase of your Master's dissertation. A useful distinction that can be made to help people get a grasp of the range of possibilities is to contrast open, or unstructured, forms of research with pre-coded or structured ones. All this distinction means is that in the former case the answers people are likely to give to the researcher's questions are not anticipated. The researcher is open to whatever people say. In the latter case the researcher has a good idea of the likely range of answers and is more interested in the relative frequencies with which the various options are expressed. In this type of research the researcher can provide respondents with a previously prepared list of options to choose from or respond to. Each of the major research methods, questionnaires, interviews, observation and so on can be used in an open (exploratory) or pre-coded (surveying) manner. Table 4.1 shows how this can be done.

The approaches shown in Table 4.1 need explanation, some more than others.

Interviews

The ways in which interviews can be conducted in an open or in a structured manner can be easily explained:

Table 4.1 Unstructured and structured approaches to the main research methods

	Exploratory research *Unstructured*	←————————→	*Survey research* *Structured*
Interviews	In-depth and open	Critical incidents	Interviewer keeps to a script and there are answer options
Panels	Focus groups		Delphi technique
Questionnaire	Lots of white space on the page		Tick boxes
Observation	Keeping a research diary	Checklists and categories	Completing an observation schedule Activity sampling
Documentary	Rhetorical analysis		Statistical analysis of themes

- The idea of an open interview is straightforward. The interviewer engages in informal conversation with the respondent about a particular area of interest. The interviewer may steer the conversation a little, by picking up on the cues and themes raised by the respondent, but generally the respondent leads the direction of the interview.
- Pre-coded interviews in contrast are controlled by the researcher. In these interviews the interviewer generally reads from a prepared script and is expected not to deviate from it. The questions asked are organised into a logical sequence, and for most questions the respondent is given a series of options and asked to choose a given number of them.
- Semi-structured interviews are in between these two extremes. Generally the interviewer has a schedule to remind them of the main issues and topics that need to be covered by the respondent. However, the respondent has much latitude to respond to the questions in the ways that seem sensible to them. The critical incident approach will be discussed later in this chapter but it is mentioned here because it is a form of semi-structured interview. The respondent is asked to think of occasions in their working life when they had to deal with a particular kind of issue, for example managing problem staff. The interviewee chooses an incident and then is encouraged by the interviewer to explain the incident in full detail.

Panels

Panels are a very common research method. As with interviews, they can be used in an open or in a pre-coded manner. When in open mode they take the form of focus groups. A group of people are brought together to have a free flowing, but focused, discussion on a particular topic. Gordon and Langmaid (1988) provide an accessible guide to focus groups. Figure 4.1 lists some of the issues that have to be considered when planning a focus group.

Decide what themes and issues are to be discussed

Develop protocols for use of information:
– you need to tell participants how the information they give will be used and the extent to which their anonymity will be preserved.

Decide the ideal group size:
– normally somewhere between 4 and 12 people in each group;
– add 20% for no-shows.

Choose the categories of people to take part in focus groups:
– make sure that there are no great differences in status or any other feature that might cause some participants to feel nervous or insecure and so not contribute to the discussion.

Determine how long the focus group should meet for. Normally they take between half an hour and an hour and a half. Any longer than a two-hour maximum would overstretch people's powers of concentration.

Facilitation:
– do you need someone to chair the focus group and keep the group on task? The answer is probably yes. The person chosen will need the skills and confidence to be able to manage the task.

Focus groups are normally tape-recorded, with the permission of the panel members of course. Make sure you have a good-quality microphone that can pick up the voices of people sitting around a table.

Figure 4.1 Setting up a focus group

The Delphi technique

The Delphi technique provides a contrast to focus groups because it uses panels in a structured manner. It was developed as a tool for futurology. It can be used to develop a consensus about the likelihood of future scenarios. It can also be used to develop a consensus on any issue that involves judgement and competing priorities.

In its classical form, a panel of experts in the subject being researched is formed. It is not necessary, indeed it is not a good idea, that this panel ever meets. A set of options or scenarios is developed (this is the pre-coding bit) and written into a questionnaire that is sent to all panel members. The panel members complete the questionnaire by entering their preferences or their judgements about the probability of each scenario. They might think a scenario has a 10 per cent chance of coming true for instance, or think that, on a percentage scale, it scores 70 per cent as an outcome to be desired. When the questionnaires are returned, the figures given by the experts are summarised as averages. The results are then fed back to the experts, in a second-round questionnaire, and they are invited to reconsider their judgements and make a new return. The idea is that by going through a series of such iterations the experts may arrive at a consensus about the issue in question.

Questionnaires

The difference between pre-coded and open questionnaires is simple. The pre-coded ones have lots of tick boxes for respondents to fill in, whereas open questionnaires have a few open questions and lots of white space for people to make their responses in their own words.

Documentary research

Research using documentary material can also take an open and a pre-coded form. In an open approach to texts and documents the researcher may be trying to understand, for example, how rhetorical techniques are used to try and persuade the reader to a point of view. Look at exercise 6.4 in Chapter 6 for an example of this type of analysis. Other open analysts may be looking for common narrative structures that are shared by many similar documents. Silverman (1993: Ch. 4) provides an interesting account of this style of analysis. In a pre-coded study of documents the researchers may well use electronic document files or electronic textual databases to count the frequency and context of the appearance of certain key words or phrases. Sometimes, for example, the popularity of management fads can be compared by counting the number of articles and papers (using bibliographic databases to do the counting) about them that are published. For example, as the number of papers on the learning organisation has diminished, so the number on knowledge management has increased, perhaps providing evidence that the latter is eclipsing the former.

Observational research

The degrees of openness or pre-coding that can be used in observational studies will be considered in more detail. This is partly because observation provides good examples to illustrate the differences between open and pre-coded research, but also because it may encourage people to use observation, which is a relatively underused method in Master's projects, more often. A number of illustrations will be given to explain the differences between open and pre-coded research.

Unstructured observation – a very open approach with a low degree of structure

At the open end of the scale, the researcher sits, watches and listens. If the researcher were interested in customer service in a doctor's surgery, they might obtain agreement to observe and then spend a morning's session sitting quietly in the corner of the waiting room observing. The researcher should try to keep alert to the events that happen. At the end of the session they should write down in a research diary all that they saw and heard and their reactions to it. They might need to junk the early observation because it would take a while for those being observed to lose their self-consciousness about being watched. Of course some researchers might use video or audio recordings of phone calls (if the research were being done in a call centre, say) to observe their subjects clandestinely. In the 1960s, when researchers were less ethically aware, a lot of educational research into children's learning and behaviour was done by filming children in classrooms through one-way mirrors. Great care needs to be taken with the interpretation of material gathered thorough open approaches. These issues are discussed in Chapter 5.

Checklists – a low degree of structure

A move away from open observation to a semi-structured form of observation can be achieved by using checklists such as the one shown in Figure 4.2.

This example is taken from a much larger document designed to help someone trying to research the culture of an organisation by observation. The checklist follows the stages in a visit to an organisation. It begins with

---

Some things to look for

Approaching the building

1. As you approach it, what does it look like, what does it make you think of?
2. What are the surroundings like?
3. Have attempts been made to improve the building's appearance?
4. What are the access and the signposting like?
5. How easy is it to get lost?

Etc.

The visual messages inside the building

1. What impression does the reception area give?
2. What sort of furniture and soft furnishings are used?
3. How clean is it?
4. What sorts of things are stuck on the walls?
5. How recent and relevant are the posters and notices?
6. How are rooms labelled and signposted?
7. Are there any signs that users of the building have personalised it?
8. Do different ranks or types of users have different spaces – how do they differ?

Etc.

Watching and listening to people

1. How do people acknowledge or ignore each other as they pass?
2. How do staff speak to the public, clients, each other?

Etc.

Figure 4.2 An observational checklist

finding the building and the look of the building and proceeds in later pages to include how staff talk to each other, whether they have their coffee breaks together and so on. The checklist is not prescriptive. The researcher is not required to answer every question in it. It is merely an aide-memoire to jog the researcher into noting the things they might be looking for.

Categories – a medium level of structure

A slightly more structured approach to observation would be to use categories. Some of the most famous categories for observational studies are used for studying the interactions between people in meetings. Bales' (1950) scheme of categories (Figure 4.3) is one of the earliest.

To use the categories, the researcher needs to sit somewhere where they can observe the participants in the meeting. As people make contributions to the meeting, the researcher classifies the interventions under one of the 12 categories of behaviour and uses the 'five-barred gate' system to allocate the intervention to the correct participant (who have all been given identification numbers). The researcher can subsequently analyse the range of behaviours used by different participants. Different categorical schemes

Type of contribution	Person									
	1	2	3	4	5	6	7	8	9	10
1. Shows solidarity										
2. Shows tension release										
3. Agrees										
4. Gives suggestions										
5. Gives opinion										
6. Gives orientation										
7. Asks for orientation										
8. Asks for opinion										
9. Asks for suggestion										
10. Disagrees										
11. Shows tension										
12. Shows antagonism										

Source: Bales (1950)

Figure 4.3 A scheme of observational categories

exist for different research topics. It is also possible to develop your own scheme of categories.

If a more structured type of observation is necessary, a pre-coded observation schedule can be used. Rutter (1979) used the schedule shown in Figure 4.4 in a study of the impact of academic ethos on schools' achievements. This is only part of the observational schedule but it gives a flavour of the overall style. By observing the minutiae of school life the researchers were able to form a measure of the rigour of academic expectations in a school's ethos (or culture as we would more likely term it today).

Activity sampling – very highly structured

Perhaps the most highly pre-coded form of observation is activity sampling. This technique can stand as an example of the opposite of open observation. To use activity sampling, researchers have to identify a limited number of conditions that they wish to research and then define them very precisely. Let us imagine that it was important to make a study of the use of peripatetic teaching styles by university lecturers. In plainer language, this is about whether lecturers teach standing up or sitting down. To research how often lecturers are on their feet when lecturing and how often they are sitting down, it would first be necessary to define the two conditions. Would a lecturer leaning against a table, for example, constitute sitting or standing? When the definitions have been sorted out the researcher would

---

This is a list of some of the things the observers had to record when they observed a lesson in a classroom:

1. The number of pupils in the class and the number who arrived after the start of the lesson.

2. The number of pencils borrowed from the researchers during the administration of the questionnaire.

3. The number of children not in correct school uniform (as defined by the school).

4. The number of children in outdoor coats or anoraks.

5. The number of broken chairs in the classroom.

6. The number of broken or cracked windows.

7. The decorative condition of the room: one point was given for each of five items and a total score assigned to each room.

8. The amount of children's work on the walls, coded from 1 to 4.

   0 = none; 1 = one-quarter of available wall space; 2 = one-half of available wall space;

   3 = three-quarters of available wall space; 4 = all available wall space.

9. The amount of graffiti, coded using the scale shown in item 8.

Source: Rutter (1979)

Figure 4.4 A structured observation schedule for the classroom

then have to take instantaneous observations of the lecturer at random points in time. Typically a researcher would have a little electronic gadget that beeped randomly but at a pre-set mean interval. Each time an observation was made the researcher would record whether the lecturer was standing or sitting. At the end of the research period the observations would be tallied and converted into percentages. If there were 500 observations and the lecturers were found on their feet in 300 of them, then the general conclusion that lecturers spend 60 per cent of the time standing can be drawn. Activity sampling enables researchers to measure the use of time to defined levels of statistical accuracy (of which more later – see p. 174). There are many issues in management (for example, the use of expensive plant and premises) where it is helpful to know how time is spent.

Discourse analysis is becoming used more frequently in management research and it is based on the observation and recording of conversations within organisations. Most commonly researchers work from a transcript of the recordings and try to understand the processes of communication that occur within organisations. The techniques of discourse analysis are varied and include classifying utterances into categories and counting their frequencies to much more open and exploratory forms of analysis. Tietze *et al.* (2003) provide a good introduction to discourse analysis.

Deciding whether to use open or pre-structured methods

The choice of research methods, whether to use interviews, questionnaires, documentary sources, and so on, was discussed in Chapter 1, and the choice between open and pre-structured was anticipated. In this chapter the issue has been given a more detailed treatment because the techniques for designing and conducting the two sorts of research approach are different. There are a number of factors that should be taken into account when deciding which approach to take:

- If you do not know what kinds of answers you will get from respondents or sources, then you should take an open approach.
- If you are looking for new ideas, then adopt an open approach.
- If you want to quantify the research material, then it is best to use a pre-coded approach.
- If you want to compare the views and experiences of a great many people, then it is easiest if pre-coded approaches are used.

Planning and setting milestones

Collecting research material is time consuming. Not just because it takes a lot of your time to do the work but also because there will be lost time, such as when you are waiting for people to return questionnaires, which can delay the project. Problems in carrying out the material collection phase of a project can be the critical factor that leads to a failure to meet the deadline for submitting the dissertation. It is a good idea therefore to plan this stage of the project and to set milestones that tell you when various parts of the research phase have to be completed.

Jankowicz (1995: 76) provided estimates of standard times for some of the activities you may have to do during the project. In the case of pre-coded, survey-based work, some of the critical items are as follows:

- informal pre-testing of a questionnaire by five respondents on one site – one day;
- reaching a postal questionnaire audience by mail – one week;
- time for respondents to complete a questionnaire – two weeks;
- time for questionnaire to be received back – one week;
- time to post, complete, return 'chase-up' letters and questionnaires – three weeks;
- transcribing questionnaire results into a database (20k characters) – five hours;
- learning how to use SPSS – three days.

Do not assume that open and unstructured research is quicker:

- preparing a ten-item interview schedule – one day;
- pre-testing the schedule on two guinea pigs – one day;
- setting up ten interviews and sorting out cancellations – one day;
- number of interviews a day – four (five possible but tiring);
- reviewing a tape of an interview and making notes – two to three hours;
- transcribing an hour of tape-recorded interview – seven hours.

In view of these time estimates the need to plan your research work is great.

● ● ● ● Exploratory research methods

Collecting the material

Exploratory research may involve the use of a battery of research methods – interviews, observation, documents and so on. However, interviewing is the most commonly used method in Master's level research into business and organisations and it will be used to provide examples of good practice in open and semi-structured research. After interviewing has been discussed there will be a review of a range of more specialised semi-structured techniques that can be used in exploratory research.

Interviewing

To do research interviewing successfully requires as much planning and organising as any other form of interview. The main steps in planning interviews are shown here:

- Roughly sort and list areas of questioning.
- Edit and prioritise questions.
- Consider the methods that will be used to analyse the questions.
- Decide on which questions are going to be open and which closed.
- Put questions into sequence.
- Check the questions for relevance to your research topic – do not ask questions that are impertinent.

The first stages involve identifying the areas you could ask questions about and organising them into priority order. It is never possible to cover as much ground in an interview as you had hoped. It is helpful to know beforehand which issues are less important and can be abandoned if time runs out. Once it is known what you want to find out, it is as well to check whether there might not be a better way of seeking the answers. If you want to find out about specific cases that might be embarrassing to the respondents, past strategic decisions that went wrong, for example, you might be well advised to find the material in contemporary documentary sources and so avoid the spin that interviewees will give to their accounts of past actions.

Even if the interview is going to be very open, it is worth considering using some pre-coded elements. In-depth and open interviews can be intensive. The use of pre-coded questions occasionally, with perhaps the options printed on a card that can be shown to the interviewee, can provide a welcome change of pace and style.

Some questions have to be diplomatically phrased. In these circumstances it is sensible to draft the questions before the interview. Reading them from a cue card, at least until you have done enough interviews to memorise them, avoids any stumbles or lengthy circumlocutions. Finally, bringing the planning stages to an end, it is worthwhile considering how you want to analyse the material to make sure that you are asking the right questions to produce material that can be used in the way intended.

The next stage is organising the interview:

- Script the initial questions and any that are difficult to phrase.
- Check that the language you use is simple and unambiguous.
- Prepare an interview schedule.
- Decide upon the recording method.
- Pilot an interview with someone friendly and make any necessary changes.
- Select interviewees.
- Negotiate access.
- Arrange time and place.

It is useful to write an interview schedule that contains all the main points you want to raise. If the details about the interviewee, time and place of interview are also included, and if you leave space between the main headings where you can jot down notes during the interview, then the schedule can double as a written record of the interview. In addition to any written note, the tape-recording of the interview should also be considered. I do not think I have ever had a respondent who refused to have the interview recorded. Some agreed only on the understanding that if they asked for the tape to be turned off at any time I would do so. The trouble with tape-recording is not so much the interviewee as the equipment – inadequate microphones, expiring batteries, jacks inadequately inserted in sockets and so on. Always check the equipment before the interview. If the respondent refuses to be recorded, or if the equipment fails, write up your notes as quickly as possible after the interview. Memory fades very quickly.

It is sensible to pilot the interview schedule on some friendly respondents before conducting interviews in earnest.

Who you interview is normally decided by purposeful sampling. This involves identifying the people who have the answers to the questions you want to ask. Often snowball sampling is used to identify people to interview. This begins by using your personal contacts to identify respondents. The people interviewed are then asked to nominate people they know who would also be good respondents. The process then snowballs, collecting more and more interviewees until you have done all the interviews you need. Even using this method, finding interviewees and negotiating their agreement to be interviewed can be a lengthy job. You also have to negotiate the terms of engagement, the subjects of the interview, how the information is to be used, what guarantees about confidentiality are to be offered and whether there will be any benefit for the interviewee. This latter may be no more than a promise to give interviewees a summary of the research when it is written up.

The place at which the interview takes place needs organising. Often, however, you will have no choice in this matter. The respondent will want to be interviewed in their office, although this is seldom ideal. It does, however, have the advantage that people will be more comfortable in their own space and you may pick up interesting clues by observing their workplace. When people work in open-plan offices it is often possible to book an interview or meeting room. These are ideal because removing people to a neutral space can encourage them to open up and to challenge their own assumptions. In the end choosing the place in which to conduct an interview is a matter of judgement constrained by practicalities. Ask people to turn off their mobiles during the interview.

Telephone interviews

Sometimes it is appropriate to interview people over the phone. The advantages are that you can often obtain access to people by phone who would never find the time to give you an interview. It is also an efficient method to find out how a number of people respond to a specific issue. If you wanted to find out what companies thought about Investors in People, then a telephone survey of local companies would quickly give you an overview of the situation. However, phone interviews have to be kept short, and it is not sensible to use them to ask questions about complex matters or questions that require detailed or long answers.

After organising the interviews the next stage is to conduct them. The interview should include the following phases:

- Explain the project.
- Offer confidentiality, anonymity and feedback.
- Explain the timing of the interview.
- Do the interview.
- Close with thanks – ensure there is an opportunity for follow-up.

Even if the interview is open or semi-structured it is still the responsibility of the researcher to manage the flow of the interview and bring it to a satisfactory close when the agreed time is completed. The means by which a researcher can control an interview through the types of questions they ask are listed below.

Steering a semi-structured interview

- Non-committal utterances and head nods.
- Repeating interviewee's last statement with a questioning inflection.
- Probing the last utterance.
- Probing the idea just before the last utterance.
- Probing an idea expressed earlier in the interview.
- Introduction of a new question on the same theme.
- Introducing a new theme.
- Summarising conclusively.

The researcher needs to employ the normal range of question types to understand fully what the respondent is telling them. Normally a section of an interview should be begun by the researcher asking an open question. An open question invites the respondent to talk expansively rather than to deliver a monosyllabic response. Sometimes a closed questions can be used as long as it is followed by an open supplementary. 'Should the company have agreed to the merger?' ... 'Why do you say that?' As the interviewee responds to the question the researcher should ask probing questions to explore areas the interviewee is skirting around and closed questions to check upon matters of detail. It is important to be aware of the respondent's body language. If the respondent begins to show emotion when giving their answers then researchers should use reflective questions. A reflective question reflects the speaker's emotions back to them and gives them a chance to talk further about them: 'So you felt very angry and frustrated at that point in the negotiations?' These questions are often restatements of what the interviewee said but are delivered by the researcher with an inflection at the end of the sentence that makes it into a question. When the topic has been dealt with, at least to the researcher's satisfaction, it can be closed, with the researcher summarising the main points of the interviewee's response and a question about whether the summary is accurate. Be careful in the use of non-committal nods and utterance (often no more than an 'Uh-huh'). They might seem non-committal to the researcher but they may convey to the interviewee that the researcher agrees with the interviewee's point of view.

Research interviewers should show enough vivacity and interest to keep the interviewee talking but should not give away too much of their own feelings and beliefs about the subjects under discussion. This is in part to avoid leading the interviewee to give the answer the interviewer hopes for. There is a danger if the interviewer reveals their position that the interviewee will accommodate their answers to it. It follows that when interviewing you should not express your opinion or challenge your respondent's opinion, except in so far as probing helps you to understand it. Neither should you give advice or express agreement with the respondent. This can be difficult as oftentimes the person is only too keen to enlist you as an ally in some internal battle they are fighting in their organisation.

The following bullet points identify some common problems with interviews:

- *Don't over-schedule* If you try to do more than five interviews a day you will be so exhausted at the end of the day you will not hear what the final respondents tell you.
- *Make the interview with the top boss the dessert rather than the starter* Do not start by interviewing the big boss. They will be impatient, and until you have talked to others in the organisation you will not know enough to be able to evaluate and respond to what the boss tells you.
- *Find a pleasant place for the interview* The room in which you do the interview should be quiet and uninterrupted and have comfortable chairs if possible. Do not have a desk between you and the interviewee. It is often good to sit at 90 degrees to each other with perhaps a table or coffee table, sitting in the angle, that you can both put an elbow on.
- *Do your homework* Find out all you can about an organisation before you interview people in it – search the World Wide Web to find out what is happening to the organisation.
- *'Please give me an example'* Interviewees mostly want to give you opinions. It is essential that you ask for examples that back up interviewees' views with details of actions and behaviours. Otherwise you may misunderstand what they are saying.

- *Don't be afraid to ask the stupid question* In my last research project, I found myself interviewing accountants. Not being an accountant I often did not understand what they told me. The natural inclination was to pass over the misunderstanding to avoid looking like a simpleton. But when doing research interviews you have to be prepared to look ignorant or foolish. If you do not understand, ask for more explanation, and keep on asking until you do understand.
- *The devil is in the details* You do not understand anything until you understand the detail. This is especially true if you are asking about procedures, systems and channels of communication.
- *Interview a range of stakeholders* Make sure you interview people from all the interested parties and not just senior management.
- *Three typical statements* It is a good idea to have an interesting question to end on that gives the respondent a chance to summarise all that they have said. It could be something like 'Will you give me three statements that characterise [the subject of the interview]?'

The end of an interview is often the most interesting part. If a tape recording has been made of the interview, the point at which the researcher declares the interview closed and turns off the cassette recorder is the moment when the interviewee relaxes and opens up to the researcher. These last-minute insights should be remembered and written down as soon as you are alone.

Interpretative approaches

There are many devices that can be used to tease out evidence about how people interpret and react to their organisational and work worlds. Here are the main ones that will be discussed here:

- diaries/shadowing – a life in the day of …
- life histories
- storytelling
- metaphors
- critical incidents
- personal constructs
- deframing – videos, photos, thought experiments.

Most of these techniques can be used in the context of interviews, focus groups or observation. However, they are not all suitable for all projects. You could, for example, make a collection of the metaphors that people use in describing a particular aspect of their work or organisation by doing the following:

- observing and listening to them at meetings;
- interviewing participants;
- asking members of a focus group to think of a metaphor;
- analysing the documents produced at work.

These techniques and their applications are not fixed or rigid. They can be adapted to suit circumstances. You must use judgement to decide which, if any, might be helpful to your project.

The possibilities for the use of interpretative techniques are vast. The techniques listed above will now be discussed in more detail.

Diaries/shadowing

The use of diaries to gather qualitative research material has a long pedigree. In the 1960s and 1970s many studies of the managerial role were based on diaries in which researchers asked managers to record their daily activities. Sometimes these diaries were highly quantitative and recorded how time was used. In other cases they were narrative accounts of a day's work. It may be objected that the authors can deliberately distort the content of diaries. An alternative is to shadow managers. This is time consuming and merely moves the problem from worrying about the respondents' subjectivity to doubts about the researcher's biases. David Lodge's (1989) novel *Nice Work* gives an amusing perspective on shadowing.

Diaries are a favoured technique of participant observers. Donald Roy was an early user of the technique. He worked on a factory floor to provide research material for his studies in industrial sociology. He kept a diary of his experiences. The following is a brief extract:

> On April 7th I was able to enjoy four hours of 'free time'. I turned out 43 pieces in the four hours from 3 to 7, averaging nearly 11 an hour (or $2.085). At 7 o'clock there were only 23 pieces left in the lot, and I knew there would be no point in building up a kitty for Monday if Joe punched off the job before I got to work. I could not go ahead with the next order … because the new ruling made presentation of a work order to the stock-chaser necessary before material could be brought up. So I was stymied and could do nothing for the rest of the day. I had 43 pieces plus 11 from yesterday's kitty to turn in for a total of 54. (Roy 1952: 432)

Writing one's own research diary, as Roy did, can be valuable. There can be practical problems in asking others to write diaries for you. They might not be inclined to give the time and care it would demand.

Life histories

This is a useful technique for eliciting qualitative information from managers and professionals. The respondents are asked to tell the story of how they got to where they are in their careers and organisations. Good examples of this technique can be found in Watson and Harris (1999).

Exercise 4.1

Keeping a diary

Let us assume you are researching the management of meetings. Keep a diary for a number of days in which you record your impressions of all the meetings you have attended. You might like to note your thoughts on the following matters:

- the outcomes of the meeting;
- examples of good meeting management;
- examples of poor meeting management;
- particular behaviours by participants and whether you thought them helpful;
- clichés and jargon that the groups seem to be developing.

Storytelling

One consultancy project I was involved in concerned the introduction of performance-related remuneration in a medium-sized firm of solicitors. We devised a scheme for distributing a proportion of the partnership's profits to the partners according to their contribution and performance. One of the reasons the senior partners wanted performance management was because they thought many of the partners were more concerned with doing interesting work than with doing profitable work. This tension was identified by an analysis of the many stories that we heard the partners tell

Exercise 4.2

Timelines

Let us assume you are researching career patterns and the development of managers. Identify someone to interview and ask them to draw a timeline on Figure 4.5 that plots the highs and lows of their career. Once they have drawn it, ask them to describe and explain the high and low spots. If you cannot find anyone to interview, you could draw your own timeline.

Figure 4.5 A timeline

The techniques could also be used to research people's perceptions of the changes in their organisation's culture over time.

about each other. One particular partner figured strongly in most of the stories; but, strangely, he had different roles in them. In some stories he was cast as the villain, sometimes he took the role of the hero and sometimes he was seen as a fool.

The partner had developed a new line of business for the firm that centred around uninsured losses on vehicles. The work required little legal expertise. As it could be processed administratively, the cases could be dealt with in a high volume/low margin manner. This business generated the bulk of the partnership's profits. In a partnership, partners traditionally receive a portion of the profits in relation to their percentage ownership, not according to their efforts. So for some people the partner of whom all the stories were told was a hero because he generated profits that they all benefited from. But sometimes the other partners saw him as a villain because his indispensability to the firm meant he could blackmail the partnership into doing what he wanted. He would just threaten to leave the partnership and take the lucrative business with him. Other partners saw him as a fool because he had neglected his professional legal expertise and made himself into a mere administrator. An analysis of these stories confirmed the tensions that existed within the firm between those who took an entrepreneurial and commercial perspective and those who had a traditional, quasi-academic outlook on their profession. Stories and anecdotes can provide excellent windows into organisational cultures (Gabriel 2000).

Metaphors

One way in which you can discover the metaphors people use when thinking about something is to ask them to draw a picture or a symbol that represents, for them, the subject of the research. Some students doing a management

---

Exercise 4.3

Heroes, villains and fools

This exercise is based on one developed by McClean and Marshall (1991). It is intended to help identify some of the key features of an organisation's culture.

Ask the respondent to recall a story, shaggy dog story, joke or anecdote that they have heard or told about the organisation. It must be one that concerns the organisation and refers to its personnel and habits. Ask them to tell you the story. Then ask them to tell you the following:

- what they think the moral of the story is;
- which of the characters in the story are seen as heroes, and why;
- which of the characters in the story are seen as villains, and why;
- which of the characters in the story are seen as fools, and why;
- what they think the stories reveal about the values and culture of the organisation.

project on managing the transition of school pupils from junior school to secondary school used this technique very successfully. First they asked pupils who were about to move to secondary school to draw a picture of their new school. At this stage the pupils had visited the new school so they knew it to be a bright, modern building. Nevertheless what they drew were dark halls – brooding, grey and spooky. They were again asked to draw a picture of their new school in their first week there. The pictures were still predominantly grey and grim. Only after three months, when they drew their final pictures, were the representations more realistic, light and cheerful. The team found that the drawings, through revealing the children's metaphors for their new school, threw much light on the problems of transition to secondary schools.

The same technique can be used with people in organisations. Respondents may be a little embarrassed at being asked to draw a picture and they may need a little encouragement. Alternatively you could use the 'If the organisation were an animal what sort of animal would it be?' approach. Students have used this successfully but I must admit I find this method a little toe curling.

Gareth Morgan's (1989) book *Imagin-I-Zation* is a good source for material on the use of metaphors.

Critical incidents

The critical incident technique (Flanagan 1954) has a long pedigree in social science research. In a critical incident study the respondent is asked to think of occasions on which they dealt with the subject of the research,

---

Exercise 4.4

Images and metaphors

This exercise can also be used to gain insight into people's thoughts about their organisation's culture. This one, too, is based on an original exercise in McClean and Marshall (1991):

- Draw a picture that represents the culture of your department.
  - Avoid drawing an organisation chart; choose an image instead. It might be a jelly, a dustbin, a lumbering articulated truck or whatever. Trust your intuition.
- Identify the adjectives that the chosen metaphor or image suggests – slow, responsive, efficient, cold and so on.
- Then repeat the exercise for another department with which the first department interacts.
- Compare and contrast the metaphors that describe the two departments.
- How well do the two departments work together?
- Can the smoothness or the choppiness of the relationship between the two departments be explained by the comparison of the metaphors used to describe them?

and things went well, and other occasions when things went not so well. In one typical study, the researchers used the technique to discover the impact that Medline, a medical bibliographic database, had on doctors' treatments of their patients. They asked the following questions:

> I'm interested in recent Medline searches that were especially helpful in your work or that were unsatisfactory. I'm especially interested in searches that have had an impact on patient care.
>
> I'm going to ask you a series of questions about such searches, one search at a time. I want to know what circumstance led you to do the search, what the context was, what specific question or issue you had in mind, what information you wanted and why. I'll need you to be as specific as you can. If I don't understand the situation or certain terminology, I'll ask you to explain it further. (Wilson *et al.*: 1989)

More commonly, in management research, the critical incident technique is used to identify the critical job requirements that are the difference between doing the job correctly and doing it incorrectly. This use of the critical incidents can lead, amongst other things, to the development of competency frameworks (Boyatzis 1982). As will be seen later in the chapter, critical incident information can also be analysed quantitatively.

Initially the technique was used as a means of identifying behaviour alone; but in modern uses an attempt is often made to recover the construction of meaning involved in the respondents' efforts to make sense of the issue. Ellinger and Watkins (1998: 228) describe this as a constructivist approach to critical incidents that aims to understand respondents' interpretation of their lived experience.

I have used critical incidents to research the following:

- Supervisory behaviour – 'Can you think of an incident involving managing staff that you thought you handled well/not so well?'
- Ethical dilemmas at work – 'Can you think of an incident at work that caused you a pang of conscience?'
- Evaluating management development programmes – 'Can you think of an incident at work that you thought you handled well/not so well because of things you learnt from the management development programme?'

There are of course many other possibilities.

Personal constructs/repertory grids

Personal construct theory was developed by Kelly (1963). It is a theory of personality that concerns the mental models, representations or hypotheses that people use to make sense of the world. He termed these notions 'constructs'. Repertory grid was an interviewing technique he developed to identify an individual's personal constructs. The theory assumes that each

Exercise 4.5

Critical incidents

If you were investigating an organisation's culture, here are some questions you might ask to elicit critical incidents. Try them on someone:

- Can you think of a situation at work when you knew what you would be expected to do but were unsure that this was right?
- Can you think of a situation at work when the novelty of a situation meant that there were no conventions or typical behaviours to guide your actions?
- Can you think of a situation at work when your values appeared to conflict with those of other groups in the organisation?

For each situation they can remember, ask the respondent to describe the following:

- the situation
- their thoughts and feelings about the situation
- what they did and why
- what others did
- the consequences and outcomes of the situation.

What clues do the incidents give about the culture of the organisation?

individual has different constructs. The basic technique is to ask someone to compare three things – people, products, whatever – and to think of a feature or dimension on which they show differences and similarities. If you have nine elements (nine customers for example), then you will go through the construct elicitation process for each possible combination of three from the nine. By going through a large number of comparisons, a map of a person's personal constructs can be developed.

If you were interested in MBA students' responses to different modules they are studying, you might present them, in turn, with a number of cards with the names of the modules written on them. You might randomly give a respondent cards with the following written on them:

| BUSINESS ETHICS | CORPORATE STRATEGY | MANAGEMENT ACCOUNTS |

The respondent is then asked, 'In what ways are two of these similar and different from the third?'

The respondent might reply that two involve number crunching and the third does not. The answer identifies a construct in which 'involves numbers' and 'does not involve numbers' form the opposite ends of the dimension. In this way the respondent's constructs are teased out. Sometimes you might want the respondent to focus on a particular issue.

You could ask the respondents, for example, to identify what two modules have in common that makes them different from a third 'in terms of the quality of teaching'.

In the example given in Figure 4.6 the process is used to rehearse some constructs about different managerial functions. However, in this example the process has been simplified by using a comparison of two objects only to elicit the constructs. In Figure 4.6 the first column, which in practice would be longer, lists the objects (in this case, the management functions that are being studied). The arrows point to boxes in the second column. Each row is used to record the differences between two groups as indicated by the arrows. The first row compares marketing and finance people; the second compares finance and production personnel, and so on. The second and third columns are used to record the extremes on a dimension that the respondent believes distinguishes people in different management functions. When I (acting as respondent) compared marketing people with production people I thought that fashionableness was something that distinguished them.

Stewart and Stewart (1981) is an old book but it contains a very practical guide to the use of repertory grid. In practice this basic mechanism becomes a complex and statistical process. It is best to use software to do the analysis. An introduction to repertory grid techniques and associated software can be seen at http://www.enquirewithin.co.nz.

In recent years the technique has been used, amongst other things, to evaluate training programmes and to identify managerial competences.

Figure 4.6 The basic mechanism of repertory grid

Deframing

Deframing is a technique that, like repertory grid, assumes that people construct their view of the world through mental models. It is a way of distancing a person from their everyday experience. It requires them to look at something afresh; as if they were an alien visiting from a different planet. Video and photos can sometimes perform this role. As already mentioned in Exercise 2.2, I once went to a seminar on quality improvement in residential services for people with learning disabilities. The seminar leaders had been to many residential centres and taken photos of the buildings. They projected a slide of a room on to the screen during the seminar and asked the audience what they thought the room was used for.

Exercise 4.6

Construct elicitation

- Choose three elements.
- Elicit your constructs using the following grid.

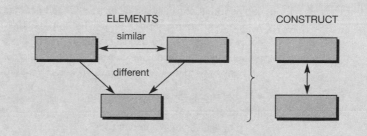

You can photocopy the grid to identify constructs from different combinations of elements.

The room was large and light and cheerfully, if garishly, decorated. There were cuddly toys dotted about and the walls were covered with big posters showing chimps getting up to naughty tricks such as stuffing toilet rolls down the WC pan. The audience all said they thought it was a nursery. The truth was that it was a day room in a home for adults with learning difficulties. No doubt the staff had decorated the room with the best intentions to make it attractive to the users. But the photo was used to deframe the staff and to get them to see the room as clients and outsiders would see it. The photos were to help staff see how the room could reinforce damaging stereotypes that the adult users were just like children and were more trouble than a cartload of monkeys.

A common way of deframing is to look at something with fresh eyes. This is most easily done by making comparisons. Exercise 4.7 uses a comparison between perceptions in the past and current perceptions. But there are many other ways of making comparisons. Visiting similar organisations is an easy method. It forces people to challenge their own organisations because it reminds them that things can always be done differently.

Analysing the material

Imagine the situation. You have done your open-ended, in-depth interviews, you have carried out unstructured observations or whatever. As a result, you have a large pile of raw material in front of you. How do you start to make sense of it? There are two contradictory things people often discover about analysing unencoded research material. The first thing is *the law of the missing middle*. This states that students who move straight from collecting their research material to writing up the dissertation,

---

Exercise 4.7

The newcomer exercise

This is another exercise that is based on one in McClean and Marshall (1991). It works because over a period of time we become used to the culture of an organisation and what originally struck us as strange becomes commonplace. It is only when we force our memory back to our first impressions that we realise what we have come to accept. As, by definition, culture is the values and habits we accept without thought, then this technique is excellent for making cultural values visible.

Think back to your first few days in your current organisation.

- What struck you as odd about its:
  - work practices
  - physical location and premises
  - patterns of relationships between people
  - values and priorities?
- How did it differ from your previous organisation?

---

thereby missing out the intermediate stage of sorting and sifting the material, tend to end up in a mess and a muddle. But, *the dilemma of drafting* says that researchers never really understand their material until they write it up. It is the process of writing that forces people to make sense of the material, and the significance of the material only emerges when sentences are put together.

If both of these premises are true (and they are only the result of anecdotal observation of students), then making sense of research material involves a repeated cycle of sorting and sifting, followed by writing, followed by more sorting and sifting, and so on. There are a number of devices that people use to assist them in this process (Riley 1996).

- *Memos to self* You write memos to yourself when you have a flash of insight (otherwise known as an epiphany or a 'Eureka! moment'). These can occur at any time, when reading, driving, interviewing, checking your research notes. It does not matter if the thoughts are fragmentary or incomplete. Jot them down informally and revisit them when you are writing up the dissertation.
- *Keeping a researcher's diary* A researcher's diary is a very similar process to writing memos to yourself. It has the advantage that a diary is chronological and so you can use it to give an account of how your thinking has developed during the project. A diary is essential to anyone doing action research.
- *Imaginary letters to a friend* Fix upon a friend who has no knowledge of your field of research and write them a letter in which you explain your project. Take it seriously even though you have no intention of

posting it. The letter format makes you boil down your thinking about the project to a few interesting and short sentences. Because you are writing to a friend and not to an academic colleague, you will be forced to write in an informal, non-academic style. This should help to clarify your thoughts.

Coding

Before you start writing you need to draw out the usable material from all the stuff you have collected. The process for doing this has the formal name of coding. It involves identifying themes, dividing the research material into chunks or units (and excluding the great bulk of the interview material that you decide is of no value) and allocating the units to the themes. Essentially this is an indexing process. It can be done manually or it can be done using software (see the last part of this chapter – Software for analysing research material).

There is an important practical difficulty if your research material includes tape-recorded interviews. It is whether to transcribe the material or not. The problem is that transcribing a taped interview is very time consuming (see p. 140). The process can be especially slow if you are unused to transcribing and if you do not have the proper equipment. It is obviously best to conduct your analysis using transcripts of the interviews, but many students doing MBA and Master's dissertations will simply not have the time to prepare them. In this case it is perfectly possible to write a set of notes on each interview based on listening to the taped interviews several times.

If you have used interviews, and if you have transcripts of the interviews, you can go through the sheets using a highlighter pen, or by marking the margins in scribbles, to identify the material that you think will be useful. If you have a tape and/or written notes, but no transcript, the simplest procedure is to listen to the tapes or scan the notes to identify the major themes or issues. In either case, create a sheet of paper for each theme and then listen to the tape again, or read the notes more carefully, and transcribe useful material from the interviews on to the appropriate sheet. Figure 4.7 shows one sheet from the analysis I carried out when I researched the role of district managers in a large service organisation.

The codes or themes can be identified by either skimming your research material, as already illustrated, or by reading the literature. You can also code for different things. For example, you could use substantive codes. Figure 4.7 uses substantive codes that concern the subject matter of the research. Alternatively 'code domains' (e.g. actions, meanings, relationships, settings, etc.) could be used. These relate to the levels at which the material can be analysed rather than the subject of the research. However the codes are defined, it is important that they remain open to modification and change. As the research progresses, understanding improves and it is necessary to modify and develop the framework.

Figure 4.7 A coding sheet

Two other pieces of advice about coding structures:

- Organise the codes into a hierarchical order. This can be done using an 'organisation chart' form. This enables the researcher to show how some codes are subsets of others and allows content analysis to be done at different levels of aggregation.
- Use cross-references between codes. These are useful to make connections between disparate elements in the code structure that might otherwise be ignored. One simple way of doing this is to allocate units of material to a number of appropriate codes.

This might seem like a lot of work but it makes writing up the dissertation much easier. This is important at a stage in the project when deadlines loom. As you write each section of your findings, turn to the appropriate coding sheet and there you have all the information you need – the most common views taken of a matter, the extreme views, the juicy quotes – all ready for you to write up. If you have to continuously refer back to your original research notes when writing up, the process is cumbersome and you are more likely to forget important points.

Content analysis

Content analysis is an additional step you can take when you have finished coding the material. It adds a quantitative element to the analysis of qualitative material. In a content analysis the frequency with which issues or themes appear in the material is measured.

David Silverman (1993: 165) provides an interesting example of a content analysis that is summarised in Table 4.2. He was studying the differences between private health care and NHS health care. In particular he wanted to find out how the relationship between doctor and patient differed in the two systems. He focused on ceremonial order. Two aspects of this order were whether a doctor opened a consultation with general conversation, to build rapport with the patient, and whether future appointments were made to suit the patient's diary. The research was done by observation. The consultations were recorded and then analysed. The frequencies with which the doctors chatted with the patients and took their prior appointments into account were coded, with the results that can be seen below. The use of percentages rather than words such as 'mostly' and 'infrequently' to describe the material gives the findings more punch.

Table 4.2 Content analysis: ceremonial orders in health care

	% occurrence of feature in private clinics (*n* = 42)	% occurrence of feature in NHS clinics (*n* = 104)
Appointments set at patients' convenience	36	10
Social elicitation	60	30

Source: Silverman (1993: 165)

Content analysis can be very useful when you have a large number of critical incidents to analyse. In a recent study I, with colleagues from Nottingham Business School, carried out a critical incident study of the ethical difficulties financial and HRM managers reported they experienced at work. A total of 240 incidents was collected. A classification of ethical problems was developed from the material in the incidents and then the incidents were classified accordingly. The results are shown in Table 4.3. In the case of this research, a content analysis is a very efficient method of

Table 4.3 Categories of ethical issue reported by accountants and HRM specialists

Problem type	Financial and accounting specialists (%)	Human resource management specialists (%)
Distributive justice	12.2	12.2
Economy with the truth	28.5	9.4
Confidential and privileged information	8.4	6.5
Conflicts of interest	6.9	3.7
Bullying and pressure	13.0	9.4
Bending the rules and ethical risk taking	16.8	27.1
Matters of principle	6.1	17.8
Giving and withdrawing trust	8.4	14.0
Total number of critical incidents	131	109

highlighting the differences between the ethical problems reported by financial and human resource management specialists.

The difficulty with this form of content analysis is that the allocation of incidents to the categories is subjective. It is done according to the researcher's judgement. Other researchers might put some of the incidents in different categories. This is known as the problem of inter-rater reliability. One way of diminishing this problem is to ask several people to allocate the incidents to categories and to exclude from the analysis any incidents that the raters cannot agree upon.

Writing case studies and accounts

If content analysis is not appropriate for your research material, it can be written up as a case study. In a case study you give a narrative account of the subject of your study. You can draw your material from your coding sheets or your index of codes, but the skill is in blending it into a coherent story that draws together all the complex interactions and processual coincidences that constitute organisational life.

● ● ● ● Survey research: pre-coded and structured research methods

Collecting the material

In this section the development and use of a questionnaire-based survey that is largely pre-coded, completed by a sample taken from a particular population, and to be analysed quantitatively, will be used to illustrate the use of pre-coded and structured techniques. The issues will be dealt with by going through the stages from deciding on the sample size to analysing the results of the questionnaire.

Sample size

The first question that worries people designing a questionnaire is 'How many should I send out?' Students' concerns about whether they can achieve a big enough sample are often a key factor when deciding whether to do a survey. As it is a critical matter, this question will be dealt with first. The answer depends on a number known as the limit or margin of error. The purpose of taking a sample is to obtain a result that is representative of the whole population being sampled without going to the trouble of asking everyone. The problem is that no sample can be guaranteed to be representative. If you could take a large number of different samples from the same population, some would overestimate and some underestimate the true figure. The margin or limit of error is a measure of this uncertainty in the representativeness of the sample.

You may not have been aware of the term 'margin of error'. But you are almost certainly aware of its importance. The US presidential election of 2000 provides a good example. In the opinion polls before the elections the results were often Gore 48 per cent and Bush 50 per cent. The margin of error on these opinion polls was +/– 2 per cent. That is to say the percentage of the population likely to vote for Gore could have been anywhere between 46 per cent and 50 per cent, most likely 48 per cent. The proportion who would vote for Bush could be anywhere between 48 per cent and 52 per cent, most likely 50 per cent. The margin of error was the same or greater than the difference between the candidates. The poll results therefore could not be used to predict who might win. In the event, this proved to be a very accurate forecast.

The size of sample you need depends in part on the size of the margin of error you are prepared to accept and the size of the population from which you are going to take the sample. If there were 1000 employees working in an organisation that you wanted to sample, and if you were prepared to accept a margin of error of +/–5 per cent, then Table 4.4 can be used to discover the number of completed questionnaires necessary.

The figures in Table 4.4 are the number of completed questionnaires you need to have returned. The number of questionnaires you send out will have to be larger. In the case of a general questionnaire, a return rate of 30 per cent would be very good. If the questionnaire was being distributed to employees in an organisation, it might be easier to chase up the questionnaires and then a return rate of 70 per cent or more might be achievable.

Sampling frame

To send questionnaires to people you need a list of the names and addresses of all the people in the appropriate population. Such a list is called the sampling frame. Finding a sampling frame may be a major obstacle. People are not inclined to give researchers access to mailing lists for free because the information they contain is valuable, and doing so may

Table 4.4 Estimating margin of error on sample survey results

Population	Margin of Error			
	5%	3%	2%	1%
50	44	48	49	50
100	79	91	96	99
150	108	132	141	148
200	132	168	185	196
250	151	203	226	244
300	168	234	267	291
400	196	291	343	384
500	217	340	414	475
750	254	440	571	696
1000	278	516	706	906
2000	322	696	1091	1655
5000	357	879	1622	3288
10 000	370	964	1936	4899
100 000	383	1056	2345	8762
1 000 000	384	1066	2395	9513
10 000 000	384	1067	2400	9595

Note: At 95 per cent level of certainty – this means that in 95 out of 100 times the true result will be within the range of the margin of error. There is, however, a five per cent chance that the true value will be outside of the range. It is possible to set different confidence levels. If a 99 per cent confidence level were needed, then many more completed questionnaires would be necessary.

Source: Saunders *et al.* (2002: 156)

contravene data protection legislation. If you are doing the survey within an organisation, then the payroll is the most reliable sampling frame. Once the sampling frame is available, the normal process is to take names from the list randomly until you have as many as you need in the sample. This is known as probability sampling. It is the best form of sampling because all elements in the population have an equal chance of being included in the sample. It minimises the possibility of an unrepresentative sample. It can be a time-consuming process and so a systematic sample is sometimes used. This means taking elements at fixed intervals from the sampling frame, taking every tenth person on the payroll for example. In the case of activity sampling (see p. 138), systematic sampling could be achieved by taking observations every half an hour, say. Of course if the subject being studied had a natural cycle that lasted half an hour (taking a cigarette break, for example), then the sample of observations would be highly distorted. Quota sampling is a technique that aims to ensure that the sample is representative of the major groups in the population. If the proportion of women and men employees is 30:70, then a quota sample would try to reproduce this ratio in the sample. In practice it is difficult to achieve. You may send questionnaires to men and women in the desired proportions, but there is no guarantee that the completion rates will be the same for the two groups and therefore the final sample of questionnaires will not be in the correct ratio.

Many people doing Master's dissertations resort to purposive sampling because their problem is simply getting enough questionnaires filled in. This is a grand way of saying that the researcher puts into their sample whoever they can obtain access to or whoever they think may be appropriate respondents for the questions they want to ask. Students often have to resort to this technique for practical reasons. The downside is that the lack of randomness in the sample means that any calculation of the margin of error that might be done would be unreliable.

One interesting development in the use of research questionnaires is the use of email and the World Wide Web to deliver questionnaires and to receive the responses. This is most easily done if you want to survey employees in a single organisation who all have access to email and the organisation's intranet. One colleague conducted a survey of employees' opinions about a new office building they had moved into. He was able to obtain the email addresses of all the employees based in the building and he sent them an email explaining what the research was about. The email contained a hyperlink to a World Wide Web page that held the questionnaire. Respondents clicked on to the link and completed the questionnaire on the screen. They were then asked to click on a button that emailed their responses to an electronic database (also on a web page) where all the returns were collected. This approach is more difficult to use for a public population because not all respondents may have access to email or the Internet and there can be problems in sending the results back to the researcher because of the different capabilities of hardware and software. Another problem of using email to return completed questionnaires is that the email will come with the sender's email address and so it is more difficult to promise confidentiality convincingly.

Designing a questionnaire

There are a number of general issues to bear in mind when designing a questionnaire. They are all concerned with maximising the response rate:

- Keep them as short as possible. Two or four sides of A4 paper would be good for research for a Master's dissertation.
- Design them to look attractive by using the capacities of your word processor.
- Give them a logical and sequential structure so that the respondent can easily see what the questionnaire is about and can follow its themes as they develop.
- Divide the questionnaire into parts that correspond to the various issues you are asking questions about. If you are going to ask for demographic information about the respondents, (such as age, sex, job

title or whatever), ask for it at the end of the questionnaire. People are more likely to answer personal questions if they have already invested time and effort in completing the rest of the questionnaire.

● Ask the easy questions first and the hard ones last.
● Keep any personal questions (as long as they are justified) until last.

Many students ask for too much demographic information in their questionnaires. They ask questions about age, sex, ethnicity, socio-economic classification and so on as a habitual response rather than from a genuine need for the information. There are two reasons for asking for demographic information. The first is to provide a way of checking the representativeness of the people who respond to the questionnaire. If, for example, an organisation that has been surveyed has 20 per cent of its staff working in technical jobs but only five per cent of those who completed the questionnaire hold technical positions, then it may be necessary to take this into account when interpreting the results. The second reason is to allow you to do cross-tabulations. This is dealt with later in the chapter, but in brief cross-tabulation allows you to enquire of the questionnaire replies whether people with differing demographic characteristics responded in a similar manner or not to the main questions asked.

Question formats

The next step in designing a questionnaire is to choose the question formats that are appropriate to the information being sought. A number of formats will be rehearsed here.

Dichotomous questions

These are questions that offer the respondent only two alternatives to choose between. These can only be used when the issue is clear-cut. To ask 'Is globalisation a force for good or bad in the world … Yes/No?' is to reduce a complex issue to an absurd demand for a simple answer. The question is a large and difficult one and respondents may object to having to give a simplified response to it. The examples given below are appropriately set as dichotomous questions:

Are you   Male ☐   Female ☐

The law requires all employees to have a
contract of employment   True ☐   False ☐

Multiple choice questions

These questions normally provide respondents with a choice of three to five options and ask them to choose one. There is normally a final 'Other (please specify)' option. The skill in drafting these questions lies in giving unambiguous options that are mutually exclusive:

What sort of domestic animal would you choose as a pet?

Dog ☐   Cat ☐   Bird ☐   Fish ☐   None ☐

Other (please specify) ....

Checklists

These are the same as multiple choice but the respondents are allowed to tick as many items as they wish:

What aspects of the staff cafeteria do you think are unsatisfactory?

Menu choice ☐   Prices ☐   Quality of food ☐   Style and design ☐

Rating scales

These questions ask respondents to rate or evaluate a service, policy or option according to a carefully graduated scale. The respondents indicate the nature of their opinion by marking the appropriate place on the scale:

What is your opinion of the service provided by the call centre?

Excellent   Poor

    1   2   3   4   5

The scale can be entirely in words. If you use verbal scales it is necessary to be careful in writing them. A sample of patients in a hospital was asked (Thompson 1986: 95) to complete a rating scale question on the degree of boredom they experienced during their hospitalisation. Here are the results:

I was thoroughly bored throughout my stay	13%
I normally found something to occupy my time	66%
There was never a dull moment in such a busy ward	21%

The first and last statements in the scale were very extreme, of utter boredom or total exhilaration. It was not surprising that most respondents chose the mid point on the scale. The researchers redrafted the scale and gave it to the same respondents, with the following results:

I was quite bored during my stay in hospital	18%
Although I didn't have much to do in the ward I wasn't particularly bored	36%
I normally found something interesting to occupy my time	31%
There was never a dull moment	14%

This revised scale shows a much wider spread of results and differentiates between the degrees of boredom experienced by those in the middle of the distribution of opinion. These examples show how sensitive the results from a rating scale question are to phrasing used in the scale.

> ### Exercise 4.8
>
> # Verbal and numerical scales for rating
>
> *Jim Stewart*
>
> **Step 1**
> Give a numerical value between 0 and 9 (where 9 = the greatest frequency) to indi-cate the frequencies suggested by each of the following words and phrases.
>
> | | | | |
> |---|---|---|---|
> | Often | ... | Quite often | ... |
> | Always | ... | Frequently | ... |
> | Sometimes | ... | Rarely | ... |
> | Never | ... | Almost always | ... |
> | Usually | ... | A lot | ... |
> | Most of the time | ... | Seldom | ... |
> | Occasionally | ... | | |
>
> **Step 2**
> Ask a few friends or colleagues to do the same. Compare and discuss the ratings.
>
> **Suggested answer**
> The exercise normally indicates that the meanings of words about frequencies are not fixed and that it can be dangerous to use words in rating scales in questionnaires. It is likely that you and your colleagues agreed that 'always' is 9 or thereabouts and that never was a '0'. However, the chances are that you and your colleagues disagreed about the value to be placed on the other words and phrases.

It is possible, by using a technique called Behavioural Anchored Rating Scales, to attribute a numerical value to positions on verbal scales (Mohrman *et al.* 1989). Such scales are often used in appraisal systems.

A further possibility is to use graphic symbols. You could use a smiley face ☺ to represent the positive end of a scale and a series of increasingly scowling faces for the other end of the scale.

Ranking questions
These questions ask respondents to put a number of statements or options into rank order:

> Indicate your order of preference for the kind of nursing you would like to do after graduation. Show your first choice as 1 and your least favoured choice as 4.
>
> Acute care.....   Occupational.....   Community.....   School.....

Ranking questions are important because they are more useful for explor-ing difficult questions of priorities than are rating questions. If you wanted to find out which of five departments should bear the brunt of a major budget cut, then a rating question would probably reveal that respondents thought that none of the departments could manage with a swingeing cut. However, if respondents were asked to put the departments into rank order, according to their ability to bear a cut, most respondents would be able to discriminate between the departments.

Likert scales

These are a form of rating scale that is commonly used to ask people about their opinions and attitudes. The basic structure is to provide a series of statements, some negative and some positive in tone, and to ask the respondent to choose a position on a five-point scale between strongly agree and strongly disagree. It is this scale that Rensis Likert invented.

Statements	Strongly agree	Agree	Uncertain	Disagree	Strongly disagree
1. Training in office management improves one's promotion prospects					
2. Off-the-job training is usually too theoretical and impractical					
3. Off-the-job training is usually more like a holiday than work					

The straightforward way to use these questions is to analyse them one at a time. However, as long as the statements all relate to the same subject it is possible to use them to measure the overall opinion of an individual, or of a sample of respondents, to a particular issue. In the example shown above the issue in question is attitude towards training. This is done by deciding whether statements are positive or negative towards training. Let us agree that statement 1 is positive and statement 2 is negative. It is then necessary to decide whether 1 or 5 on a five-point scale is going to represent a positive attitude. Assume the number 1 is chosen to indicate a positive attitude. As statement 1 is positive, a respondent who ticked 'strongly agree' will score a 1 and a respondent who ticked 'strongly disagree' will score a 5. Statement 2 is negative and so the scoring is reversed. Once all the statements have been scored, then a respondent's overall score on the statement can be calculated as a mean. If a respondent scored 20 on five statements, then her or his average, or mean, score would be 4. The researcher can then claim that, on a scale from 1 to 5, where 1 equals a positive attitude and 5 a negative attitude, this person has a score of 4 and therefore has a broadly negative opinion of the issue. If the scores of all the respondents are averaged, then the result is an overall and representative measure of attitude amongst the population surveyed.

The use of Likert statements to measure attitudes is only valid as long as the statements relate to the subject of the research. There are a number of reasons why this might not be the case. One possibility is that the researcher thinks that a statement relates to an issue but that many of the respondents see it as unrelated. Another possibility is that some respondents may see a statement as positive while others see it as negative. Statement 3 in the example shown is a case in point. Some people might think seeing training as a holiday a bad thing. Others might think it perfectly acceptable that training should be seen as a perk or a reward. If either of these situations is true, then the statement should be removed from the questionnaire because it is not a reliable indicator of the opinion being studied. There is a technique for checking the reliability of statements, known as Cronbach's Alpha, and it is available in SPSS (Bryman and Cramer 1997: 63–65). An introduction to SPSS is given in the final part of this chapter.

Needless to say, interpretivist researchers find the whole idea of measuring attitudes laughable. They would argue that attitudes are too complex to be reducible to a single number on a scale. Billig (1996: 207–208) points out that most people are in a constant state of debate with themselves about their views on any issue and therefore their attitudes are subject to constant change and revaluation.

Semantic differential

In a semantic differential question respondents are asked to rate a single object or idea on a series of bi-polar scales. Each scale is formed from adjectives (words, which are a semantic matter) that are opposites (i.e. differential):

To me, electronic mail means:

Boring	---:---:---:---:---:---:---:	Interesting
Relevant	---:---:---:---:---:---:---:	Irrelevant
Exciting	---:---:---:---: ---:---:---:	Unexciting
Nothing	---:---:---:---:---:---:---:	A lot
Appealing	---:---:---:---:---:---:---:	Unappealing
Fascinating	---:---:---:---:---:---:---:	Mundane
Worthless	---:---:---:---:---:---:---:	Valuable
Involving	---:---:---:---:---:---:---:	Non-involving
Not needed	---:---:---:---:---:---:---:	Needed

As with the Likert scales the respondents' ticks can be given a numerical value and means calculated, always making sure that the scoring of the questions is adjusted to account for the mixing of positive and negative adjectives at both ends of the scale.

Open questions

It is nearly always a good idea to have a number of open questions in a questionnaire otherwise dominated by tick boxes. It is an irritation to people when they are required to respond to pre-determined categories. The provision of space for them to give an answer from their own perspective and in their own words diminishes the frustration:

Open questions are vital when the researcher is interested in new ideas or novel points of view or cannot anticipate the likely answers.

There are a number of types of question that you should avoid. These restrictions mostly apply to asking questions in interviews as well as to designing questionnaires.

Leading questions

A leading question is one that, by its content, structure or wording, leads the respondent in the direction of a certain answer. Sometimes, as in 'Wouldn't you say…' the ploy is obvious. In other questions the leading is more insidious.

	SA	A	U	D	SD
Teachers should be praised for their managerial skills, particularly in view of the large class sizes	☐	☐	☐	☐	☐

Hypothetical questions

Hypothetical questions ask people what they would do in a particular circumstance. What people say they might do and what they actually would do are often quite different. Hypothetical circumstances are without constraint and so people answer them in terms of what it might be nice to do or in terms of what they think others believe they ought to do. It is at least possible that the overestimate of 12 million visitors to the Millennium Dome was a result of market researchers asking hypothetical questions.

Presuming questions

A presuming question is one that assumes something about a respondent. Frequently questionnaire designers make assumptions that the respondent will both understand and know the answer to their questions.

Drafting and piloting the questionnaire

If anyone manages to write a perfect questionnaire on first draft, it must be the result of sheer good luck. Most people draft questionnaires that are full of mistakes, illogicalities and howlers. The following is a good example of the mistakes people can easily make in their first drafts. It is about the staffing resources in a college of further education:

Are the staff that teach you (please tick one box only)

Male ☐   Female ☐

Half male/half female ☐

More male than female ☐

More female than male ☐

It is just possible to see what the drafter meant.

The only way to prevent such problems is to pilot and test your questionnaire.

Distributing the questionnaire

Here are a few tips for distributing your questionnaire:

- Send out the questionnaire with a covering letter that includes a 'thank you' and gives instructions for returning the questionnaire.
- Repeat the 'thank you' and the return instructions at the end of the questionnaire.
- If the questionnaire is sent out by post include an SAE.
- Most of the paper on people's desk is white. Print your questionnaire on coloured paper. It will stand out and increase the chances of it being completed. Apparently pastel colours are the best ones to use.
- Seek sympathy, but do not grovel. If you have sent the questionnaire to employees many of them will have done courses that required them to send out questionnaires. Appeal to their sympathy for your plight to encourage them to fill in the questionnaire.
- Offer to send people who request it, perhaps by completing a tick box and contact details question on the questionnaire, a summary of the findings from the questionnaire.

Checking the margin of error

When the questionnaire has been piloted it can be useful to check the margin of error on the results. Each question will have its own margin of error and there will not be time to check every one. Choose an important question that gives a nominal answer, i.e. the answer can be expressed as a percentage. The following formula can be used to calculate the margin of error at a 95 per cent confidence level:

Exercise 4.9

The attitudes towards staff appraisal questionnaire

Review the following fictitious questionnaire and identify as many mistakes and bad things about it as you can. Treat it as a first draft.

Survey into staff attitudes on the performance appraisal scheme

The organisation's Investors in People (IiP) accreditation is coming up for renewal. As part of the preparation for the visit of the inspection team this questionnaire is being sent to all staff to complete. You can return the completed questionnaire in the envelope provided to your line manager. The questionnaire is anonymous. When the results have been analysed it will provide the information necessary to show that the organisation's appraisal scheme is effective and supports our investment in you, our employees.

The questionnaire is also available on the organisation's intranet at www.skegmouthindustries.com/investorsinpeople/appraisal/survey/Ab2593602/responses/289993355/html. If you fill it in on the screen you can email it to the HRM department.

It takes just a few minutes to fill in the questionnaire and the managing director is looking for a very high response rate. Please tick the boxes as appropriate.

Part 1

1. What is your role in the organisation?

Top management team	1	Senior manager	6
Upper middle manager	2	Middle manager	7
Senior team leader	3	Team leader	8
Core worker	4	Casual worker	9
Blue-collar worker	5		

2. What age are you?

Under 12	13 to 15	15 to 21	22 to 30	30 and over
10	11	12	13	14

3. Are you   male ☐ 1   female ☐ 2

4. How would you describe your ethnic and cultural origins?

UK ☐   Indian ☐

European ☐   Pakistani ☐

African ☐   Other Asian ☐

Caribbean ☐

Other (please specify) ....

5. Have you applied for a job outside the organisation within the last year?   Yes ☐ 10   No ☐ 11

Exercise 4.9 *continued*

Part 2

6. How many days absence have you had in the past two years? [   ]

7. Do outside interests take up much of your time?   Yes [ ]   No [ ]

8. Have you had an appraisal this year?   Yes [ ]   No [ ]

9. My appraisal was   Exceedingly helpful and beneficial [ ]

    Quite helpful [ ]

    A complete waste of time [ ]

10. Did you find

The preparatory documentation	very satisfactory	satisfactory	acceptable
The appraisal interview	very satisfactory	satisfactory	acceptable
Your performance ratings	very satisfactory	satisfactory	acceptable

    How often do you?

	frequently	sometimes	occasionally
11. Review your performance against targets and objectives	[ ]	[ ]	[ ]

	regularly	frequently	sometimes
12. Review your personal development with your manager	[ ]	[ ]	[ ]

	often	occasionally	rarely
13. Discuss your career ambitions with your manager	[ ]	[ ]	[ ]

Part 3 Please read the statements below; decide whether you strongly agree, agree, disagree or strongly disagree, and then circle the number below your choice.

	Strongly disagree	Disagree	Agree	Strongly agree
14. An effective appraisal scheme improves the organisation's performance.	1	2	3	4
15. The performance pay element of the appraisal scheme is fair and motivates me to perform better	1	2	3	4
16. Without an appraisal interview my staff development needs would not be met.	1	2	3	4
17. If a peer mentoring scheme were introduced it would help me become better at my job and I would take part with enthusiasm.	1	2	3	4

Exercise 4.9 *continued*

Part 4

18. The appraisal system benefits me and the organisation because...
    (please complete the sentence in not more than 50 words)

19. What changes would you like to see made to the appraisal system?

Suggested answer

- The introduction to the questionnaire presupposes that the results will support the organisation's reaccreditation. This makes the questionnaire a series of leading questions because the respondents will know which answers they are expected to give.
- The instructions on what to do with a completed questionnaire are confusing. The lengthy URL for the web version of the questionnaire is far too complex for anyone to wish to type into his or her web browser. It would be all right if the notification of the questionnaire had been sent by email and people had only to click onto the hyperlink.
- Never suggest how long it takes to fill in a questionnaire. Some people will do it quicker and think they must have missed something. Some will take longer and think themselves 'thick'.
- The general instruction to 'tick the appropriate boxes' does not apply to all questions. Some require answers to be circled.

  Q1. This is a multiple choice question but the options presented are ambiguous. Terms such as 'upper middle' have no commonly agreed definition. Other options (casual worker, blue-collar worker) could be seen as disrespectful. There is also a technical problem. The logic of the possible answers is hierarchical and it zigzags from left to right and back again; the numbers however proceed first down the left hand column and then down the right hand column. The numbers are unnecessary in any case. They are probably data input field numbers to help the staff who type the completed questionnaires into computer databases. However, they are of no relevance or interest to the people filling in the questionnaire.

  Q2. The options provided leave out 12-year-old people and leaves 15-year-olds a choice of two categories to check. People over 30 years old may regard the options as a little insulting.

  Q.3. This is probably acceptable.

  Q.4. The options in this multiple choice question are not mutually exclusive. A person might quite honestly tick UK (because they are a UK citizen), European (because we are part of the European Union), Caribbean (because they were born there) and Indian (because they are Hindu and live by Indian social customs). The options do not cover enough of the range of possible responses. Several groups may feel less than pleased at being thrown together in the category of 'other Asian'.

  Q.5. This is the sort of question people may be uncomfortable answering unless they feel very confident of anonymity. The phrase 'within the past year' is ambiguous. Does it mean the calendar year, within the last 12 months or within the past financial reporting year?

  Q.6. It is most unlikely that the respondent will know the answer to this question unless it is very simple one, such as having had no days off. Questions ought not to be asked if it is suspected that the respondents will not know the answer.

  Q.7. This is an impertinent question. Both in the sense that it is not relevant to the subject of the questionnaire and it is also a question to which the employer has no right to know the answer. There was probably some hare-brained notion behind the question, such as that people with strong outside interests will be less committed to work and will have a lower opinion of appraisals.

Exercise 4.9 *continued*

Q.8. There is a phenomenon in the literature on appraisal known as the 'disappearing appraisal'. If you ask appraisers whether they have conducted an appraisal, they will answer yes far more often than the staff they are supposed to have appraised. The issue is whether different groups might have different understandings of what appraisal is.

Q.9. This question can only be answered if the respondent has reported that they have had an appraisal interview. The three options presented do not give a graduated set of responses to the question. The middle option is likely to be the mean position whereas the other two options are very extreme and are likely to occupy positions at the far end of the normal distribution 'bell' curve. In other words, the options are not very sensitive to the likely range of responses to the question.

Q.10. This rating scale is so crass as to be unbelievable. I have seen it used in a feedback questionnaire on customer service in a hotel.

Q.11. The rating scales in this block of questions are very loosely drafted so that the same words appear in different places on a three-point scale.

- **Part 3**. This section uses Likert scales. However, the mid point in the scale has been left out. This raises a contentious point of debate in questionnaire design: whether it is acceptable to have an even number of points on a scale or whether it is always proper to have an odd number of points. The argument for even-numbered scales is that it forces respondents to take a view one way or another and this gives managers useful information. The argument in favour of odd-numbered scales is that most people take a neutral or a 'not sure' position on most issues and therefore the mid point of 'uncertain' on the Likert scale is necessary to record their position. As I heard someone say on the radio when talking about how he had felt when responding to a pollster's questions, 'What I actually thought is that there were points in favour of the thing and points against it and that both sets of arguments were open to questioning'.

  Apart from this general point it should be noted that the scale is presented 'strongly agree' first in the instructions and 'strongly disagree' first in the places for the respondents' answers. This leads to a further problem. The Likert scale is presented in an order that is the reverse of that normally used. The normal order is given in the rubric to this block of questions but is reversed for the questions themselves. There is a danger that people might respond according to the anticipated, normal order and not to the actual order of the scale.

Q.14. This question is tautological – an *effective* appraisal scheme can only improve an organisation's performance: if it did not it would not be effective.

Q.15. This is a double question. A performance pay element could be fair but not motivate, or motivate because it is not fair, or be both fair and motivating.

Q.16. This question contains a double negative. This always increases the ambiguity of a statement or question. People often assume that if people say yes to a double negative question, then the opposite must also be true; i.e. if they agree with the statement in Q.14 then they must believe that with an appraisal interview their development needs would be met. This is not necessarily so.

Q.17. This is a hypothetical question. Seldom give credibility to the answers to such questions.

Q.18. This statement belongs only in a quiz on the back of a cereal packet.

Q.19. This is OK but there is not enough space given to answer it.

- **General**. The sequencing of the questions is wrong. The first questions should be about the subject of the questionnaire – not, as in this case, about the respondent. Demographic questions about the respondent should be at the end of the questionnaire. There are in any case too many demographic questions. They outweigh the questions about appraisal. There is no particular reason that the questionnaire should be divided into four parts.

  The questionnaire is also unattractive and poorly designed. It would be nice if there were a 'thank you' at the end.

$$L = 2 \sqrt{\frac{p(100-p)}{n}}$$

Where L = the margin of error, p is the percentage answer to the question in the questionnaire (e.g. 30 per cent of respondents ticked 'strongly agree') and n = the number of questionnaires (the sample size).

If you do not like formulae you can use the nomogram shown in Figure 4.8. Take a ruler and place it on the correct point on the 'number of observations scale' (using the 95 per cent confidence side of the scale); pivot the ruler until you have it on the appropriate point of the 'percentage occurrence' scale and read off the margin of error on the middle scale.

Figure 4.8 The nomogram

Source: Moore (1980: 250) and also Whitmore (1975: 126)

This formula, and the nomomogram, can only be used on their own where the population that was sampled was very large or, what may be the same thing, the sample was less than 10 per cent of the population. They can, for example, be used for identifying the margin of error on activity sampling results (see p. 138). In this case n = the total number of observations made. As the number of points in time at which observation might be made is very large (you might observe every second), so we can assume that with activity sampling the sample of observations will always be a small proportion of the total time. However, with the kind of surveys and questionnaires MBA and Master's students typically do, it is quite likely that the sample will be a large percentage of the population, especially if the survey population is within a department or an organisation. There may be 400 employees in a department, for example, and it would be quite easy to survey more than 10 per cent of them. This is good news for MBA researchers. Where the sample is a relatively large proportion of the population the limits of error will be smaller than those suggested by the formula and the nomogram. Looked at obversely this means you can get the same margin of error with a smaller sample size. To work out the margins of error in this situation you add a correction element to the formula:

$$L = 2 \sqrt{\frac{p(100-p)}{n} \times \left(\frac{N-n}{N-1}\right)} \quad \text{This is the adjustment element}$$

In the adjustment element N = the size of the total population and n = the sample size.

If the margin of error is unacceptably high you will need to have more questionnaires completed to reduce it to a proper level. The following formula can be used to calculate the total number of questionnaires needed. You can of course also use the nomogram to avoid doing the mathematics.

Exercise 4.10

Margin of error

In a survey in a department of 500 employees, 200 completed questionnaires were returned. Of these 48 per cent of the respondents strongly agreed with the statement 'Tea trolleys improve morale at work'. Use the formula to calculate the margin of error.

Answer
The margin of error on the result would be +/–5.5 per cent so the true figure will lie somewhere between 42.5 per cent and 53.5 per cent, most likely around the 48 per cent mark. If you cross check this result with Table 4.4 you will see that it recommends that 217 questionnaires would be needed to get a margin of error of +/– 5 per cent.

The choice of an acceptable margin is up to the researcher, but +/– 2 per cent or +/–5 per cent would be conventional options:

$$n = \frac{4p\,(100-p)}{L^2}$$

If the sample size calculated from the formula or read from the nomogram is a large percentage of the population, then the following formula can be used to calculate an adjustment factor:

$$\text{Adjustment factor} = \frac{N}{N + n - 1}$$

where N = total population size, and n = sample size calculated from the formula or read from the nomogram.

It may well be that the numbers needed to reach a low margin of error cause panic for part-time researchers for whom it may be difficult, because of shortage of time if nothing else, to obtain and process such volumes of questionnaires. One piece of good news is that if the results are highly skewed, for example if 80 per cent of respondents 'strongly agreed', then acceptable margins can be achieved with relatively smaller sample sizes.

Exercise 4.11

Sample size

Assuming a margin of error of +/–5 per cent is acceptable, what is the total number of completed questionnaires that would be necessary to achieve it if there were 200 employees in the population and in a small pilot study 48 per cent had agreed with a statement and 52 per cent disagreed?

Answer

The total number of observations necessary to achieve a margin of error of +/–5 per cent would be 133. Let us see how this is arrived at. If you use the nomogram a proportion of 48 per cent (or as close as you can get it on the scale) and a margin of error of +/–5 per cent, this gives a sample size of 400 or thereabouts (the figure is 399 if you calculate it using the formula). As this sample size is a high proportion of the whole population – in fact, of course, it is much bigger than the size of the entire population, which is only 200! – you can apply the adjustment formula. If you put the figures into the formula you get:

$$\frac{200}{200 + 399 - 1} = 0.334$$

When you multiply the suggested sample size of 399 by the adjustment factor (0.334) it gives you a sample size of 133. If you check this with the figure suggested in Table 4.4 you will find it very close (132).

You can discover this for yourself by using the nomogram. The minimum sample sizes given in Table 4.4 are 'worst case' figures because they are calculated on the assumption that the sample is equally split, 50:50, on issues.

Do not let trouble with margins of error put you off using questionnaires. The dissertation markers are conscious of the problems of obtaining large numbers of completed questionnaires, especially when the project is only part of the demands made by a part-time course on students who also have jobs to manage and friends and families to talk to. If the margins are low dissertations are not marked down if you have made reasonable efforts to get questionnaires filled in and if you recognise the limitations that a small sample places on the results.

This section has concentrated on questionnaires as an example of pre-structured research methods. There are, of course, as suggested in the first part of this chapter, many other means of collecting quantitative material. You may have used activity sampling or obtained material from organisational or publicly available databases. The next section provides some of the basic statistical tools you might need to analyse the material.

Analysing the material: basic statistical analysis of data – *Diannah Lowry*

Introduction

'Oh no, not statistics!' we can hear you say. Do not be put off by the thought of statistical analysis. You may not be aware of it, but you are probably using statistical thinking in your everyday life. Any time you use phrases such as: 'On average I drive 65 miles a week' or 'We can expect snow at this time of year' or 'The earlier I start work on my dissertation, the better I am likely to do' you are making a (rough) type of statistical statement.

Statistics has its genesis in the somewhat contentious philosophical view that our observations of the world can never be totally accurate. Statistics thus arises out of 'caution in the face of uncertainty' (Rowntree, 1991:18), and enables us to estimate the extent of our errors when making observations and generalisations.

Moreover, statistics is not an invention of the so-called 'modern' era. Statistical thinking in one form or another has been around throughout the ages. The Old Testament tells us that the Pharaohs of Ancient Egypt had a keen interest in collecting data about how many people they had available to build pyramids and fight wars, and how much wealth they could extract in taxation. The Domesday Book assembled for William the Conqueror is another example of a compendium of statistics about the population and available resources. Statistics also has some origins in gambling. In the seventeenth century the French mathematician Blaise Pascal tried to assist a gambling friend to 'figure out the odds' on the dice table. Such musings resulted in 'the theory of probability', a theory that has since revealed its explanatory and predictive powers in diverse areas such as business, astronomy, genetics and even warfare.

The examples of statistical thinking described above reveal two different types of statistical thought. The statement 'On average I drive 65 miles a week' is essentially descriptive. The statements 'We can expect snow at this time of year' and 'The earlier I start my dissertation, the better I will do' go beyond description and infer what is likely to happen in the future. There is thus a distinction between *descriptive statistics* and *inferential statistics*. The former is concerned with generalising from a sample, while the latter is concerned with generalising from a sample to make estimates and inferences about a wider population. How safe is it to make generalisations from a part to a whole? This is what statistics is all about: quantifying the probability of error. It is this issue that is covered in the next sections. Bear in mind that this is a section on *basic* statistical analysis, and is therefore confined in its scope to the forms of analysis you may wish to undertake. We do not expect you to become statistical masters as a result of conducting a single piece of research. If you require more detail in any of the areas discussed, feel free to consult a more in-depth guide to statistical procedures.

Now, take a breath and *relax* – it's really not that hard!

Types of variable

Samples are made up of individuals. The individuals (or 'members') in the sample may be humans, squirrels, pay rates, alcoholic beverages or whatever. All members of the sample will share some common attribute or characteristic we are interested in. In the case of employees, we may be interested in salary level, level of job satisfaction, hours worked, number of hours spent training, etc. Furthermore, each member will differ from one or more of the others on these characteristics. In looking at members of a sample we ask how they *vary* among themselves on one or more of such characteristics. Because of the variation among members, such characteristics are called variable characteristics or, more simply, **variables**.

Suppose you are thinking of purchasing a second-hand car. Can you list some of the variables that you would consider in choosing a vehicle? No doubt you would consider some or all of the following as variables of interest:

- price
- make (e.g. Peugeot, Fiat, Rover, Toyota)
- type (e.g. estate, four-wheel drive, soft top)
- colour
- age
- condition (excellent, acceptable, poor)
- mileage
- transmission type (automatic or manual)
- size of engine.

How do you evaluate each individual car, in the sample available to us, in terms of these variables? This depends on the *type* of variable.

With variables such as price, age, mileage and size of engine we are looking at quantity variables. Such variables can be either *discrete* or *continuous*.

A *discrete* variable is one in which the possible values are clearly separated from one another. Take family size for example: a family can have one child, or two or three, etc., but it cannot have 2.5 or 3.75.

Continuous variables, however, do have possible values between them. Take the variable of height as an example. A child may be three feet high this year and three feet six inches next year. In the meantime, however, they will have not just been three feet one inch and three feet two inches, but an infinite number of heights in between: 3.0001 feet … 3.00015 feet … and so on.

Discrete variables imply counting, while *continuous* variables require a measurement system.

Now, let us go back to the variables involved in the purchase of a second-hand car. Amongst our car variables 'price' is discrete, since the asking price of the vehicle could be £4000.00 or for some incredibly unlikely reason it may be £4000.01; but there is no possible price between these two, or between any other two that are more than 1 pence apart. Also, given the car registration system in the United Kingdom, 'age' could also be considered a discrete variable (all 'G'-registered cars are 1990 models, etc.). Size of engine is also a discrete variable – 1.4 litre engines are distinct from 1.6 litre engines, and so on. Mileage on the other hand is *continuous*: the mileage may be 30,000 or 120,000 miles or an infinite number of possible miles in between.

With a variable such as 'make of car' we set up categories, e.g. Toyota, Rover, Peugeot and so on. Then we categorise each car simply by noting its name. This type of variable is called a *category* variable. A category variable such as 'make of car' is sometimes called a *nominal* variable (from the Latin *nominalis* = of a name). Other variables listed above include 'type of car', 'colour' and 'transmission type' and these are also category variables (they are also *nominal* variables).

You may have considered 'condition of car' to be a category variable, and indeed it is, since there are three categories of condition mentioned: excellent, acceptable and poor. This is, however, a different type of category variable. Since the categories can be ordered according to condition, this type of category variable is called an *ordinal* variable.

Figure 4.9 summarises the types of variables discuss here:

As you shall soon see, different variable types require different statistical analysis, the main difference being between category and quantity variables. Before we move on, however, it is important to note that data about quantity variables *can* be converted into category data. For example, cars under 1.4 litres can be converted into 'small engine capacity', those between 1.6 litres and 1.8 litres as 'medium engine capacity', while

Figure 4.9 Types of data

anything over 2 litres could be categorised as 'large engine capacity'. The drawback to this sort of method is that loss of information occurs. If the numbers in each category are recorded, we lose data about exact (actual) information. This sort of sacrifice is sometimes worthwhile in order to make data easier to handle. However, the sacrifice should not be made without weighing up the pros and cons.

There is another important aspect in analysing variables. You will need to differentiate between the *independent* variable(s) and the *dependent* variable(s). The *dependent* variable is the variable of interest to you in your research question. Suppose, for example, that you were researching pay differentials between full-time employees and part-time employees. In this study the variable of interest is amount of salary, and this is then the *dependent* variable. It is dependent on employment status; hence employment status is termed the *independent* variable in this particular piece of research. Your software package will ask you to identify your independent and dependent variables in the course of the statistical tests you choose to use.

Summarising data and making them useful

Available software packages these days make it easy to summarise large amounts of data in diagrammatic form. For example, the most common methods of summarising categorical data include tables, histograms and pie charts. Excel and SPPS can easily facilitate these summary statistics. However, you will need to become acquainted with the software of your choice in order to produce the diagrams. Do not be concerned – these sophisticated packages include 'tutorial sessions' that clearly demonstrate how to generate the desired summary.

Summarising categorical data

Tables display data either in their 'raw' form or in percentages. From a table, it is often possible to determine the 'mode' of the sample. The mode of a distribution is the category that occurs with the greatest frequency. It is the most 'fashionable' or popular value. For example, size 7 is the mode, or modal value, in women's shoes – it is the size that most shoe shops sell in the greatest quantity.

Histograms and pie charts provide a diagrammatic view of differences in proportions. An example of a histogram is provided in Figure 4.10.

Histograms are particularly useful if you wish to compare one category with another (by comparing the heights of the columns). However, if you wish to compare each category (piece) with the total, a pie chart is more illustrative. An example of a pie chart is provided in Figure 4.11. There is a tendency to overuse pie charts in dissertations. If half the respondents to a questionnaire are male and the other half female, a pie chart illustrating the fact adds little.

Summarising quantitative data

The techniques for summarising quantitative data include the methods of determining measures of central tendency, as well as measures of dispersion. Statistical packages will calculate these measures for you. Measures of central tendency include the median and mean, while measures of dispersion include the range and standard deviation. Lets look at these a little more closely, without going into too much mathematical detail.

The *median* value (from the Latin for 'middle') is a kind of representative value that indicates the centre of a distribution. The median is the value that splits the distribution of data into half. There should be as many observed values greater than the median as there are less. Thus, if the following were the number of miles driven by seven postgraduate students per week:

0   16   18   20   33   48   68

the median here would be 20 (miles per week). That is the value with equal numbers of observations greater and lesser. When the number of observed values is even, the median is quoted as the value halfway between the two middle values. Thus, if our sample looked like this:

0   16   18   20   33   48

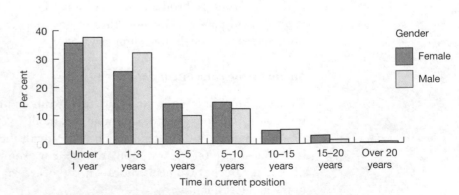

Figure 4.10 Time in current position by gender

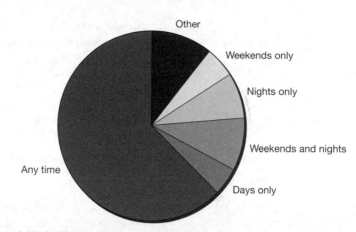

Figure 4.11 Availability for work of casual employees

the median here would be halfway between 18 and 20 (18 + 20)/2 = 19; and 19 is thus the value that has equal numbers either side of it (even though no student actually drove just 19 miles)[1].

A more commonly quoted representative value is the arithmetic *mean*. As you are probably aware, the mean is simply the average of the sample. It is calculated by adding together all the observed values and dividing by the number of observations. As a measure of central tendency, the mean has an advantage since it is usually stable from one sample to another. However, if there are extreme outliers (see footnote), these extreme values will distort the mean. In such cases the median is preferred as a measure of central tendency.

The *range* is an elemental form of a measure of dispersion. It is a simple calculation where the lowest value is subtracted from the highest value. While it is a simple measure to calculate, we cannot put too much faith in it. It depends on just two values – the two most extreme cases. These may be outliers, and not typical of the sample. Thus, the range may provide a distorted view of the sample.

A more comprehensive measure of dispersion is the *standard deviation* of the sample. Identifying the standard deviation is a way of indicating a sort of 'average' amount by which values deviate from the mean. The greater the dispersion, the bigger the deviations and the bigger the standard deviation of the mean. Consider the following sets of values:

(a)   6   24   37   49   64   (mean = 36)

(b)   111   114   117   118   120   (mean = 116)

---

[1] The median is a good way of summarising data when there are a few extreme (high or low) values observed (these are termed 'outliers'). Their effect would be to distort the mean.

The values in (a) are more dispersed (i.e. they deviate more from the mean) than those in (b), so it is likely that the standard deviation is larger. Let us see why, by calculating how each value in (b) differs from the mean of 116:

Value:	111	114	117	118	120
Deviation from 116:	–5	–2	+1	+2	+4

We cannot take an average of these deviations, since there are negative values. In order to overcome this, we square each deviation, and thus get rid of the minus signs:

Deviations:	–5	–2	+1	+2	+4
Squared deviation:	25	4	1	4	16

The mean of these squared deviations is called the **variance**:

Variance = (25 + 4 + 1 + 4 + 16)/5 = 50/5 = 10.

The variance is a measure with some good uses. However, if the original values were, say, 'heart beats per minute', then the variance would be so many 'square heart beats per minute'! So, in order to get the measure of dispersion back into the same units as the observed values (and the measures of central tendency), we take the square root of the variance – and this is termed the **standard deviation**:

Standard deviation of distribution (b) = $\sqrt{10}$ = 3.16

The same process of calculation for (a) above reveals a standard deviation of 20. We can thus comment that the distribution of (a) is much more dispersed.

The remaining discussion on significance and specific statistical techniques is, at best, basic and brief. The intention here is not to overwhelm you with statistical theory or formulae. The remaining subsections merely serve to introduce you to some of the issues and methods you may like to consider in analysing your data. As stated above, you will need to supplement the materials provided here with reference to slightly more detailed texts on statistical methods, or alternatively consult the handbook that accompanies your statistics software package of choice.

Comparing samples and tests of significance

It may be the case that you wish to compare two or more samples in your research. Suppose, for example, you were interested in comparing the annual salaries of permanent and part-time workers. You may do this by comparing the mean salaries of each group. However, how do we know whether the mean salaries are *significantly* different from each other? In statistical thinking, 'significant' does not just mean 'interesting' or 'important'. A significant difference is one that signifies a real difference in populations. We will get back to this point in a minute. For now, we must consider another concept.

Researchers are expected to be cautious, and they have thus developed a cautious convention. The convention is that we test for a significant difference by asking: 'Could it be that the difference is *not* significant?' So we start out by assuming there is *no* real difference between the salary levels of permanent and part-time employees. This assumption or hypothesis is called the **null hypothesis**. This hypothesis is under attack in all research. If the difference between means turns out to be too big to be explained away as chance variation, then we must reject the null hypothesis, and we must replace it with an alternative hypothesis. The alternative hypothesis is that there is a difference between the salary levels of permanent and part-time employees.

Now, we may further hypothesise that permanent employees receive higher annual salaries than part-timers. If we are testing this, we have a *directional* research question. We are suggesting a direction of findings. This type of testing involves a one-tailed test, and you must select this option on your software package in your process of analysis. I will not go into the mathematics of one-tailed tests – it is beyond the scope of this discussion. Just remember to choose the option in your analysis. If, however, you are not suggesting any direction in your research question (i.e. suggesting the results could go either way), you will need to use the two-tailed test option in your computer analysis.

Let us get back to that somewhat significant matter of 'significance testing'. It was stated earlier that a significant difference shows a real difference in populations. But how big does a difference have to be in order to be considered significant?

The two common cut-off points in statistical analysis are the five per cent level and the one per cent level (written as 0.05 level and 0.01 level). This type of information will be displayed in the results of your computer analysis on your statistical software. A difference is less significant at the 0.05 level than at the 0.01 level. Any result of a test of significance greater than 0.05 would result in acceptance of the null hypothesis (i.e. there is no difference between the samples). A difference at 0.05 is called 'significant', while a difference at 0.001 is called 'highly significant' (both lead to acceptance of the alternative hypothesis, i.e. there *is* a difference between the samples).

Statistical tests for quantitative data

Comparing two means – the t-test

If you have two groups and you would like to test the difference in their mean scores, an appropriate test is the t-test. This test of means will be included as a simple option (just click the option) in your statistical software package and as such the rather complicated formula underlying the test statistic will not be included in this discussion. (Refer to a statistics text if you require the mathematical logic and formula underlying the test.) Suppose, for example, that a researcher wants to test the different levels of job satisfaction (converted into quantitative data) between permanent and casual employees. The t-test would be an appropriate test in this case. Your computer will provide you with a t-statistic and a significance level. Remember, if the significance level is 0.05 or less you can reject the null hypothesis, and conclude that one group *does* differ from the other in terms of job satisfaction.

Comparing several means – ANOVA (F-statistic)

Let us say the same researcher wanted to compare three groups in terms of their job satisfaction – permanent employees, fixed-term contract employees and casual employees. In this case, with more than two groups, the t-test cannot be used. Instead we use what is called an analysis of variance test (or ANOVA). As the name suggests, the test involves comparing variances to make inferences about the means. The logic of this test goes something this – the variance of the means of the three groups will be large if the groups differ from each other in terms of satisfaction level. If the variance *within* groups is compared with the variance *between* groups, it can be determined whether the means are significantly different. You *are* lucky that your computer will do all this for you! The ANOVA test results in what is called the F-statistic (named after the British statistician R.A. Fisher). The larger the ratio of variance, the greater the value of the F-statistic. A high F-statistic usually indicates that the results are significant. Once again, however, your computer will provide you with significance levels. Remember, if the significance level is 0.05 or less you can reject the null hypothesis, and conclude that the groups differ in terms of job satisfaction.

Analysing relationships – correlations

Correlation analysis is a measure of association (relationship) between two or more variables, and is calculated from standardised measures of covariance (but do not worry too much about this latter piece of information). There are three kinds of correlation: positive, negative and zero. With **positive correlation** changes in one variable are accompanied by changes in the other variable and in the *same direction*. In other words, larger values in one variable tend to go with larger values in the other. This is illustrated in the scatter diagram shown in Figure 4.12.

However, in equally strong relationships, the two variables change in the *opposite* directions. Larger values on one will tend to go with smaller values on the other. This is called a negative correlation. For example, there may be a **negative correlation** between age and willingness to learn about statistics within a group of students, i.e. younger students may be more willing to learn about statistics, and older students may be less willing to do so.

Figure 4.12 Positive correlation

If there were no clear tendency for the values on one variable to move in a particular direction (up or down) with changes on another variable, then it could be said that we are approaching a **zero correlation**. For example, the relationship between age and height of female postgraduate students may well approach zero correlation. A zero correlation is illustrated in the scatter diagram of Figure 4.13.

As alluded to above, correlations vary not only according to direction (+ or −) but also in strength. Your computer will calculate a numerical measure to indicate strength of the relationship, and this is called the **correlation coefficient**. It is represented by the letter r. The correlation coefficient (r) cannot lie outside the range between −1 and +1. Those two values of r represent, respectively, perfect negative and perfect positive correlation. When $r = 0$ there is no correlation at all. The closer the correlation gets to +1 or −1 the stronger the correlation; the closer it gets to 0 the weaker it is. Table 4.5 is a rough guide to interpreting correlation coefficients:

Your computer package will be able to display a correlation matrix for you if you are investigating the correlation between a number of variables.

Figure 4.13 Zero correlation

Table 4.5 Interpreting correlation coefficients

Correlation coefficient	Strength
0.0 to 0.2	Very weak, negligible
0.2 to 0.4	Weak, low
0.4 to 0.7	Moderate
0.7 to 0.9	Strong, high, marked
0.9 to 1.0	Very strong, very high

Source: Rowntree (1991:170)

An example of a correlation matrix is provided in Table 4.6.

To illustrate correlation from Table 4.6, management skills is related to promotion satisfaction, organisational commitment is related to management skills, and organisational commitment is related to job satisfaction.

A serious word of caution needs to be included here: correlation does *not* imply causation. If variables X and Y are correlated, this may be because X causes Y, or because Y causes X, or because some other variable is affecting both X and Y, or for a mixture of these reasons, or the whole relationship may be a coincidence.

This perhaps requires further explanation. Consider the following: no matter how highly correlated the rooster's crow is to the rising sun, the rooster does not cause the sun to rise. Another example is that it has been found that there is a high correlation between lecturers' salaries and alcohol consumption over a number of years. This does not indicate that lecturers drink, nor does it indicate that the sale of alcohol increases lecturers salaries. A more likely explanation is that both salaries and alcohol *co-vary* because they are *both* influenced by growth in national income and/or population. So, variables can be statistically related, but not causally related (when this is the case, they are usually termed *spuriously related*).

Table 4.6 Correlation matrix of size, location and work context factors with satisfaction, organisational commitment, intent to stay and performance commitment

	1	2	3	4	5	6	7	8	9	10	11	12	13
1. Size	1.0												
2. Location	.07	1.0											
3. Work scheduling	.14	.01	1.0										
4. Wage satisfaction	.15	.02	.47 *	1.0									
5. Social integration	.02	.04	.26	.28	1.0								
6. Promotion satisfaction	.05	.13	.48 *	.32 *	.33 *	1.0							
7. Management skills	.03	.09	.62 *	.41 *	.34 *	.61 *	1.0						
8. Involvement	.11	.10	.02	.01	.12	.08	.03	1.0					
9. Intent to stay	.06	.02	.34 *	.20	.11	.20	.25	.13	1.0				
10. Organisation commitment	.01	.06	.46 *	.34 *	.31 *	.49 *	.64	.07	.39 *	1.0			
11. Satisfaction	.03	.01	.44 *	.34 *	.33 *	.34 *	.44	.04	.39 *	.61 *	1.0		
12. Work commitment	.00	.01	.19	.09	.08	.18	.31	.08	.18	.45 *	.26	1.0	
13. Performance commitment	.00	.03	.17	.09	.13	.20	.23	.05	.27	.35 *	.35 *	.18	1.0

Statistical tests for categorical data

Comparing proportions – the chi-squared test (χ^2)

This is one of the most widely used categorical variable tests in the social sciences. The symbol is the Greek letter *chi*, pronounced 'kye' as in 'sky'. This test informs us as to whether the collected data are close to the value considered to be typical and generally expected, and whether two variables are related to each other. Suppose we are wishing to see if there were any signs of correspondence between an applicant's gender and whether or not they have had prior work experience. Essentially the data obtained in a study (observed frequencies) are compared with expected data (expected frequencies), and the actual differences determine the level of significance. An example of these is provided in Table 4.7.

Table 4.7   A contingency table

Obtained frequencies: work experience

	Yes	No	Total
Male	70	30	100
Female	50	50	100
Total	120	80	

Expected frequencies: work experience

	Yes	No	Total
Male	60	40	100
Female	60	40	100
Total	120	80	

The steps involved in the chi-squared test go something like this (again, do not worry – your computer does it for you). First, a contingency table is constructed. Then observed frequencies are identified and expected frequencies are ascertained. Expected frequencies are subtracted from the observed frequencies – these differences are then squared and divided by the number of expected frequencies. Your computer will provide you with a chi-squared statistic and will indicate its level of significance.

Cross-tabulation is often used to analyse questionnaire results and chi-squared can be used in association with it. Cross-tabulation is the comparing of respondents' answers to one question in a questionnaire in relation to their answers to other questions. Most commonly respondents' replies to questions on the substantive theme of the research are compared with the respondents' demographic characteristics such as their age, sex, length of service and so on. Cross-tabulation can best be explained by example. Let us imagine a staff satisfaction survey in a large organisation. One question might ask whether people thought they experienced discrimination at work because of their ethnic origin, sex or disability. The question might use a rating scale.

I am treated fairly on
grounds of sex, race
or disability

I have been treated
unfairly on grounds of
sex, race or disability

1	2	3	4	5
69.2%	14.7%	10.9%	3.2%	1.9%

The results (shown above) would probably be regarded by management as positive. It might, however, be thought interesting to cross-tabulate the results with answers to the question about the sex and ethnic origin of the respondents. Table 4.8 gives the results when analysed according to whether respondents saw themselves as a member of an ethnic minority group.

An inspection of Table 4.8 suggested that people who considered themselves to be in an ethnic minority ticked the 'treated fairly' end of the scale less often than those who did not consider themselves to be in an ethnic minority. When the other parts of the scale are considered, which all imply a degree of unfairness, the 'ethnic minority group' always scored higher than the non-ethnic minority group. While the survey may show that discrimination is not a major problem, the cross-tabulation suggests that the ethnic minority group sees, it as rather more of an issue than the non-ethnic minority groups do. But are these differences statistically significant? The chi-squared test can be used to provide an answer.

The use of chi-squared begins with a *null hypothesis*, which is that there is no association, or difference, between the responses to the two questions in the cross-tabulation. A null hypothesis means that the responses to one

Table 4.8 Cross-tabulation

				Q. 78 Do you consider yourself in an ethnic minority?		Total
				Yes	No	
Q. 56	Fairly	1	count	41	868	909
			% within Q. 78	53.2%	70.5%	
	Fair treatment	2	count	14	178	192
			% within Q. 78	18.2%	14.5%	
		3	count	14	127	141
			% within Q. 78	18.2%	10.3%	
		4	count	6	36	42
			% within Q. 78	7.8%	2.9%	
	Not fairly	5	count	2	22	24
			% within Q. 78	2.6%	1.8%	
	Total		count	77	1231	1308
			% within Q. 78	100%	100%	

question are not associated with differences in responses to the other question. SPSS reports the value of a chi-squared test for the above data as 13.557 with a significance level of 0.009 (on a probability scale of 0–1). The significance level is the probability that the null hypothesis is true. In this case the probability is 0.009, or 0.9 per cent. The significance level of 0.009 is smaller than 0.05 and smaller than 0.01. The differences are therefore significant at the 0.01 level. In other words, we can say that at the 99 per cent confidence level the null hypothesis is probably not true. There is a less than one per cent chance that it might be true. As researchers we would be willing to say that the null hypothesis is not true at the 0.05 per cent confidence level, which would mean there was a five per cent chance of the null hypothesis being true. It can be concluded with a known degree of statistical confidence that there is an association between being, or not being, a member of an ethnic minority and the degree of discrimination respondents believed they suffered. If you want to know more about chi-squared, and SPSS, see Bryman and Cramer (1997: 168–72).

Exercise 4.12

Cross-tabulation

The table below shows the results of a cross-tabulation between answers to the question 'Are you female or male?' and answers to the rating scale question on discrimination on grounds of sex, race or disability. Inspect the figures and decide whether men and women have responded differently to questions about discrimination. You do not need to do a chi-squared test but you might want to calculate a few percentages.

				Q.74 Are you male or female?		Total
				Female	Male	
Q.56	Fairly	1	count	713	189	902
	Fair treatment	2	count	150	44	194
		3	count	110	31	141
		4	count	33	10	43
	Not fairly	5	count	19	6	25
	Total		count	1025	280	1305

Answer

Inspection suggests that the null hypothesis is true. When the percentages of men and women responding to each of the categories in the rating scale are calculated it is clear that there is little difference between the two sexes. Neither group feels more discriminated against than the other. The chances are that the null hypothesis is true. This is supported by the chi-squared test. When the chi-squared test is used the probability of the null hypothesis being true (the significance level) is 0.973, or 97 per cent. It is much higher than the 0.05 level and so the differences are not significant at that level.

There is a rough and ready, but quicker, way of looking for statistically significant differences between percentages. In Appendix II of Oppenheim (1992) is a set of three nomograms that can be used for making a quick check on whether there are any significant differences between percentages. This would be perfectly adequate for many applications in Master's dissertations.

Final word

This section on basic statistical analysis has attempted to cover a lot of material in a fairly short space. Hopefully it will provide a neat introduction to some tests available to you on current statistical software packages. Just another gentle word of caution. Over the years it has been pointed out that 'there are lies, damned lies, and statistics'. Daryll Huff's (1991) book title *How to Lie with Statistics* conveys this message rather well. So let us finish off this section with a succinct quote from Rowntree (1991:190):

> As a consumer of statistics, act with caution; as a producer, act with integrity.

● ● ● ● Software for analysing research material

Jankowicz (1995: 76) argued that the break point at which it becomes sensible to use software to analyse your results is 100 questionnaires. I might prefer to use software if there are more than 30 questionnaires. Certainly, if you anticipate doing cross-tabulations, then the use of software is almost a necessity. Doing cross-tabulations manually is very time consuming as the questionnaires have to be frequently sorted into different subcategories and the percentages recalculated. There are a number of pieces of software that you might use to analyse the results from your questionnaires or any other quantitative material. If you were only interested in simple and descriptive statistical analysis of your material, then Excel would be perfectly adequate. If you wanted to carry out cross-tabulations, then Excel is not so useful. It can handle cross-tabulation by using pivot tables, but it would probably be easier to use one of the other packages. MINITAB is described in some detail and explains how many of the things discussed in the previous section can be done using it. It also explains time series analysis, which is a useful technique for many people doing their dissertations. A briefer guide is given to SPSS.

Software is also available to help with the analysis of qualitative material. Most people using qualitative material for MBA and Master's dissertations do not use such specialist software. However, a brief guide to QSR-NUD*IST, one of the software tools for exploring such material, is included in this part of the guide.

MINITAB – *John Buglear*

MINITAB is a general-purpose statistical package originally developed for academic use but also widely used in business. The package offers a wide range of facilities, from modest bar charts to sophisticated multivariate analysis, yet it is straightforward to use thanks to its educational origins.

The most recent version of the package is Release 13, which is in Windows format. Data can be input directly into MINITAB worksheets, or read from (and written to) Excel, Quattro Pro, Lotus, Symphony and dBase files. Output can be printed directly or pasted into Word or PowerPoint. The package enables the user to customise and edit output.

More information about MINITAB can be obtained from the design company's web site, http://www.minitab.com. At the time of writing the company offers a free 30-day trial of the package.

The cheapest way to buy a copy of the package is to purchase a copy of McKenzie and Goldman (1999), which is supplied with a CD containing the student version of the package. This version, actually the previous release MINITAB 12, is sufficient for most academic data analysis requirements. A number of statistics textbooks illustrate and explain MINITAB output, including Buglear (2001) and Cramer (1997).

The three sections below are designed to demonstrate some of the procedures and facilities of the package to the new user.

Data entry and storage, statistical diagrams and summary measures

When you enter MINITAB there is a short loading sequence, following which you should see a screen that has two sections. The upper half of your screen is the *session window*. It should display the date and a welcome message. The session window is where the output that you request will be shown, with the exception of graphs, which will be displayed in their own windows.

In the lower part of the screen there is the *worksheet*, where you can enter and store data. This worksheet looks like a spreadsheet since it consists of numbered rows and columns, but there are important differences. In a spreadsheet you can enter titles, names and formulae freely because you define the data you wish to analyse by their column and row location. In MINITAB you will be defining the location of data you want to analyse using only their column location. This is easier but it does mean that you have to ensure that only the data you want to analyse are entered into the column. You can give the data a name or title but you have to enter the name in the *unnumbered cell* at the very top of the column where you want to store your data, immediately beneath the column number (C1, C2 and so on). The unnumbered cells at the top of the worksheet columns are shaded in version 13 of the package.

Keeping names out of data columns is especially important when you are dealing with numerical data that you want to analyse arithmetically, such as calculating the mean of the data. If you put the variable name in one of the numbered rows of the column, the column designation **T** (for text) will appear next to the column number at the head of the column. If you ask the package to calculate the mean of such a column, you will find that it will not allow you to do so. To avoid this happening, do not put any letters or punctuation marks other than full stops (for decimal points) in a column containing numerical data. Be particularly careful not to insert commas in data consisting of large values; you may think of the number as 23,456 but you must enter it as 23456.

At the very top of the screen you will see a menu bar of function headings (File, Edit, Manip and so on) which open pull-down menus when clicked.

When you have identified these features of the screen, enter the data in Table 4.9 into the first four columns (C1 to C4) of the worksheet. Put the names of the four variables in the unnumbered columns at the top of the columns. Two of the variables are non-numeric (gender and promotion); as you enter the first values of these variables, you should see the column designations of C1 and C4 change to C1-T and C4-T.

When you have entered the data, the top of your worksheet should now look like this:

C1	C2	C3	C4
Gender	Age	Salary	Promotion
M	43	36	Y
M	29	25	Y

If you make a mistake in entering the data, you can amend the contents of a cell by clicking on the cell and typing in what you want to store in the cell. If you miss out a value, click on the worksheet cell you want to be below your insertion, click **Editor** on the menu bar and select **Insert Cells**. A new cell will now appear into which you can type the missing value. If you want to delete a cell, click on the cell concerned then click **Edit** and **Delete Cells**.

The letters F and M in the first column stand for female and male. While it is convenient to enter the data in this form, we can alter them to 'Female' and 'Male' for storage and analysis. Click **Manip** on the menu bar and on the pull-down menu select **Code**. Pick **Text to Text** from the sub-menu. In the command window specify C1 as the column to **Code data from** then click in the space below **Into columns** and type C1. Enter the **Original values** (F and M) and **New** values (Female and Male). Repeat the procedure for the promotion data, replacing 'Y' and 'N' with 'Yes' and 'No' in column 4.

Table 4.9 Example data

A researcher is interested in the career progression of members of a professional institute. A random sample of members was selected and each received a questionnaire that contained questions about their career development, specifically their gender, age, current salary, and whether they had been promoted within the last five years. Thirty completed questionnaires were received. The results have been tabulated as follows:

Gender	Age	Salary (£000)	Promotion
M	43	36	Y
M	29	25	Y
M	55	47	N
M	31	28	Y
M	37	42	Y
M	58	30	N
M	49	50	N
M	30	22	N
M	26	24	Y
M	35	30	Y
M	42	35	N
M	51	46	Y
M	29	20	N
M	47	32	N
M	62	35	N
F	37	31	N
F	25	20	N
F	42	37	Y
F	28	24	Y
F	33	26	N
F	39	35	Y
F	26	22	N
F	45	30	N
F	27	25	Y
F	38	37	N
F	49	33	N
F	36	40	Y
F	31	27	N
F	44	32	N
F	39	28	N

Now the data have been amended it is timely to save them. Click **File** on the menu bar and choose **Save Current Worksheet**. In the **Save Worksheet As** window that appears click ★ to the right of the **Save in:** box and pick the appropriate drive and folder. Type an appropriate file name in the box to the right of **File name:** and click the **Save** button.

Construct a simple bar chart for the gender data. Select the **Graph** menu and choose **Chart**. In the command window, click in the box below **X** in the top right hand corner then type C1 and click the **OK** button. After a short delay your bar chart should appear. It should look like the one shown in Figure 4.14. Delete the graph and repeat the procedure to obtain a bar chart for the promotion data in C4.

Figure 4.14 Simple bar chart of the gender data

Construct a stack bar chart for the gender and promotion data by clicking **Graph** then **Chart**. In the box below **X** type C1. Lower down in the command window you will see a heading **For each**, click the ▼ button and select **Group**. Type C4 in the box below **Group variables**, and then click the **Options** button and click the button to the left of **Stack**, and then click in the space to the right of **Stack** and type C4. Click the **OK** buttons on both the **Options** and command windows. The chart will appear after a short delay. It should look like the one shown in Figure 4.15. To obtain a cluster bar chart, delete the graph and repeat the procedure leaving all the instructions as they were but this time click the button to the left of **Stack** in the **Options** window to remove the tick then click the button to the left of **Cluster** and type C4 in the space to the right of **Cluster**. Click **OK** in both the **Options** and **Chart** windows.

Produce a histogram for the ages data. Select the **Graph** menu then **Histogram** and type C2 in the box below **X** then click **OK**. You should see a diagram like Figure 4.16.

Delete the graph and repeat the procedure to obtain a histogram of the salary data. Try it once again but this time click the ▼ button to the right of **For each**, select **Group** and type C1 in the box below **Group variables** then click **OK**. The histogram should be like the one in Figure 4.17. The default setting for histograms involves plotting class midpoints along the horizontal axis. If you want to use class endpoints, or 'cutpoints' as they are called in MINITAB, repeat the procedure but this time click the **Options** button in the **Histogram** window. Under the **Type of Intervals**

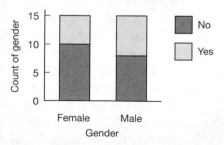

Figure 4.15 Stack bar chart of the gender and promotion data

Figure 4.16 Histogram of the ages data

heading click the button to the left of **CutPoint**. You can specify the cut-points you want to use by clicking the button to the left of **Midpoint/cutpoint positions** and typing in the cutpoints you want to use, separated by spaces. You might try typing in 20 25 30 35 40 45 50 for these data and comparing the graph you get with Figure 4.17.

Figure 4.17 Histogram of salary by gender

The histogram in Figure 4.17 portrays both the distributions of female and male salaries. Unfortunately, they blot each other out and this makes it difficult to compare the distributions. A more useful alternative for comparative purposes is the boxplot, which is based on order statistics: the median, quartiles, and minimum and maximum values.

Produce a boxplot for the salary data. Select the **Graph** menu then **Boxplot** and type C3 in the box below **Y** then click **OK**. The diagram you see should be like that in Figure 4.18.

Figure 4.18 Boxplot of the salary data

In Figure 4.18 the distribution of salaries is depicted against a vertical scale by means of what is known as a box and whiskers plot. The box at the heart of the diagram has a line across the middle. This line represents the median of the distribution, about 30 in this case. The upper and lower edges of the box mark the positions of the upper and lower quartiles, respectively. The vertical line above the box extends to the maximum value, 50, and the line below the box extends to the minimum value, 20.

Delete the graph and repeat the procedure to obtain another boxplot but this time click on the space below the **X** button and type C1. Click **OK**. You should see something like Figure 4.19 with two boxplots plotted on the same pair of axes, one representing salaries of females, the other salaries of males.

Figure 4.19 Boxplot of salary by gender

Obtain summary statistics for the salary data. Select **Stat** then **Basic Statistics**. Pick **Display Descriptive Statistics** from the sub-menu. In the command window type C3 in the **Variables** space then **OK**. The output that appears in the session window should look like Table 4.10.

In Table 4.10, N is the number of values in the distribution, Mean is the arithmetic mean, TrMean is the trimmed mean (the mean of all values except the highest five per cent and lowest five per cent, which is intended to correct the distortion that any extreme values exert on the mean), StDev is the standard deviation and SE Mean is the standard error of the mean. In the lower row Q1 and Q3 are the upper and lower quartiles.

Repeat the procedure but now click the button to the left of **By variable** in the **Display Descriptive Statistics** command window and then click the space to the right of **By variable** and type C1. Click **OK**. The analysis that

Table 4.10 Summary measures for salary data

```
Descriptive statistics: salary
```

Variable	N	Mean	Median	TrMean	StDev	SE Mean
Salary	30	31.63	30.50	31.23	7.92	1.45
Variable	Minimum	Maximum	Q1	Q3		
Salary	20.00	50.00	25.00	36.25		

appears in the session window should show summary measures for the salaries of females on one line and males on another.

Produce a 95 per cent confidence interval for the mean salary of all institute members. Select the **Stat** menu then choose **Basic Statistics**. Pick **1-Sample t** from the sub-menu then type C3 in the space below **Variables** in the command window and click **OK**. You should find output like that shown in Table 4.11 in the session window.

In Table 4.11 the figures in brackets under 95.0% CI indicate that we can be 95 per cent certain that the mean salary of all institute members is somewhere between £28,680 and £34,590.

Leave the package by clicking **File** on the menu bar and choosing **Exit**. Since this is only an exercise you may choose not to save the output you created.

Data retrieval, bivariate analysis and random sample selection

Enter MINITAB and retrieve the data you saved in the previous section. Select **File** from the menu bar and click **Open Worksheet**. In the command window that appears, click the Y button to the right of the **Look in:** box and select the appropriate drive, folder and file. Click **Open** and **OK** on the subsequent message informing you that the data will be added to the worksheet. Your data should appear in the on-screen worksheet.

Produce a contingency table for the gender and promotion data. This will allow you to assess the association, if any, between these two variables. Select the **Stat** menu and choose **Tables**. Select **Cross Tabulation** from the sub-menu. In the space under **Variable** in the command window type C1 and C4 then click **OK**. In the session window in the upper part of the screen you will see a two-way tabulation of the gender and promotion data. Repeat the procedure but this time click the button to the left of **Chi-square analysis** then the button to the left of **Above and expected count**, then click **OK**. You should see a table like Table 4.12 in the session window.

In Table 4.12 there are two numbers in each cell. The upper number, the count, is the number of respondents giving those gender and promotion details, for instance ten respondents were females who had no promotion. The lower number is the expected frequency, the number of respondents that we would expect to have those gender and promotion details *if gender and promotion were independent*. The chi-squared figure is an aggregate measure based on the differences between the counts and the expected frequencies for all the cells in the table. The larger the differences

Table 4.11 Confidence interval for population mean salary

One-sample t: salary

Variable	N	Mean	StDev	SE Mean	95.0% CI
Salary	30	31.63	7.92	1.45	(28.68, 34.59)

Table 4.12 Contingency table of gender and promotion

Rows: Gender		Columns: Promotion	
	No	Yes	All
Female	10	5	15
	9.00	6.00	15.00
Male	8	7	15
	9.00	6.00	15.00
All	18	12	30
	18.00	12.00	30.00

Chi-square = 0.556, DF = 1, P-Value = 0.456

      Cell Contents --
               Count
               Exp Freq

between the expected values and the counts, the bigger the value of chi-squared. The larger the differences, the more evidence there is for association between the variables. The P-value to the right of the chi-squared figure is the probability that these sample results occur *if there is no association between the variables in the population*. You can interpret it simply as the probability of no association between the two variables. In this case the P-value is 0.456, so there is a 45.6 per cent chance of no association suggesting that gender and promotion are independent. In practice only when this figure is less than five per cent (0.05), and by implication the chance of association is more than 95 per cent, would it be legitimate to conclude that there is association.

Produce a scatter diagram to show the age and salary data. Select the **Graph** menu then **Plot**. In the command window type C3 in the space below **Y** then C2 in the space below **X**. Click **OK**. The scatter diagram that appears should look like the one in Figure 4.20.

You might like to embellish your scatter diagram. Delete the graph and repeat the procedure to produce a scatter diagram but this time click on

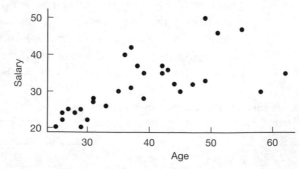

Figure 4.20 Scatter diagram of salary and age data

the ▼ to the right of the **Annotation** button. Select **Title** from the sub-menu. In the window that appears type an appropriate title in the space provided, then click **OK**. Click the ▼ to the right of the **Frame** button then select **Min and Max** from the sub-menu. In the window that appears type 20 in the space to the right of **Minimum for X**, 70 in the space to the right of **Maximum for X**, 0 in the space to the right of **Minimum for Y**, and 60 in the space to the right of **Maximum for Y**. Click **OK** then **OK** in the main command window. The graph that appears should incorporate your title and both axes should start at zero. You can use the same design tools to embellish boxplots.

Find the (Pearson) correlation coefficient for age and salary. Click **Stat** on the menu bar then **Basic Statistics** from the menu and **Correlation** from the sub-menu. Type C2 and C3 in the space below **Variables** then click **OK**. The coefficient, 0.684, should appear in the session window.

Obtain a regression model for the relationship between age and salary. Select the **Stat** menu then **Regression**. Choose **Regression** from the sub-menu. In the command window that appears type C3 in the space to the right of **Response** and C2 in the space to the right of **Predictors** then click **OK**. You should see output like that shown in Table 4.13.

In Table 4.13 the regression equation is the equation of the straight line that best fits the data. The R-Sq figure tells us the proportion of the variation in salary that can be explained by age, 46.8 per cent. The unusual

Table 4.13 Regression model of salary and age data

```
Regression analysis: salary versus age
```

The regression equation is
Salary = 10.7 + 0.539 Age

Predictor	Coef	SE Coef	T	P
Constant	10.729	4.350	2.47	0.020
Age	0.5392	0.1087	4.96	0.000

S = 5.881   R-Sq = 46.8%   R-Sq(adj) = 44.9%

Analysis of Variance

Source	DF	SS	MS	F	P
Regression	1	850.59	850.59	24.59	0.000
Residual Error	28	968.37	34.58		
Total	29	1818.97			

Unusual Observations

Obs	Age	Salary	Fit	SE Fit	Residual	St Resid
6	58.0	30.00	42.00	2.35	12.00	−2.23R
7	49.0	50.00	37.15	1.55	12.85	2.26R
15	62.0	35.00	44.16	2.74	9.16	−1.76 X

R denotes an observation with a large standardised residual.
X denotes an observation whose X value gives it large influence.

observations at the end of the output do not fit the regression model particularly well: the first two are outliers, and the third is detached from the general location of the data.

You might like to try and identify these unusual observations on a plot of the regression model. Select the **Stat** menu then **Regression**. Choose **Fitted Line Plot**. In the command window type C3 in the space to the right of **Response (Y)** and C2 in the space to the right of **Predictor (X)**. The graph that appears will be like that in Figure 4.21.

Select a random sample of 12 from the sample of 30. Select the **Calc** menu and choose **Random Data**. From the sub-menu select **Sample From Columns**. In the command window specify that you want to **Sample 12 rows from columns** C1–C4 and **Store samples in** C5–C8. Click **OK** then check that your sample of 12 is stored in columns 5 to 8.

Leave the package by clicking **File** on the menu bar and choosing **Exit**.

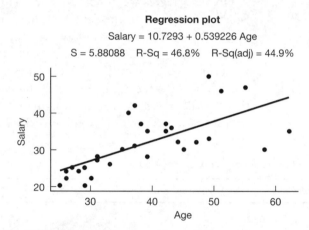

Figure 4.21 Fitted line plot of salary and age data

Basic time series analysis

Table 4.14 contains the sales in units of a certain brand of cold and 'flu remedy at a pharmacy.

Enter the data in Table 4.14 into C1 of the MINITAB worksheet *in chronological order*. Type an appropriate title, for example Sales, in the unnumbered cell at the top of the column.

Table 4.14 Pharmacy sales data

	Quarter			
Year	I	II	III	IV
2000	312	181	142	260
2001	325	174	158	277
2002	346	185	149	293
2003	322	191	137	268

Figure 4.22 Time series plot of pharmacy sales data

Select **Time Series Plot** from the **Graph** menu. The column name should appear in the space on the left of the command window. Double left click on it and it should appear in the space under **Y**. Click **OK** and you should see a graph such as the one in Figure 4.22 appear.

Figure 4.22 is a rather crude graph of the series that can be improved, so delete it and return to the **Time Series Plot** command window. Check that your variable name still appears under **Y**. Click on the ✿ button to the right of **Annotation** and select **Title** from the sub-menu. In the window that appears type a suitable title in the space provided, then click **OK** to return to the command window. Click the ✿ button to the right of **Frame** and select **Min and Max** from the sub-menu. In the window that comes up type 0 in the space to the right of **Minimum for Y** and 400 in the space to the right of **Maximum for Y**. Click **OK** to return to the command window and in the section headed **Time Scale** click the button to the left of **Calendar** and choose **Quarter** from the pull-down menu. Click **OK** and your graph should now look like that in Figure 4.23.

Figure 4.23 Amended time series plot of pharmacy sales

Delete the graph then click **Stat** on the menu bar, choose **Time Series** and then **Decomposition** from the sub-menu. Next type C1 in the space to the right of **Variable**, and 4 in the space to the right of **Seasonal length**. Select **Additive** as the **Model Type**; check that **1** appears in the space to the right of **First obs. is in seasonal period**. Type an appropriate title in the space provided if you wish, then click **OK**. Three layers of graphs should appear, delete the two uppermost graphs. The remaining one should look like that shown in Figure 4.24.

Figure 4.24 shows the original series (the solid fluctuating line), the trend estimates (the smooth line through the middle of the series), and the series values we should expect based on the trend and regular seasonal effects (the broken fluctuating line). The differences between the series and the expected values are the irregular components. We might look at large irregular components and try to find factors that may account for them, for instance sales in the first quarter are rather lower than expected. Perhaps the product was out of stock for some of the time and sales opportunities were lost. The figures to the bottom right of the graph – MAPE, MAD and MSD (mean absolute percentage error, mean absolute deviation and mean square deviation, respectively) – are measures of the accuracy of the model. They are useful in assessing the appropriateness of different model types for a given set of data.

To obtain forecasts for future values of the series, repeat the procedure outlined in the penultimate paragraph but this time in the **Decomposition** command window click the button to the right of **Generate forecasts**, type 4 (for forecasts for the next four quarters) and click **OK**. You will see a set of graphs appear. The forecasts will be plotted in the bottom graph of the set and will appear in the session window as shown in Table 4.15.

In Table 4.15 the periods given are 17 to 20. The original series values were values 1 to 16, so these forecasts are for the four quarters of the subsequent year, 2004.

Leave the package by clicking **File** on the menu bar and choosing **Exit**.

Figure 4.24 Decomposition plot of pharmacy data

Table 4.15 Forecasts of pharmacy sales

Forecasts		
Row	Period	Forecast
1	17	327.325
2	18	172.834
3	19	145.218
4	20	264.976

SPSS

The current version of SPSS for Windows is 10.0. SPSS stands for Statistical Package for Social Sciences. It is in Windows format and so much of it will be familiar to students used to using Windows. The software can be set up to analyse data from your own questionnaire or it can be used to analyse databases that have been imported from existing secondary sources. It is possible to import data files from other software programs such as SNAP or from a spreadsheet.

If you are going to analyse data from your own questionnaire, it will be necessary to set up the variables in the SPSS data editor. This is normally not too big a job. As with all such programs the real effort is inputting the data from your questionnaires. Once this has been done you can start to analyse your data with a wide range of statistical tests. Certainly all those mentioned in this chapter, including chi-squared and correlation, are easily applied using the package. The data editor looks like a spreadsheet and so it is easy to read. There is a detailed tutorial guide and help function with the package.

When you open up SPSS you are faced with the data editor. The first task is to set up the variables you need to analyse your questionnaire results. To do this you need the **variable view**:

- To switch to this click on the **variable view** tab at the bottom of the sheet. In the variable view sheet each row represents a variable and you use the rows to define the variables you want. If the first variable, for the sake of illustration, is the respondents' ages, click on the first cell in the first row and type in 'age' as a variable name.
- The second cell in the row is used to define the type of data that will be put in the variable. Click on to the cell and a button will appear in it. Click on the button and use the menu to choose **numeric** because the data you will be inputting are the respondents' ages as numbers.
- The next two cells are used to define the width and the number of decimal places. Mostly these will be left at the default setting.
- The cell headed **variable label** is an optional space in which you can write a fuller description of the variable.

- The next cell **values and value labels** is important. It allows you to further define the values given to any variable. If you were setting up a variable to record the responses to a Likert statement, you would want to define five value labels as follows:

    1 = strongly agree
    2 = agree
    3 = uncertain
    4 = disagree
    5 = strongly disagree

- To do this click on the button in the cell and use the box that pops up. Where it says **value**, enter (in this case) the number 1 and in the box for **label** enter 'strongly disagree'. Press the **Add** button and that label will appear in the display box. Then repeat the routine for the other four values.

- The next cell is for dealing with missing values where a respondent has filled in a questionnaire but left some of the boxes empty. SPSS can happily deal with missing values as long as you tell the software how to recognise them. Decide on a number that you will use to signify a missing entry; 0 is often the sensible one. Click on the button in the 'missing value' cell. Press the **discrete missing values** button and type '0' in the first of the three boxes. The next two cells you can mostly ignore.

- When you click on the final cell you can define the type of data you are using by choosing between scale, ordinal or nominal data (see p. 178).

- Go through this process for every question in the questionnaire you want to analyse. Then make sure the file is saved.

The next stage is to input the data. To do this go to the **data view** by clicking the appropriate tab at the bottom of the screen. You will be faced with a spreadsheet in which each variable is now represented by a column. The name of the variable is shown at the top of each column. Every row in the spreadsheet is used to represent one completed questionnaire. The results from the questionnaire can be entered into the spreadsheet by typing in the appropriate figure in the appropriate cell.

The remaining task is to analyse the results. The first task will be to do frequency analysis. Start from the **data view** sheet and use the menu buttons along the top of the sheet:

- If you want to do a basic frequency analysis click on **Analyse ... Descriptive statistics ... Frequencies**.

- A frequencies box will appear. Choose the variable you want to analyse by highlighting it in the list. Press the **arrow** box to move it to the preview area that shows which variables will be analysed.

- Click the **statistics** button and choose which statistics you want (mean, mode or median, for example), and press **OK**.

- Click the **charts** button and choose any graphs and charts that you want and click **OK**.
- Then press **OK** on the **Frequencies** box and the analysis will be done and presented to you.

If you want to do a cross-tabulation proceed as follows:

- Using the menu buttons click on **Analyse ... descriptive statistics ... Cross tabs.**
- Choose the two variables you want to cross-tabulate and move them into the preview areas, one to be the rows in the cross-tabulation and one to be the columns.
- If you want chi-squared to be calculated press the **statistics** button and click the **chi^2** button and **OK**.
- Press the **Format** button to give you the option of having the percentages presented in the cross-tabulation output as well as the raw figures. Press **OK** when you have made your choice.
- In the cross-tabulation box you can also choose whether or not to have charts.
- When you have chosen your options press the **OK** button and the cross-tabulation analysis will be presented.

This is a very brief guide but it is sufficient to allow you to make an initial foray into SPSS. The World Wide Web page for the student edition of SPSS can be found at http://www.spss.com/education/student.htlm.

QSR NUD*IST – Carole Tansley

Data analysis and the use of QSR NUD*IST software

QSR stands for Qualitative Solutions and Research, a software development company in Melbourne, Australia, and NUD*IST stands for Non-numerical Unstructured Data Indexing Searching and Theorizing. QSR NUD*IST research software is a useful computer software package designed to aid users in handling non-numerical and unstructured data in qualitative analysis, by supporting processes of coding data in an index system, searching text or searching patterns of coding and theorising about the data. The NUD*IST software has a full command language for automating coding and searching and supports a wide range of research methods. Its command files and import procedures make research project set-up very rapid, enables a link between qualitative and quantitative data and is tolerant of large data sets.

To use the package the first thing that has to be done is to import the material. This might be any of the following:

- interview transcripts or notes;
- transcripts of conversations and discussions;
- observation notes;
- participant observer notes;
- organisational documents – minutes, reports, advertising material;
- any other text-based information.

This is normally done by importing word processing files. Just write the document in your word processor, save as plain text and import. Or 'batch in' as many new documents as you like in one action. Apart from using word processors to get text, you can also copy and paste text as a new or appended document into your project from the Web, email or a database, automatically converted to plain text, or save a growing memo as a document so it can be coded and searched. Documents are imported singly or in batches, in plain text with automatic formatting to the chosen unit of text. When you want to import text QSR NUD*IST takes over from your word processor the task of formatting them for your project. Text units, the basic unit for coding text, can now be lines, sentences, paragraphs, or any unit you end by hitting **Enter**. Set a preference, and QSR NUD*IST takes over, ensuring new documents have the right text unit type and the right line length.

Once the material is ready the analysis can be started. There are a number of stages:

1. The material is divided into 'chunks'. These are the basic units of analysis and you decide what it should be. Mostly it will be sentences or paragraphs.
2. Next 'nodes' must be identified. These are the key themes (see p. 155) against which the material will be coded. Nodes can be thought of as if they were the items in an index.
3. The researcher must then go through the research material and allocate the 'chunks' to the 'nodes'.
4. The nodes can be divided into two kinds – free nodes and structured nodes. Free nodes are just a random list of themes. Structured nodes are when the researcher links the themes in a hierarchical structure of themes, sub-themes, sub-sub-themes and so on. The development of such theme structures is the process by which researchers use the software to begin to theorise about their material.
5. When the researcher wants to write about a particular theme the software will bring together all the material that relates to it.
6. The software provides an opportunity to experiment and explore the links between the research material and the themes or nodes. Coding on-screen, with immediate access to the code system, the researcher can monitor and manage the emergence of ideas. Coded material is displayed for reflection, revision of coding and coding-on to new

categories. With searches of coding or text accessed by new, visual displays, the researcher can test hypotheses, locate patterns or pursue a line of enquiry to a confident conclusion.

QSR NUD*IST is on the PC platform, has low system requirements and comes with a detailed online Help, new tutorials and user guides.

There are tools for handling large surveys or small, in-depth and analytical projects. Access to import and export facilities for statistics, database and table-handling programs (such as SPSS, Excel and Access) ensure easy and comprehensive interaction between quantitative and qualitative aspects of the project – if needed. The Merge program allows multiple researchers to bring their work together (including those using older versions of the software). If graphic visualisation is important to your project, export to the extremely powerful analytically oriented Decision Explorer.

QSR NUD*IST is a highly effective means of storing and interpreting a variety of qualitative research material, including interview transcripts, researcher's notes, diary entries and other word processed documents. As well as providing an 'electronic filing cabinet' of text documents that provides the researcher with a database of material to analyse and interpret, QSR NUD*IST facilitates the generation of theory by providing the capability to code the transcripts, to search for words and phrases quickly, and enables the retrieval of coded text segments, related memos and reports.

QSR NUD*IST is extremely useful in interpretative approaches to research. Val Caven of Nottingham Business School found NUD*IST invaluable in her research about the career progression of women architects. She provides a useful description of how she used NUD*IST in her analysis:

> Whilst NUD*IST has proved to be a useful tool in carrying out the text searches and in the creation of coding categories, it is not to say that none of this would have been possible without NUD*IST. What is provided by NUD*IST is greater speed and sophistication in much the same way as using a tape recorder can assist the process of carrying out interviews. Ideas can be tested and nodes created in attempts to establish whether there is any significance in preliminary themes and hunches. If subsequent examination finds them to be of no relevance then little time has been lost. Alternatively, because such ideas can be contained within the index tree as 'free nodes' they can be saved and perhaps referred to at a later date. The coding system is emergent and can be created and changed throughout. The researcher also remains very close to the data as the possibility of the context of passages of text being lost by becoming isolated from their source is removed by the 'jump to source' function which takes the researcher to the actual text within the original interview. Nevertheless, it must be stressed that using software such as NUD*IST does not supplant the input of the researcher, nor does it 'think' on behalf of the researcher. The true value of NUD*IST is in the speed and ease of its use that in turn, can give the researcher greater freedom and flexibility in developing theory.

For further information about QSR NUD*IST and other software packages to aid your research, go to Scolari's web page for details: http://www.scolari.co.uk/frame.html?http://www.scolari.co.uk/qsr/demo. For information on Decision Explorer go to: http://www.scolari.co.uk/frame.html?http://www.scolari.co.uk/de/de.htm.

Summary

- Decide whether you will be researching as an explorer or a surveyor, or both.
- Make a careful choice about the degree of openness or pre-coding that you need to apply to the research methods you are using.
- If you are using an open or semi-structured approach you still need to plan and organise your research methods carefully.
- If you are using pre-coded techniques choose the best question format, from those available, for each of the questions you want to ask.
- Whether you use open, semi-structured or pre-coded techniques always pilot your research tools, schedules, aide memoires, questionnaires or whatever before using them on your main research subjects.
- If your research material is qualitative use a coding method to summarise and précis the material. Frame the account of your material in a case study format, which helps you to identify the connections between the themes within your material.
- If your research material is quantitative, analyse it using descriptive and summary statistics. Use graphs and charts where they ease explanation but avoid overusing them.
- Use appropriate statistical tests to check the significance of your analysis.
- Consider using software packages to help you analyse your material qualitatively or quantitatively – but be careful. Deciding whether the effort needed to master the software and input the research material is justified within the short amount of time available for a part-time Master's dissertation is a fine judgement.

Suggested reading

Saunders *et al.* (2002) is the best option if you want a general guide to all the techniques covered in this chapter. For open and semi-structured research I recommend Silverman (1999). The classic work for those designing a questionnaire is Oppenheim (1992). For statistics and quantitative methods read Buglear (2000). Sapsford and Judd (1996) is a good alternative. Bryman and Cramer (2001) is based on SPSS and explains the statistical techniques well but probably goes into too much detail for most Master's students. Sapsford (1999) is helpful survey research.

Bryman, A. and Cramer, D. (2001) *Quantitative Analysis with SPSS release 10 for Windows: A Guide for Social Scientists*, London: Routledge.

Buglear, J. (2000) *Stats To Go*, Oxford: Butterworth Heinemann.

Sapsford, R. (1999) *Survey Research*, London: Sage.

Sapsford, R. and Judd, V. (1996) (eds) *Data Collection and Analysis*, London: Sage.

Silverman, D. (1999) *Doing Qualitative Research*, London: Sage.

References

Bales, R. F. (1950) *Interaction Process Analysis*, Reading, MA: Addison-Wesley.

Bayly, C. A. (1996) *Empire and Information: Intelligence Gathering and Social Communication in India, 1780–1870*, Cambridge: Cambridge University Press.

BBC (2003) 'Row over NHS star ratings', BBC News [Online] 16 July, available at: http://news.bbc.co.uk/1/hi/health/3069121.stm [accessed 16 July 2003].

Billig, M. (1996) *Arguing and Thinking: A Rhetorical Approach to Social Psychology*, 2nd edn, Cambridge: Cambridge University Press.

Boyatzis, R. (1982) *The Competent Manager*, New York: John Wiley.

Bryman, A. and Cramer, D. (1997) *Quantitative Data Analysis with SPSS for Windows: A Guide for Social Scientists*, London: Routledge.

Buglear, J. (2001) *Stats Means Business*, Oxford: Butterworth Heinemann.

Cramer, D. (1997) *Basic Statistics for Social Research*, London: Routledge.

Ellinger, A. D. and Watkins, K. E. (1998) 'Updating the critical incident techniques after forty-four years', in Torraco, R. J (proceedings ed.), *Academy of Human Resource Development 1998 Conference Proceedings*, Baton Rouge, LA: Academy of Human Resource Development, Conference held Chicago, March.

Flanagan, J. C. (1954) 'The critical incident technique', *Psychological Bulletin*, vol. 1, 327–358.

Freeman, D. (1983) *Margaret Mead and Samoa: The Making and Unmaking of an Anthropological Myth*, London: Harvard University Press.

Gabriel, Y. (2000) *Storytelling in Organisations*, Oxford: Oxford University Press.

Gill, J. and Johnson, P. (1997) *Research Methods for Managers*, 2nd edn, London: Paul Chapman.

Gordon, W. and Langmaid, R. (1988) *Qualitative Market Research: A Practitioners' and Buyers' Guide*, Aldershot: Gower.

Huff, D. (1991) *How to Lie with Statistics*, Harmondsworth: Penguin.

Hurston, Z. N. (1942) *Dust Tracks on a Road*, Philadelphia, PA: J. B. Lippincott.

Huxley, T.H. (1807) 'Biogenesis and abigenesis', in *Collected Works*, Vol. VIII.

Jankowicz, A. D. (1995) *Business Research Projects*, 2nd edn, London: Chapman Hall.

Kelly, G. (1963) *A Theory of Personality: The Psychology of Personal Constructs*, New York: Norton.

Lodge, D. (1989) *Nice Work*, London: Penguin.

McClean, A. and Marshall, J. (1991) *Cultures at Work: How to Identify and Understand Them*, Luton: Local Government Management Board.

McKenzie, J. and Goldman, R. (1999) *The Student Edition of MINITAB for Windows 95 and NT*, New York: Addison-Wesley Longman.

● ● ● ● Introduction

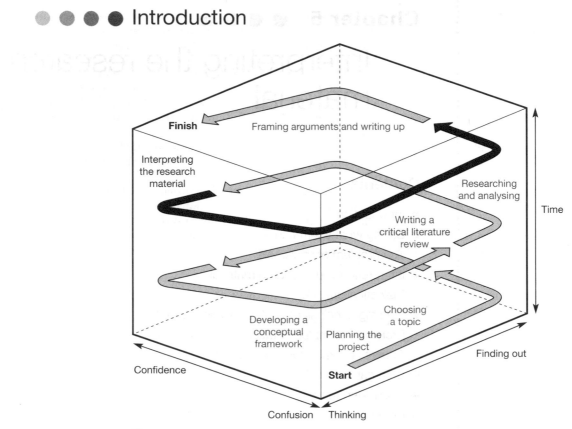

Finish

Framing arguments and writing up

Interpreting
the research
material

Researching
and analysing

Time

Writing a
critical literature
review

Developing a
conceptual
framework

Choosing
a topic

Planning the
project

Finding out

Confidence

Start

Confusion   Thinking

The processes of researching and writing a Master's dissertation

What is now proved, was once only imagined

William Blake 'The Marriage of Heaven and Hell' (1991: 46)

This chapter focuses on the processes and skills of interpreting your research findings and of drawing conclusions from your interpretations that are sensible and practicable. Interpretation in this chapter means deciding how robust and helpful your research findings are and the extent you might rely on them when exercising your judgement. It involves much thinking to help you 'find out' the meaning of your research findings. It can represent a loss of confidence after the buzz of certainty that comes with having completed the research phase of your project. It should be a stage in which you question everything before finally coming to a final statement of your interpretation and conclusions in the next, 'writing up' phase of the project.

In Chapters 1 and 2 the interpretivist and realist approaches to research were introduced (amongst a number of others). Each has its own forms of explanation. Realist research tries to explain things by modelling the relationships between variables. This might be achieved by the following:

- A high-level mathematical model that tries to replicate the ways in which a complex series of variables interact. Models of national economies or of market behaviour would be examples.
- More restricted statistical models that try to describe the interaction between a limited number of variables. The relationship between job satisfaction and work performance might be a case in point.
- A series of generalisations about the interactions of variables based on a qualitative and quantitative comparison of a number of case studies. Someone might try to identify the 'driving and restraining forces' that have an impact on projects to introduce teamworking by studying a number of plants where such a change has been introduced.

One of the major issues when interpreting such research is whether the variables that have been used are sensible and valid. There can be a danger that the variables are not as they seem.

Interpretivist research seeks to explain things by mapping the processes by which meaning is developed and changed. This might be achieved as follows:

- giving accounts of the processes of meaning formation in particular contexts. For example, in a naturalistic or pluralistic evaluation of a service an account might be given of the views the different stakeholders hold in relation to that service.
- Providing an account of how meanings at individual and at group levels are negotiated and changed by the interaction of many factors, such as power and chance. A study of decision making amongst a group of managers using the garbage can theory (March *et al.* 1972) as a framework would be an example.
- Generating high-level theory about the processes of interpretation, the means by which people create their own identities and interpretations. The processes can be illustrated by critical incidents, extracts from discourses and epiphanies obtained by observation. Weick's (1995) work on enactment would be an example.

One of the major problems in interpreting such explanations is their very pluralism. The danger is that the researcher may privilege one form of explanation over another. In action research projects, for example, which often adopt an interpretivist approach, the researcher's voice can remain predominant despite their protestations that they are listening to the voices of others.

Both of these areas, the solidity of variables and the hegemony of certain perspectives, will be considered in this chapter, which is divided into three parts:

1. **Saying what you mean**. In business and management it is easy to fall into the use of jargon in ways that disguise the fact that we do not always know, or say, what we mean. This part looks at the problems of claiming too much by saying too little in dissertations and gives you some practice in saying what you mean.

2. **Interpreting your research findings**. Contrary to popular belief research findings, whether they be interview transcripts, quantitative question-naire results or any other form of material, do not interpret themselves. This part provides some techniques that will be helpful in making sense of your material.

3. **Drawing conclusions**. Even when you have made sense of your research material and this has helped you to understand the managerial or organisational issue you are studying, the conclusions to be drawn and the recommendations you need to make may not be obvious. Making your conclusions and recommendations calls for a different type of thinking. Your analysis of the research material will not help you syn-thesise a response. In Chapter 1 (see p. 28) a distinction was made between research questions and strategic questions. It will be necessary to conclude the dissertation with an account of the answers to your research questions. It is also in the conclusions of your dissertation that you should give your judgment, and possibly your recommendations, about the strategic question. This part of the chapter looks at how to arrive at strategic conclusions and recommendations that are appropri-ate and which can be implemented.

Learning outcomes for the chapter

1 Readers will be able to write in a careful manner so that the claims they make are not greater than can be supported by their research and reading.

2 Readers will have a general understanding of the issues surround-ing claims to truth and validity when writing a dissertation.

3 Readers will be able to use a range of approaches for interpreting the research materials they have gathered during the research.

4 Readers will be able to draw conclusions based upon their interpre-tations of their research material.

5 Readers will be able to identify the problems of implementation associated with any conclusions or recommendations they might propose in the dissertation.

● ● ● ● Saying what you mean

There is a grave danger, when writing dissertations, that we lapse into bizno-bollocks speak, such as in the following example:

> It is our job continually to leverage other's performance-based methods of empowerment.

Or its scholarly equivalent, professorial pompous talk:

> The premise of capitalist narrative states that reality is used to reinforce the hegemony of capitalism. If neo-capitalist narrative holds we have to choose between the semiotic paradigm of discourse and the textual paradigm of consensus.

Both of these examples are extreme because they were written by computer programs[1] that use random methods to generate text. They look as if they mean something profound but, because they are randomly generated, they are clearly nonsense. It is easy to find examples of both conditions in management reports and in academic journals. Business and management students are more likely to suffer from bizno-bollocks speak than its academic equivalent when they write. It is easy to fall into the trap of using management jargon because it sounds impressive. However, as it involves little thought, it generally means little or nothing. The purpose of this part of the chapter is to help you to be more careful about what you say, especially when you are writing a report or dissertation.

The problem of universals

To help you avoid making claims that are not, quite, what you mean we need to take a short detour into medieval philosophy. Although it might seem to wander off from the point you will see (in Exercise 5.2) that the detour has practical consequences for dissertation writing. The argument that follows from here to Exercise 5.2 is work in progress. It is intended to help you think more clearly about what you write; but it is open to argument and challenge.

Most of management and business research deals not in tangible objects but in ideas and abstractions. If you are studying human resources management, for example, then HRM itself is an abstraction, as are many of the things you study in its name, such as motivation, empowerment and commitment. Even in the more quantitative branches of management the subjects that are studied are mostly concepts and ideas, such as strategy

---

[1] See the Dilbert mission statement generator: http://www.unitedmedia.co./comics/dilbert/career and the 'postmodern essay generator' at: http://www.csse.monash.edu.au/other/postmodern.html.

Exercise 5.1

Researching supply chains

Let us consider a conversation I had with a researcher a few days before writing this. He was planning some research into the efficiency and effectiveness of supply chains. 'We are looking for a correlation between lean manufacturing *attributes* (low stock levels, advanced software systems, etc.) and *competitive bases* (flexibility, speed, responsiveness). At first we intended to measure these things directly. Some of them however are hard to measure. So we have sent out questionnaires asking managers to assess the importance of the relationship between attributes and competitive bases. Having established the relationship between attributes and competitive bases we will be able to produce a decision model to help companies find good partners for their supply chain.'

The speaker is claiming his research will provide the basis of a new decision support system to help managers choose the best partners for their supply chain. Is there anything that causes you to question the honesty of this claim?

Suggested answer

The main criticism is that the researcher is claiming more for his research than can be justified. At first glance it looks like a good piece of hard scientific research. If it is possible to calculate the statistical relationship between attributes and competitive bases, companies will be able to work out which potential partner will be most competitive. Companies could measure the organisational 'attributes' of potential partners and use these to forecast which partners would be most competitive. But this is not what the researcher is planning to do. He admits that both attributes and competitive bases are tricky things because they are hard to measure. As he said, 'the trouble is each of these things, such as flexibility, can be measured in so many different ways'. Instead he is proposing to measure what managers ('who should know after all') *think* the relationship between attributes and bases is. Suddenly we are no longer dealing with hard facts, with things; we are dealing with perceptions. Perceptions are trickier than things. It is at least arguable that the feature that characterises experts in any field is that they disagree with one another. This would not matter if the researcher admitted he was only dealing with opinions, but at the end of the conversation the researcher talks as if he will have established the relationship between attributes and bases, when he will have done no such thing.

If we look a little more closely we can see that the speaker is claiming that 'attributes' and 'competitive bases' are things. They are seen as being as real and as solid as the table I am working at. They are seen as real because, in this researcher's world, there is a general acceptance of their definition and importance. But neither of these things is real. They are just names that the author has chosen to group together, a number of other terms which he, and possibly others, think are important. Other people might choose different lists of things to put under each label. Different people may choose to define terms, such as 'flexibility', differently. The acceptance of this truth is implied in the researcher's admitted difficulty in measuring his variables. We might need to consider whether abstract terms, such as competitive bases, are ever real.

In summary the research is proposing to study people's opinions on things that are more fuzzy concepts than factual, tangible objects. This does not mean the research will not be useful, as much management research appropriately concentrates on perceptions and opinions. However, it is easy to claim that this type of research is more than it is.

and consumer preferences. Ideas, concepts, abstractions are names that we give to a number of things that we believe form a set or group because they are thought to have some important feature in common. The medieval philosophers called these sets *universals*. Think of a number of chairs you have sat in. Each and every one of these is a real thing, but the concept of *chair* is an idea formed from the conjunction of all the chairs.

Medieval philosophers were the first to distinguish between universals and substance. A chair has real substance. It objectively exists. If the substance of the chair you are sitting on breaks you get a sore backside when you fall to the floor. However, the concept or the idea of a chair, which refers to all possible chairs and not to any one particular chair, has no substance. It is a concept, an idea, or, in medieval terms, a universal. Identifying the common features that link all the chairs that can exist within the universal concept of 'chair' is often difficult. The concept is something we know intuitively rather than something we can easily articulate. You might think that all chairs have four legs; but no, there can be three-legged stools. Some chairs are built as a cube and have no legs at all. The difficulty of defining the core characteristics of a universal explains why their common use in management studies makes for difficulty: people will not agree on their definition. A universal can also be understood by comparing it with its opposite, which is a proper name. A proper name is given to a thing or person, each of which is the only thing to which the name in question applies, for example the sun, France and Napoleon. Universals such as 'chair', 'cat', 'dog' and 'humankind' apply to many different things.

It is easy, when writing about management, to use terms such as 'strategy' and others shown in Figure 5.1 as if they had clear meanings and unambiguous reality. But while it is easy to claim that a substance is real, it is not so easy to make the same claim for a universal. The document I hold which says 'A Strategy' on its cover is real enough. But whether the general idea of a strategy is as real is at least open to question (Franklin 2001).

The question that faced medieval philosophers, and still faces us, was and is: are universals real? Do they have a concrete and objective existence?

- Research into business, organisational and managerial matters tends to be research into abstract ideas.

- The technical term is 'universal'.

- Do universals have a concrete, objective existence?

Figure 5.1 Universals

As universals are the subject of much of the research into management and business it is an important question for us too. The medieval philosophers had two opposing answers to the question: realism and nominalism.

The realists thought that universals were real and had an existence separate from people's thoughts about them. The nominalists thought that universals were not independent objects and were simply convenient names or labels. These ideas need to be explained before their implications for writing dissertations are revealed.

Epistemological realism

The epistemological realist believes that universals have a reality that is independent of how people talk about them. Therefore, the concepts we use when talking about management can be real. They believe that universals (or concepts) mirror what exists in the real world. Epistemological realism is the belief that the structure of the real world is 'cognitively accessible' to those who investigate it (Johnson and Duberley 2000: 151). In other words, not only does the world have an objective existence, but also it is possible for people to know about it objectively.

Typically, an epistemological realist who was researching HRM would claim that there are things in organisations such as the following:

- human resource management practices,
- policies and procedures,
- patterns of behaviour, and
- the planned outcomes of HRM activity

that can be described and delineated. They would also claim that when all these features are put together they form something that all sensible people would agree is called HRM. Quite likely they would write about HRM as if it were an unambiguous thing. So they might claim that 'HRM is the key to competitive advantage', or something similar. Figure 5.2 illustrates the epistemological realist approach.

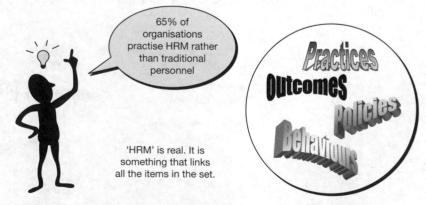

Figure 5.2 The epistemological realist position

With this belief, epistemological realists can talk about HRM in a certain way. As it has an independent existence HRM is fixed and can be measured and defined. Realists can research organisations to see which ones have HRM and which ones do not. They can draw conclusions about whether it is a good thing or not.

Nominalism

The nominalists, however, see universals in a different light. When they research an organisation they do not see undisputed facts; they see accounts and interpretations. They see themselves as researching what people say about the subject of research, in this case HRM. They study the accounts, arguments and statements that people make about HRM in their organisations. As people will inevitably have different opinions, it follows that a concept, a universal, such as HRM, will at best be a confusion of many images. The subject can only be seen hazily as if it were being viewed through a dark glass or in a distorting mirror. This situation causes some people to be so uncertain about what they are seeing through the glass that their names for these things (i.e. the universals) cannot have a reality of their own. They are not arguing that what is being researched is not real, just that the names we give to the things we research are not real. Modern philosophers of science often make a similar distinction. Bhaskar distinguishes intransitive objects (the things and events being studied), which are real, from transitive constructions (the shifting ways in which we understand those events and things), which are social constructions (Johnson and Duberley 2000: 152).

Nominalists therefore are much more careful about the claims they make based upon their research. Such researchers, investigating HRM in organisations, would not say that some organisations **do** and others **do not** have HRM. They would only go as far as to claim that most, or a certain percentage of managers in organisations, **say** that they practise HRM. This statement leaves open the question of whether what people say is mirrored by external reality. Questions about HRM, say the nominalists, cannot be answered straightforwardly because HRM is not a real thing. HRM is just a convention, a shorthand, that we use in conversation. One immediate consequence of writing in a nominalist mode is that sentences are longer because the ambiguities about the concepts being discussed have to be specified (as in Figure 5.3).

Critical realism

There is a third position on the question of universals. But you need only consider it if you have found the discussion so far interesting. It is the critical realist stance and it is an attempt to bring together realism and nominalism by transcending their differences. The idea that there is an objective world,

Figure 5.3 Nominalism

and the notions that our understanding of it can only be subjective and never objective or definitive, are shown not to be mutually exclusive.

Critical realism is a stance developed by Bhaskar (Johnson and Duberley 2000: 150–156). It proposes three levels of reality (Collier 1994: 42–45):

● *Experiences* – This is what we see and experience of the world. This can be subjective and limited. We may 'see' things from an odd perspective or may not see things at all. This level is nominalist. Our experiences are not mirrors of reality.

● *Events* – Events are the things that happen in the world that we perceive through our experiences of them. They are the things that happen and the things that are said and they are the second level of reality. This level represents a metaphysical realism, which is the view that the external world has a physical reality.

● *Mechanisms* – However, events do not occur out of nothing: they must have a cause. Mechanisms are the causes of events and are the third, and deepest, level of reality. The critical realists argue that there are many mechanisms existing at this level. They could be, for instance, the assumptions that constitute someone's personality, a clash of economic interests or the constraints of an organisational culture. Triggers switch on such mechanisms in complex combinations and they bring about the events that we experience. A crucial feature of mechanisms is that they cannot be directly experienced. They can only be logically inferred from events. This might be seen to make mechanisms nominalist but the critical realists argue that because they are the generative mechanisms that cause real events then they too must be real. The apparent contradiction between nominalism and realism is overcome at this deep level of reality. This third level is the 'real' reality that researchers ought to discover.

Critical realists studying HRM might observe (experience) that there are certain events that are typical of HRM. To understand these events they have to infer the mechanisms that might cause them. A good starting point might be to focus on any oddities or contradictions seen amongst the events, as they might indicate different mechanisms coming into play. For example, the concern for empowering employees, which HR managers often express, might sit oddly with their concentration on labour efficiency and downsizing. The three levels of understanding required by a critical realist approach are illustrated in Figure 5.4.

If we study these contradictions they lead us to an understanding of a deeper reality that is normally hidden from view. This deeper reality is the underlying dynamics or mechanisms that are driving changes in society in general and in organisations in particular. These underlying mechanisms are often understood as the workings of the deep contradictions in capitalist society that Marxists have identified. These underlying mechanisms, according to the critical realists, do have a solid and real existence. Critical realism therefore combines a belief in real social forces with an understanding of the socially constructed nature of the terms (universals) that we use when discussing them.

Implications for dissertation writers

When we research and write dissertations we are mostly dealing with universals. There are a number of positions we can take on universals:

- They are real and more or less reflect reality and are therefore easy to define and measure.
- They are just phrases – puffs of wind, arbitrary labels – and because of this ambiguity they are difficult to define and measure.

Figure 5.4 Critical realism

- They are real but exist below the level of our direct experience and although they can be defined and specified it is a difficult intellectual process to excavate through the levels of experiences and events to identify them,

and, no doubt, many other positions in between. How should we write about such things? Should we write about them as if they were clear and straightforward or as if they were uncertain and ambiguous? I think, and you may disagree, that it is best to assume the precautionary principle. Which of the two situations would be worse?

- To write about universals, such as strategy or HRM, as if they were real when in truth they are not,

or

- To write about them with caution, as if they were uncertain, when in truth they are real and unambiguous.

If you take the first course, you risk looking foolish; if you take the other course, then the worst you will look is overcautious. On balance it might be thought best to treat universals in your dissertation as if they were dangerous and ought to be carefully caged within caveats and warnings. After all even most modern realists do not claim that knowledge can be a perfect reflection of the real world, and so even they would be a little careful with their universal concepts. As Johnson and Duberley (2000: 151) argue 'truth must be more than outputs from a language game yet it cannot be absolute'. The nominalists and the postmoderns would of course just treat universals as playthings. The following credo is suggested as a helpful one to bear in mind when writing your dissertation:

- Reality may be real (it is made up of intransitive objects). There is a real world out there.
- But our understanding of it is socially constructed. People will apprehend it differently according to their assumptions and values (intransitive constructs).
- Because our understandings are based on universals that are 'confused images', we need to be very careful not to claim too much when we write up our interpretations of our research material.
- We need to write in an 'as if' mode when we write about things that are socially constructed otherwise we will fall into the trap of treating ideas as things when they are not.

Interpretation is a complex matter, as Exhibit 5.1 might suggest.

So much for the philosophy; what about the practice? Well, realists can get away with sentences that nominalists or critical realists would be chary of, as can be seen in Exercise 5.2.

Exhibit 5.1

Source. 'Therapeutisch Bruegelconcert voor een Magrittiaanse toehoorder' by Jos De Mey.
Reproduced with the permission of the artist

It is possible to take this cautious approach to writing too far. If you were to add too many cautions and caveats to your sentences,2124 they would become cumbersome and you would not be able to express what you wish to say. The purpose of Exercise 5.2 is not to freeze you into immobility but to warn you against being too sweeping in your claims.

Exercise 5.2

Framing sentences honestly

Review each of the following sentences. They all assume a realist stance. Redraft them into a form of words that would be acceptable from a nominalist stance. Another way of putting it is to ask you to rewrite the following statements so that they are more honest.

1. The organisation's culture is acting as a brake on growth.
2. The majority of staff, according to the staff feedback survey, are satisfied with the leadership they receive at work.
3. HRM increases bottom line performance.
4. Does TQM work?
5. Around this time 'hard' and 'soft' HRM emerged.

Exercise 5.2 *continued*

Suggested answer

1. The sentence treats 'organisation', 'culture' and 'growth' as if they were all real things with clear definitions. It rather assumes, for instance, that the organisation has a single culture. It is much more likely that it has an overlapping admixture of sub-cultures. It is also unlikely that everyone in the organisation agrees with the sentiment expressed in sentence 1 of the exercise, so it is necessary to be specific about who holds this view. If we assume that this is the view of managers in the HRM department, then we might reword the sentence as follows:

    Managers in the HRM department argue that the culture of the organisation, as they see it, is preventing the type of growth they believe is necessary.

2. The main problem with the sentence is that putting a tick in a particular box on a questionnaire is assumed to represent the 'real' feelings of the staff. It may be that staff fibbed when they ticked the box. Maybe they had not settled their own views on the issue and ticked any box just to complete the questionnaire. It also assumes that there is a consensus amongst the respondents about what good leadership is.

    The majority of the respondents ticked a box that said they were satisfied with the leadership they received at work.

3. This is a bold claim. Let us assume that it is based on some survey research in which companies were asked questions about their HR management and about financial performance. Let us further assume that there was a positive statistical correlation between the two variables. There are two problems. The first is that the sentence treats HRM as an unambiguous thing. The second is that it assumes that a statistical association is the same as cause and effect.

    Companies that reported that they practised HRM tended to be the same as the companies that reported higher returns on capital expended.

4. Well it all depends on what you mean by 'TQM' and by 'work'. Again TQM is treated as if it were a real thing as opposed to being a label that is used with greater or lesser exactitude by a wide range of people. The question is so wide that it is probably not possible to answer it in its present state.

5. The problem here is that 'soft' and 'hard' are being treated as if they have an independent existence from the academics and HR professionals who write and talk about them.

    At about this time academic writers began to use the terms 'hard' and 'soft' when analysing the approach to managing people known as HRM.

●●●● Interpreting your research material

It follows from the argument presented in the previous part that researchers need to take care when making sense of their research material. Richard Winter (1989) has proposed a number of principles that can be applied when trying to find out what interpretations may be placed on research material:

- reflexive critique
- dialectical critique
- collaborative resources

- risk to one's own values
- plural structure
- theory, practice and transformation.

The jargon is a little impenetrable, but each of these perspectives can be explained in a practical way.

- **Reflexive critique** Whenever we give an account of our research findings we should accept that the account would be coloured by our values, assumptions and prejudices. That is to say, our accounts are reflexive, our judgements about things 'out there' are always bent back to focus on our internal concerns and preoccupations. In a reflexive critique we recognise and explain these concerns. A reflexive critique may also cause us to reconsider our values. At a simple level a reflexive critique allows the reader an insight into the researcher's thinking and helps the reader take this into consideration when reading the researcher's account of the research. It allows the reader to apply the 'Mandy Rice-Davies' test. Rice-Davies was involved in the Profumo sex and spying scandal in the 1960s. When she was confronted in court with a witness's allegations against her she replied, 'Well he would say that, wouldn't he?' This is a useful question to ask of any researcher's work, including your own. Van Maanen (1988) provides interesting insights on a reflexive approach to research, as do Alvesson and Skoldberg (2000).
- **Dialectical critique** The key idea of dialectical critique is that whenever we study something there are always contradictions between the formal unity of the thing and its teeming, detailed practical aspect. If we study HRM we might begin with a formal definition of it. But when we look at how it is implemented in organisations we will find that it involves many different practices. This practical diversity may well contradict the apparent unity of the thing we have called HRM. Billig (1996) calls these two processes categorisation and particularisation. As soon as we think we have put everything into neat boxes, some irritating particular refuses to be pigeon-holed. If we take the dialectical analysis a little further we may find that some of the things that are done under the name of HRM not only fail to fit neatly within the category but actually challenge the formal claims made for it. In my work, for example, I have argued that codes of ethics in organisations, which are intended to encourage staff to behave with integrity, often have the reverse effect. Staff think to themselves, 'The organisation obviously doesn't believe we can act with integrity or else they would not have asked us to commit to the code of ethics.' This perceived lack of faith in their integrity encourages staff to act as they think the organisation believes they will.

  Dialectical analysis means looking for the contradictions in your research material:

- Contradictions between the big categories that bring everything together and the multitudinous detail that pulls everything apart.
- Contradictions between the formal, stated purposes of people's actions and their practice and impact.

As Winter (1989: 53) puts it, dialectical critique means looking for 'unity concealed behind apparent differentiation and contradiction concealed within apparent unity'.

- **Collaborative resources** This principle fits well with the idea of stakeholders that is commonly used in business and management studies. It means looking at an issue from the perspectives of the various stakeholders and involving them as resources in interpreting and understanding the research material. This may involve actually working with others in a collaborative group, or in some other way feeding back your material to others to gain their insights and readings of it.
- **Risk to one's own values** A good researcher is willing to let the research process challenge their own values and ways of looking at things. In particular the things at risk are:

  - the researcher's provisional interpretation of the research material;
  - the researcher's decisions about the question at issue and what the research is about; and
  - the research plan, which may well have to change as the researcher's thinking is challenged.

- **Plural structure** If the research we have carried out recognises that there are different perspectives on an issue, then it follows that when the research is written up this diversity should be recognised in the structure of the report or dissertation. In other words, the dissertation should not present the research material as a single-minded sequence of steps from initial premise to final conclusion but should also include the arguments for and against at each stage in the development of the argument. If you were doing a dissertation that evaluated a service you should not just arrange your material so that it all leads to the final conclusion that the service is good, bad or indifferent. You should recognise that different groups of stakeholders may well have different definitions of what is good and bad and that therefore they may arrive at different conclusions about the quality of the service.
- **Theory, practice, transformation** Theoretical thought about managerial and business issues is good and necessary; but just as practice needs to be challenged by theory, theory needs to be challenged by practice. The judgements and decisions that you make based upon your research should, if possible, be tried in practice or at least be capable of being tested in practice.

Winter wrote of these six principles in relation to action research. But they are useful guidelines for any type of researcher. They form a coherent series but it is not necessary that every researcher should apply all of them. I propose that you should consider applying one or two of these principles, as appropriate, when you interpret and make sense of your research material. Exercise 5.3 gives you opportunities to try out some of these principles.

Exercise 5.3

The doctors' surgery

A researcher was studying the organisational cultures of GPs' practices. He had chosen this topic because he had for long been involved with doctors as a result of his injuries from a car crash and the subsequent litigation and frequent medical examinations. One or two GPs had become his close friends and in conversation with them he had become interested in the management of primary health care.

He decided to start his study by carrying out informal observations of surgeries. He was given permission to do the work and sat quietly in waiting rooms for the duration of clinic sessions and kept a research diary in which he noted all the things that seemed to him to be of interest. A page from his research notes is printed below. You will need to know that a Lloyd George envelope is the small manila packet into which GPs traditionally stuff medical notes. A nebulizer is a device for treating a patient suffering from a severe asthma attack.

What opportunities do the materials present for applying Winter's six principles of interpretation?

Entries from a log book written during observation of a general practice surgery

1. Driving to the practice it was difficult to identify the building, it was on a busy road, many tall shrubs were growing in front of it, and there was no obvious sign; it was also in the middle of a difficult one-way road system.
2. The waiting area (for a two-doctor practice) was 30ft by 10ft.
3. There was a noticeboard on one wall of the room giving practice information. It was cluttered and two items were over two years old.
4. Overheard conversation amongst receptionists: 'Mrs Jones has been in again, she's a nuisance. She said she was just passing and thought she would see if her repeat prescription was ready, even though we told her to come tomorrow. Well it was ready, but I told her it wasn't and to come back. They start to take liberties if you aren't careful.'
5. There is a small, but well-organised, practice library, which includes health education material as well as clinical textbooks.
6. Observed: a woman and child who had been waiting 15 minutes. The child was becoming agitated and whining, 'When are we going to see the doctor?' The mother replied, in a loudish voice, 'My love, you just have to wait till they are ready.' No response from the receptionist staff who had overheard the conversation.
7. In the record-keeping area I notice that pulling and returning medical notes from the racking seems to be a cumbersome and difficult activity, without actually being able to say why. Then it hit me, the racking was designed to take A4 records but the notes are still kept in Lloyd George envelopes.
8. As I pass along the upstairs landing I hear a GP saying to a child and his mother, 'Hang on here a moment. I'm just going to go downstairs to get the key to Dr Y's room – he's not in today – and then I'll fix up the nebulizer for you in that room and I'll come back and check on you when I've seen my next patient.'
9. The administration and clerical staff, all women, wear a uniform – smart navy suits from Marks & Sparks.

Exercise 5.3 *continued*

10. Various community nursing staff are based in a pleasant, airy office within the surgery. A GP poked his head round the door, noticed that only the school nurse was in, and exited muttering, 'Bloody health visitors, never one when you want one and then three come along together when you don't.'

11. Access to the building and the downstairs rooms is good for people with mobility problems. There is also a patients' toilet with a wide door and appropriate fitments for use by people in wheelchairs.

12. The surgery runs an open appointments system during morning surgery. People come and wait in turn either for the first doctor available or, if they prefer, for their own doctor.

13. There is a large notice pinned up that says that the practice wants to provide a personal service and that, consequently, locums or stand-in GPs will never do night calls. These will always be done by one of the two partners.

14. The practice is well below the regional average for payments for night visits per GP according to the figures the practice manager showed me.

Suggested answer

The researcher has obviously had much experience of the health service. His particular experience of it, together with his attitude towards the NHS, may affect what he chose to record in his diary and what spin he placed upon it. A reflexive critique of the material would be helpful to the reader.

The practice has a policy of doing its night visits itself and providing a personalised service (item 13). But the figures from the health authority suggest that they do fewer night visits than other GPs (item 14). This apparent contradiction might form the basis of a dialectical critique. There may be reasons, such as the following, to explain the discrepancy:

- The GPs may make the visits but forget to claim the payment from the health authority and so the visits do not show up in the statistics.
- Maybe the GPs have trained their patients not to call them at night.
- Perhaps the GPs do not put their policy into practice, and so on.

Exploring the contradiction should lead to a better understanding of the situation.

There may be room for another dialectical critique when the formal conditions provided for the patients (items 2, 9, 11 and 12) are contrasted with the manner in which patients are treated by reception staff (items 4 and 6). The physical conditions are mostly good (except item 1), but the way staff treat the patients looks less good.

One of the problems with the research material is that there is no guarantee that the observed behaviour was representative of the practice. It may have been that the reception staff were just having a bad day and that this was the reason for their lack of charm. Or it may have been that the researcher was not aware of the full context of items 4 and 6 and so he misread the situations. Given these doubts, a collaborative approach would be sensible. This would mean seeking the interpretation that other receptionists, if not those particular receptionists, would place upon the events. Of course an action researcher would argue that such research should have been carried out as a collaborative exercise in the first place with all the staff of the surgery.

As the research stands, there is not much risk to the researcher's values.

There are a number of items in the diary that are capable of being interpreted differently. Item 8 is a case in point. You could argue that this is good news because here is a doctor going to some trouble to respond to the needs of a patient. A contrary view would be that it is a bad thing that the practice does not have the rooms or the procedures for dealing with this patient in anything other than an ad hoc fashion. Which view you take will probably depend on who you are. Research material such as this would clearly benefit from a plural structure when it is written up. The question of the appropriateness of putting the receptionists in uniform (item 9) might also best be considered from plural perspectives. If, for example, the surgery were in a middle-class, suburban area, the uniforms might be seen as a mark of professionalism. If the surgery were in a deprived estate, the uniforms might be seen as a mark of the staff's superiority over the patients.

There is no intention that the research findings should be used to develop or transform practice within this particular surgery. Should they?

Dialectical critique

This way of interpreting research material is particularly interesting and will repay more detailed consideration. It is best explored by doing it and so here are two exercises.

Exercise 5.4

Management attitudes towards redundancy decisions

Below is an abstract from a transcript of a research interview. The interview was structured around the collection of critical incidents. The interviewees were asked of any incident at work they could recall that seemed to them to raise questions of right and wrong or of fairness in the treatment of people. In this extract two incidents are related.

Carry out a dialectical critique of the incidents. This will involve making a comparison of the two cases to see whether there are any contradictions or discrepancies in the way the interviewee thought and acted in the two situations. If there are contradictions, how might you begin to understand or explain them?

Can you think of a recent example?

The most recent example, yes, in terms of a retail business manager who currently works for the organisation and actually works for this division, who got a consistently high appraisal rating, high performance rating over the last few years. But what is required over the next three years, this person has the ability to be above to move forward. Therefore there is a big question mark over where that person goes.

Why does this cause you a slight pang or twinge?

Because we're talking about somebody who's perceived by the organisation as a high performer. Yet in terms of everything they do every day we can see that they have the inability to change, to be above, to move forward with the change in an emerging brand.

Right. How are things changing then?

Well, the whole style of the operation is changing. We have a new director and general manager and senior management team for a start. They have a different way of working. The emphasis is on empowering the staff.

And he's a traditional company person is he?

Yes, and the emphasis is moving away from control culture, control type management, to a more loose management culture and more sales oriented and building on development in sales. This person is not interested in development and growing sales. It's more about the old control culture. 'Hit them with a big stick and sack them if they don't do what you tell them' mentality.

But he's still a good performer?

He has an excellent performance and if you look in terms of actual year-on-year profit performance he's the best achiever in the company.

In some ways this is someone who has been a good performer and has apparently done well in the company but isn't changing, and I suppose, am I right in thinking that you have a bit of a dilemma in terms of have you got to do something?

Absolutely. And also the difficulty is because he has a reputation throughout the company for that cultural aspect and that management style nobody else wants to face him. So the fact is that we'll end up losing somebody from the organisation.

He is a symbol for the old way of doing things?

Yes, and which will also cause or create a huge employer relations issue.

Why is that?

Because he will take us to tribunal.

Exercise 5.4 *continued*

Right.

Rightly so in terms of performance.

So you are going to do something about it? What have you decided to do?

Well, we've decided he's got to go.

Yes; what sort of mechanism are you going to use?

Well, it will be a severance. He'll have to go. We've looked at the other alternatives and there aren't any.

Effectively redundancy?

Effectively, a form of redundancy.

Because his role doesn't fit in. Is this one of the areas where you feel a bit of a clash between what you need to do for the organisation and your own values?

Well, you know, I think in terms of the organisation it's absolutely right, but actually this guy has worked for the company for some time and in his own way has been committed. So I think there probably is a view that maybe over the years this person hasn't been managed properly in the past and maybe if he'd been managed better in the past then maybe we wouldn't be at this point now.

As an ex-trainer and developer have you considered that?

Yes we've worked on, we've been working on it for the last six months. It's not even a runner. We're basically saying up yours, you know, as good as.

But tricky when somebody has actually got a good official appraisal record.

Yes, absolutely, no disciplinary record, no major performance issues. It's very much about management styles and culture and change.

How do you think you're going to feel when you deal with this one?

Well, I've dealt with so many that I always think that if I go home at night and sleep, my conscience is relatively clear. I have a job to do and I believe when it comes round and it's right for the business, then it's part of the job.

In a sense it sounds like you've been giving him chances and saying OK this time you've got to change.

I think so, yes, and I believe that generally if I have to do, in fact I quite often won't do something if I don't agree with it being morally right, or I'll look for a compromise.

That's a very interesting example. What we're doing is mapping out the issues that people have to face. You just said that sometimes you just don't think they're right. Can you think of an example or a type of situation when you've had to do that?

Yes, somebody who works for me, one of the directors felt, wasn't committed enough to the organisation because they didn't work seven days a week. He told me that I needed to do something about that person and I refused point blank. I said that they actually worked more effectively than anybody else here, and now I don't intend. I refuse to do that. At the end of the day, just because you believe that we should work seven days a week it doesn't prove that they're not committed. So I actually did dig my heels in and said no, I'm not going to do it, I refuse and we've worked around that. I did then talk to that person and let that person know how he felt about it and said you know you just need to think about raising your profile and meeting part-way.

That's sort of a PR job? Is this an organisation that takes the seven-day-a-week line very strongly?

Different parts of the organisation.

All sorts of people do.

It's individuals really.

Can we explore a bit more why you thought that was an inappropriate line to take?

Well I think because that person is an extremely effective member of the team and actually the output is far higher and greater, the overall output, than the average. And really it was more about profile.

Exercise 5.4 *continued*

Do you think the senior person was being fair?
No, unreasonable, totally unreasonable, absolutely.

Legally would it have been an easy thing to have done anyway?
Well, I don't legally know but in terms of the organisation, because it's the nature of the business and because our business does operate seven days a week, then it becomes the accepted norm. If you've got pressure from a senior manager, then it makes life difficult for you and then ultimately it forces somebody out. If you get a reputation within the organisation it affects your promotion opportunities or future opportunities.

Did the team member take the, did they up their profile? Did it work?
Hmm, it did actually. It's settled down again now but it was very difficult at the time. It put me in a difficult position. I'm a great believer in sticking to your guns and I'm a spade or shovel person.

Is that how you're known?
Yes, I have very strong values.

Is it a useful reputation to have?
Yes, it helps being female with that reputation.

Why?
I think I wouldn't have got away with it so easily if I'd been a man. It's a male-dominated organisation generally and being a fairly strong female has allowed me to manoeuvre a lot better than I would have done if I'd been a man.

You can stand your ground maybe a little bit more?
Yes, with the male members of the board and things. I am able to stand my ground a lot more.

Suggested answer

The interviewee had a formal idea that, in order to sleep at night, she always acted morally in matters of redundancy, severance and disciplinary action. She went to some trouble to point out that she was responding fairly to the merits of individual cases. She gave one example where she thought severance was right and another case (where a senior manager was pushing to have someone made redundant) when she thought such action would be wrong. So in formal terms both cases fit the category of acting from a position of principle.

The claim that she was applying consistent principles in the cases is possibly contradicted because the two cases she gave, in which she acted differently, were similar if not identical situations. Both incidents involved members of staff who would not adopt the values and beliefs that management wished them to adopt. In one case the manager did not fit with the culture of the new brand, and in the second the manager did not accept the macho, long hours culture. In the first case the interviewee chose to support the action proposed, but in the second case she chose to oppose it. This raises interesting questions to be answered. Dialectical critique raises new questions and moves you into a deeper level of understanding.

The interviewee could have categorised both issues as questions of compatibility between individual employees and the corporate culture, and adopted a similar stance in both cases. Instead she took opposite views. There must have been some particulars that justified this position. There must have been some features that made her see the two situations as different. We cannot know, of course, what these particulars might be, but we can speculate, and there are a few clues in the interview. Here are some possibilities:

- The fact that the second person was a member of the interviewee's staff and the first person was not could account for the different responses.
- In the second incident the interviewee was apparently being ordered to get rid of the employee and she might see this as an unwarranted attack on her managerial autonomy and wished to prevent the director feeling he could order her about.
- She might herself accept the new brand culture but reject the long hours culture, and so she might particularise according to different aspects of culture.

Exercise 5.4 *continued*

- It could simply be a matter of personality; she may have little personal sympathy for the subject of the first incident but lots for the subject of the second incident.
- It is also tempting to think there may be an age aspect to the two incidents, the person in the first incident being older than the person in the second, but there is absolutely no evidence for this.

This analysis also points up the importance of follow-up and probing questions during the interview. Some of the issues listed might have been explored in the interview. Adopting a dialectical critique can develop a more complex and dynamic understanding of issues.

Dialectical contradictions can be seen in quantitative data as well, as illustrated in Exercise 5.5.

Exercise 5.5

Staffing nursery schools

This is an opportunity to make a dialectical critique of some quantitative research material. The issue was to decide the appropriate staffing level for nursery schools. The staff numbers needed in any particular school were decided by applying a standard ratio of staff to the number of pupils. The question was, what should the ratio be? The education advisers were consulted and they argued that the staffing should be such that for a good proportion of every nursery session staff should be able to work with small groups of children. The rest of the session should be used for whole-group activities such as storytelling and outdoor play. They argued that the more time staff could work with small groups of children, the better the quality of the education. This belief was official policy.

An activity sampling study (see p. 138) was carried out in which the percentage of time staff spent with different group sizes of pupils was researched in eight nurseries. The results are shown in the table below.

Analysis of nursery staff time (analysed according to the size of the group of pupils staff worked with)

Nursery	a	b	c	d	e	f	g	h
Group size								
1	15	29	13	33	24	60	19	10
2	12	5	8	6	–	–	8	2
3	8	5	13	9	–	–	17	6
4	2	11	1	5	16	–	12	19
5	–	–	1	–	–	–	–	–
6	–	–	1	–	–	4	–	–
7	–	–	–	–	–	12	–	–
8	10	–	7	9	–	–	–	9
≥ 9	53	50	56	38	60	24	44	54
Ratio of pupils to staff	10:1	7:1	12:1	7.5:1	12:1	6.7:1	8.7:1	13:1

Exercise 5.5 *continued*

The table shows, for example, that in nursery 'a' staff spent 15 per cent of their time working one to one with children and 12 per cent working with a pair of children.

When the results were analysed an overall pattern emerged. The amount of time that staff spent with groups of four or less children was strongly, negatively correlated with the staffing ratio. The correlation coefficient (see p. 184) was –0.86912. A regression line (see p. 199) could be fitted to a graph of the data. The intercept was 78.98 and the slope was –3.43. Once this graph was plotted it could be used to determine proper staffing ratios. If the expert defined the optimum percentage of time to be spent with groups of four or fewer children, then the graph could be used to say what staffing ratio would be necessary to achieve it.

But such patterns can be deceptive. Look at the data in the table again. Can you identify any contradictions in the ways in which nurseries worked with their pupils?

Suggested answer
One nursery (f) stands out from the others. Its staff used their time in a very different way to the others. They spent all their time either on one-to-one work with the children or on large group activities. They did not do any small group work with the children. Normally statisticians would declare such a result an 'outlier' (an unrepresentative result) and exclude it from consideration. But a dialectical critique approach emphasises such discrepancies and uses them to gain a better understanding of the subject. It would question why there might be such differences. We can only speculate, but it is likely that nursery school 'f' has a different educational philosophy from most of the others. It may be that this school puts more emphasis on individual attainment and believes that this can best be done by maximising the amount of one-to-one teaching. If this, or something like it, is true, then we have to ask questions about whether the assumptions that we initially made about what makes a nursery school effective ought to be challenged. We would then find ourselves researching different views on the nature and purpose of nursery education.

In summary a dialectical critique begins with the formal policy that schools should maximise the time staff spend working with small groups of children – no doubt to develop social skills or, in management terms, team skills. It is difficult to see whether school 'f' fits in this category. At one level it does because it maximises the time spent with children in groups of four or fewer. But its choice to spend all this time in one-to-one work, rather than in groups, contradicts and undermines the purpose of the policy.

● ● ● ● Framing conclusions and recommendations

Conclusions are not the same as your research findings or research analysis. Conclusions are your interpretations of the findings. By returning to the distinction made in Chapter 1 between research questions and strategic questions it is possible to identify three types of conclusions.

- **Research conclusions** These summarise your understanding of the processes and dynamics of the subject you have researched. They provide the explanations that answer your research questions.
- **Strategic conclusions** These summarise your judgements about what actions should be taken, about what, if anything, should be done in response to your strategic questions. The strategic conclusions should be based on the new understanding that the research conclusions provide. The research conclusions may provide a context for answering the

strategic question but it is your judgement, your ability to decide options and actions, that are critical at this stage.

- **Recommendations** These are the practical steps that need to be taken to implement the strategic conclusions. Recommendations are not always necessary or appropriate in a Master's dissertation. Whether or not they are needed will depend upon the following:

  - The aims and topic of the dissertation. Some dissertations are directly addressed to problems and issues, others are not. Only in the former case would recommendations be necessary.

  - The rules and regulations of the institution you are studying at. Some institutions may ask for recommendations in dissertations, others may not; some may discourage students from making recommendations, preferring they concentrate on issues of academic understanding.

The conclusions are the link between understanding and action. This link does not arise automatically. It is forged by the writer of the dissertation. The writer chooses the link. Two practical consequences emerge from this perception of conclusions:

- **The test of conclusions is a pragmatic one** This test holds that a belief is true if it proves useful in the long run. Usefulness is not sufficient, however. It is also important that there is a sensible explanation of *why* the belief will be useful (Mounce 1997: 50–51). Let us imagine that we have been studying the impact of a particular management technique. Our research has suggested that companies that implement this technique do better than those that do not. It would be useful, therefore, to act on this belief and use the technique in our own organisation. But before we do so it would be sensible to check whether there is a sound explanation of why this technique is successful. Perhaps the success was not due to the technique. It could be, for example, that the companies we studied were just lucky and would have done well even if they had not introduced the technique. Or it might just be that it was the quality of the managers in these companies that brought success, not the application of the technique. However, if a sound explanation can be given that shows it most likely was the technique that caused the companies to perform well, then the belief that the technique works should be accepted as true. True conclusions are those that are useful and whose utility can be explained. This is one reason why the answers to research questions help validate conclusions. They explain why conclusions are useful.

  There is a danger in taking the pragmatic view. It is that we may accept as true anything that is expedient or convenient for us. The use of a pragmatist test therefore requires a ruthless honesty with ourselves. It may be necessary to recognize the value of 'truths' that we personally find discomforting.

- Drawing conclusions require a creative leap. Henry Mintzberg (1979), as have many others, recommended an inductive approach to managerial and organisational research. This involves working from the detailed research findings to new discoveries of general interest and application. A two-stage process is involved:

1. The first stage involves detective work, tracking down patterns, consistencies and inconsistencies in the research material. This stage has been covered in Chapter 4 and the first part of this chapter.
2. The second stage involves what Mintzberg refers to as 'generalising beyond one's data', or the creative leap. 'Every theory requires that creative leap, however small, that breaking away from the expected to describe something new. There is no one-to-one correspondence between data and theory. The data do not generate the theory – only researchers do that – any more than theory can be proved true in terms of the data. All theories are false, because all abstract from data and simplify the world they purport to describe. Our choice then is not between true and false theories so much as between more and less useful theories. And usefulness to repeat stems from detective work well done, followed by creative leaps in relevant directions.' (Mintzberg 1979: 584).

Not all creative leaps are true.

Having encouraged you to make leaps of judgement a note of caution is necessary. Not all bright ideas are true. As Umberto Eco (1992: 52) wrote: 'If there are no rules that help ascertain which interpretations are the "best" ones there is at least a rule for ascertaining which ones are "bad".' Another medieval philosopher proposed one such rule, Occam's razor: 'Entities ought not to be multiplied except by necessity'. The simplest argument that fits the evidence will be the best one. Arguments that bring in too many unnecessary explanations will be bad. This explains why 'cock-up' theories are more likely to be right than conspiracy theories.

Problems of implementation

Research conclusions are useful because they give a better understanding on which to base judgements and actions. Sometimes it may be appropriate to frame the judgements as strategic conclusions and recommendations for action. If you do this, you need to make sure that you have considered the practicability of your recommendations. You will need to think about such questions as these:

- the degree of support or opposition to the recommendations;
- the availability of the money and resources needed to implement the recommendations;
- whether a business case can be made that would release the necessary resources;

Exercise 5.6

The cash register

Read the brief account given below and then answer the questions asked about it. Circle T if you think the statement is true, circle F if you think the statement is false and circle ? if you think it is impossible to say whether the statement is true or false.

The story

A businessman had just turned off the lights in the store when a man appeared and demanded money. The owner opened a cash register. The contents of the cash register were scooped up and the man sped away. A member of the police force was notified promptly.

Statements about the story

1. A man appeared after the owner had turned off his store lights.	T	F	?
2. The robber was a *man*.	T	F	?
3. The man did not demand money.	T	F	?
4. The man who opened the cash register was the owner.	T	F	?
5. The store owner scooped up the contents of the cash register and ran away.	T	F	?
6. Someone opened a cash register.	T	F	?
7. After the man who demanded money scooped up the contents of the cash register, he ran away.	T	F	?
8. While the cash register contained money, the story does *not* state *how much*.	T	F	?
9. The robber demanded money of the owner.	T	F	?
10. The story concerns a series of events in which only three persons are referred to: the owner of the store, a man who demanded money, and a member of the police force.	T	F	?
11. The following events in the story are true: someone demanded money, a cash register was opened, its contents were scooped up, and a man dashed out of the store.	T	F	?

Source: Pfeiffer and Jones (1975). This material is used with the permission of John Wiley and Sons Inc.

Suggested answer

True – 6.

Not true – 3.

All the rest are 'don't knows' or 'can't says'.

1. The businessman is not necessarily the same person as the owner.
2. It is not known whether a robbery took place. All that is known is that the contents of the cash register were removed.
4. The owner who opened the cash register was not necessarily a man.
5. It is not known who scooped up the contents of the cash register.
7. It was not necessarily the same person who carried out all three actions.

Exercise 5.6 *continued*

8. It is not known whether the cash register contained money.
9. It is not known whether there was a robbery.
10. It is not known. The owner and the businessman may not have been the same person.
11. It is not absolutely certain that the store in which the lights were turned off was the same place as the one in which the other events took place.

The lesson from this exercise is that people love to make patterns from the material presented to them. In the absence of pattern, the mind is predisposed to impose one. People often claim many of the above statements are true because their mind unconsciously provides the missing information necessary to create a satisfying narrative from the scant material provided. As a consequence it might be thought, with Francis Bacon (in the *Novum Organum* of 1620), that the intellect

> must not ... be supplied with wings, but rather hung with weights, to keep it from leaping and flying.

However, once people realise this is what is happening, they then jump to the opposite position and refuse to believe it is possible to draw a conclusion about any of the statements – even those such as questions 6 and 3 that are indubitably true or false – or are they?

When drawing conclusions you need to strike a balance between creative leaps and scepticism.

- the practical and logistical difficulties that implementation of the recommendations might entail;
- the processes by which the recommendations should be sold to interested parties;
- the timetable for implementation.

Never underestimate the difficulties of implementing recommendations. Aaron Wildavsky (1973, quoted in Anthony and Herzlinger 1975: 335) wrote a tongue-in-cheek piece about the problems of implementing IT systems. Although IT systems have changed hugely since 1973, it would appear that the problems of implementing them have hardly changed at all. Here are Wildavsky's rules for implementation; I suspect they have relevance beyond IT:

- **The rule of scepticism** No one, especially the consultants, quite knows how to do the task.
- **The rule of delay** If it works at all, it will not work soon.
- **The rule of complexity** Nothing complex ever works.
- **The rule of thumb** If the procedure book or manual is thicker than your thumb the new system will never work.
- **The rule of childlike innocence** When discussing a scheme to be implemented, always ask the childlike questions you feel too embarrassed to ask.

- **The rule of length and width** If there are more than two or three links in a vertical or horizontal chain of communication, the messages will get lost.
- **The rule of anticipated anguish** a.k.a. Murphy's Law, which states 'if it can go wrong, it will'.
- **The rule of the known evil** The existing system may be rubbish but people know how to estimate the 'fudge factor' and use it to make the system work. The new system may be better but will people know how to work it?
- **The rule of the mounting mirage** Can be seen at work in the following quotation. 'We are doing badly, we need better information to perform better. We set up a costly new system. The costs of the system appear immediately but the benefits only emerge in the medium term. Therefore in the short term we are doing worse, so we need a better information system to help us improve.' Ad infinitum.
- **The tenth rule** The hypothetical benefits of a new system should outweigh the costs by ten to one before we decide to implement.

Exercise 5.7

Potential problem analysis

This exercise is based on an old technique developed by Kepner and Tregoe (1965). It is a useful way of thinking about the practical problems of implementation that might arise from your recommendations. It could be a useful framework for discussing issues of implementation in your dissertation. The technique is applied by asking and answering the following questions in sequence.

1. What problems could occur that would hinder the successful implementation of your recommendations? Make a list of them.
2. Assess the likelihood that each of these problems will occur. Rate them on a probability scale of 0 (totally impossible) to 1 (absolutely certain).
3. For each of the most likely problems, identify a number of preventive actions you might take to reduce the chances of the problem occurring.
4. Reassess the probability that a problem will still occur even after preventive actions have been taken, again by using a probability scale.
5. If the residual probability that the problem will arise is still high enough to cause anxiety, then prepare a contingency plan. A contingency plan defines the action you will take to minimise the consequences of a problem should it happen.

Accepting the limitations of research

Michael Bassey, once a professor of education at the Nottingham Trent University, proposed the following law. There are, he argued, three characteristics of a research conclusion in the social sciences. It can be true, generalisable and simple. But Bassey's law states that a conclusion can only be two of the three at any one time. If it is simple and true, it cannot be generalisable. If it is simple and generalisable, it probably is not true. If it is generalisable and true it is not simple. However, as Bassey's law is simple, and appears to be a general law, it cannot be true.

Summary

- Avoid bizno-bollocks speak and its academic equivalent.
- Avoid lazy sentences that imply more than you claim.
- Try to apply some of Winter's six principles when making sense of your research material.
- Do not disguise the apparent contradictions in your research material; use them as doorways to deeper understanding of complex processes.
- Remember that quantitative material needs interpretation just as much as qualitative material.
- Do not be afraid to make creative leaps when framing your conclusions.
- But do not construct over-elaborate theories that are more complex than the material requires.
- Consider the practical problems of implementing your conclusions and recommendations.

Suggested reading

Richard Winter (1989) is very good on the topics covered in the second part of the chapter, but it is a demanding book. It is also set in the context of education and this makes it a little more inaccessible to management students; but try Chapter 4.

Pat Cryer (1996) has a chapter on creative thinking that might be useful when making your creative leaps. Johnson and Duberley (2000) is the best book if you want to follow up on the epistemology of organisational a managerial research.

References

Alvesson, M. and Skoldberg, K. (2000) *Reflexive Methodology*, London: Sage.

Anthony, R. N. and Herzlinger, R. (1975) *Management Control in Nonprofit Organisations*, Homewood, IL: Richard. D. Irwin.

Billig, M. (1996) *Arguing and Thinking: A Rhetorical Approach to Social Psychology*, 2nd edn, Cambridge: Cambridge University Press.

Blake, W. (1991) *Poems and Prophecies*, London: Everyman's Library.

Collier, A. (1994) *Critical Realism: An Introduction to Roy Bhaskar's Philosophy*, London: Verso.

Cryer, P. (1996) *The Research Student's Guide to Success*, Buckingham: Open University Press.

Eco, U. with R. Rorty, J. Culler and C. Brooke-Rose, ed. S. Collini (1992) *Interpretation and Overinterpretation*, Cambridge: Cambridge University Press.

Franklin, P. (2001) 'Is strategy still relevant?', *The Internet Journal of Strategy and Planning* Available online at www.strategyfirst.net. [accessed 28 July 2002].

Johnson, P. and Duberley, J. (2000) *Understanding Management Research: An Introduction to Epistemology*, London: Sage.

Kepner, C. H. and Tregoe, B. B. (1965) *The Rational Manager: A Systematic Approach to Problem Solving and Decision Making*, London: McGraw-Hill.

March, J. G., Cohen, M. D. and Olsen, J. P. (1972) 'A garbage can model of organizational decision making', *Administrative Science Quarterly*, Vol. 17, 1–25.

Mintzberg, H. (1979) 'An emerging strategy of "direct research"', *Administrative Science Quarterly*, Vol. 24, December, 582–589.

Mounce, H. O. (1997) *The Two Pragmatisms: From Peirce to Rorty*, London: Routledge.

Pfeiffer, J. W. and Jones, J. E. (1975) *A Handbook of Structured Experiences for Human Relations Training*, Vol. 5, San Diego, CA: University Associates.

Van Maanen, J. (1988) *Tales of the Field: On Writing Ethnography*, London: University of Chicago Press.

Weick, K. (1995) *Sense Making in Organizations: Foundations for Organizational Science*, London: Sage.

Wildavsky, A. (1973) 'Review of Brewer's politicians, bureaucrats and the politicians', *Science*, Vol. 28, December, 1335–1338.

Winter, R. (1989) *Learning from Experience: Principles and Practice in Action-Research*, Lewes: Falmer Press.

Chapter 6 ●●●●

Framing arguments and writing up

Contents

● ● ● ● Introduction

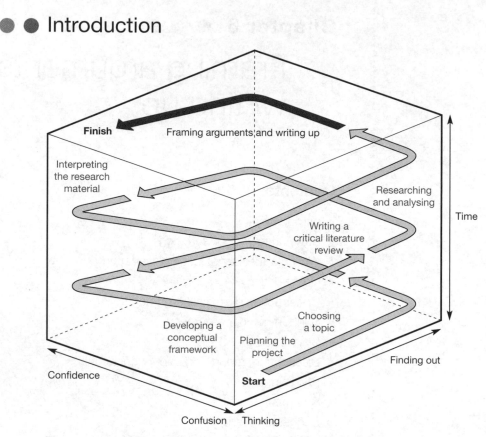

The processes of researching and writing a Master's dissertation

So, in this way of writing without thinking, thou hast a strange alacrity in sinking.

Thomas Sackville, Earl of Dorset (1536–1608)

This chapter is designed to help you write up your dissertation or paper, and to do some thinking in the process, and prepare it for submission for marking. There are three main sections:

1. Giving the dissertation structure, which gives advice about the chapter structure of your dissertation.
2. Writing a thesis, not just a dissertation, which is about making sure that the dissertation presents a clear and logical argument.
3. The style guide, which gives practical tips on writing up and presenting your dissertation.

There are more exercises in this chapter than in some of the earlier ones. This is because at this stage in the project you have gathered your material from the literature and research, and the exercises are designed to help you shape the material into good arguments that support a clear thesis.

The learning outcomes for the chapter

1 Readers will be able to give a logical and systematic structure to their dissertation or paper.

2 Readers will be able to create an overarching or narrative theme that will integrate the various parts of the dissertation or paper.

3 Readers will be able to support the main arguments presented in the dissertation or thesis.

4 Readers will be able to write the paper or dissertation in plain and clear English and in accordance with the requirements of the business school or other institution at which they are studying.

Structuring your dissertation

You need to plan the chapter structure of your dissertation. A default plan is given below, but it is not necessary or obligatory for you to follow this sequence slavishly. Feel free to develop a chapter plan that is relevant to the topic you are writing about. Papers do not have chapters and so this part does not apply to them.

If you are writing a traditional dissertation (i.e. not one based on action research), the following should provide a useful model to follow. Even if you follow this structure, you can give the chapters more imaginative titles:

(a) Introduction and objectives
- Explain the focus of the study and its object or purpose.
- Explain why the study is important and to whom.
  - Define the strategic question, if any, to be answered.
- Explain what you want to find out and why.
  - Define the research questions to be answered
- Set the scene and describe the context, but not in too much detail.

(b) Critical literature review
- Identify the appropriate academic and/or professional fields of literature.
- Describe the main themes in the literature that are important and useful to your study.
- Identify the connections or discontinuities between the themes in the literature.

- Evaluate and critique the literature.
  - Check whether the ideas you wish to use are robust enough.
  - Challenge the assumptions.
  - Question whether the literature might mean something other than it says it means.
- Create a coherent sequence of arguments from the themes drawn from the literature.

(c) The conceptual framework
- Using material from the previous chapter produce working definitions of the main concepts you will use in your study. If possible, form them into a conceptual framework, theory or hypothesis to be tested.
- Sometimes it is not necessary to have this section as a separate chapter. If this is the case, it can be included in the critical literature review chapter.

(d) Research methodology and methods
- Discuss the nature of the questions you are asking and choose an appropriate methodological stance for answering them.
- Describe, explain and justify the research methods you are using.
- Describe the practical and technical aspects of conducting the research.
- Discuss any ethical issues connected with the project.

(e) Presentation and analysis of findings
- Describe what you found out and what it means.
- Refer back to the literature review and your conceptual framework.
  - Use the literature to interrogate and evaluate your research material and vice versa.
- Presentation and analysis may require several chapters, e.g.:
  - one chapter for presentation and one for analysis;
  - several chapters, each presenting a different case study;
  - and so on.

(f) Conclusions and recommendations
- Summarise the main argument, otherwise known as the thesis, of the dissertation.
- Either discuss the validity and reliability of the findings and arguments or reflectively critique the account provided in the dissertation.
- Frame the conclusions, and recommendations if appropriate.
- Discuss any issues concerning the implementation of the conclusions or any recommendations.

This structure is designed for an academic audience, the academic staff who will mark the dissertation. It would not necessarily be appropriate for a managerial audience, especially the managers in the organisation(s) that the dissertation reports on. In any case, a dissertation is normally too long for internal management purposes. Sometimes students prepare a short version of the dissertation for organisational use. The executive summary that students have to submit with the dissertation (see Dissertation, report and paper specifications at the end of this chapter) may be sufficient for this purpose.

If you are writing up an action research project, something like the following structure might be more appropriate. A greater variety of structures can be seen in action research dissertations than in traditional ones. What they all have in common is a chronological or narrative form. In writing up action research, the story of the developing project is told from its inception, not forgetting to record the blind allies that were entered and the false starts that were made. The structures normally follow through the cycles of action, monitoring, theorising and further action:

(a) Preparation
   ● Introduction. Define the strategic and research questions the project will address. Explain the organisational and personal context.
   ● Conceptual framework. Theories, concepts and literature.
   ● Methodology and methods.
   ● First-stage action: research material collection.
   ● Reconnaissance. Collection and interpretation of evidence.

(b) Development of project
   ● Review of strategic and research questions.
   ● Review of conceptual framework and methods.
   ● Second-stage action: material collection and analysis.
   ● Interim conclusions.
   ● Issues for the final stage.

(c) Further development and conclusions
   ● Review of methods and conceptual framework.
   ● Final-stage action: material collection and analysis.
   ● Conclusions.
(d) Personal, reflexive critique.

This structure includes three cycles of action research, which is normally the most a Master's student would have time for. The first cycle would be based on a literature review and an initial reconnaissance. The second cycle (development of the project) would report on the main piece of action research. The third cycle gives an opportunity to refine the action and review the consequences.

● ● ● ● Writing a thesis, not just a dissertation

A dissertation should also be a thesis. A thesis is a proposition that a person offers to maintain, or does maintain, by argument. In a well-ordered dissertation it should be possible to identify a chain of logic and argument that can be followed by the reader. It is often a good idea to signpost this development by frequent summaries of how the argument has developed and how it is going to be developed in the rest of the dissertation. The dissertation should have a beginning, a middle and an end. In journalistic terms the dissertation should be linked by a 'hook' or a theme.

Exercises 6.1, 6.2 and 6.3 provide practise in framing a thesis.

Exercise 6.1

The press release – *Tony Watson and Colin Fisher*

- An article is being prepared on *Exciting research being undertaken by star Master's students.*
- You are to submit a press release for this article.
- The purpose of the exercise is to focus your mind on what the project 'adds up to' – a notion of a clear underlying story with a clear structure leading to a clear 'thesis'.
- Write the press release in a style appropriate for the broadsheet press.

Prepare a summary of your ongoing project that a journalist could use to write a newspaper story. Give your story **a strong narrative flow**.

- What inspired you in the first place?
- What new things are you going to tell the world?
- How are you doing it?
- What is emerging?
- What awe-inspiring difficulties are you overcoming in your crawl along the frontiers of knowledge?
- What lessons can be learned from your work?

Exercise 6.2

The pub bore test

Write an interesting account of your dissertation, in a few sentences, that you could use when someone in a pub asks, 'What's your research about?' It has to be something that would catch the listener's attention and, of course, it needs to be expressed in very simple English.

Exercise 6.3

A haiku

Write a haiku poem that captures the essence of the argument you will be presenting in your dissertation.

Haiku poems consist of, respectively five, seven and five syllables in three units. In Japanese, this convention is a must. In English this can sometimes be difficult to achieve and variations in the number of syllables are allowable. The cutting divides the haiku into two parts, with a certain imaginative distance between the two sections, but the two sections must remain, to a degree, dependent on each other. Both sections must enrich the understanding of the other. To make this cutting in English, either the first or the second line ends normally with a colon, long dash or ellipsis.

The MBA done:
With God as my witness, I'll
Not study again.

If you wish to change
And modernise companies –
Value the staff's views.

Constructing arguments

If you had difficulty in doing the exercises here is a technique for helping you sharpen up your skill in argument formation.

A four-stage sequence in developing an argument can be identified using a method loosely developed from the work of the US pragmatist philosopher C. S. Peirce (Mounce 1997: 17–18). The sequence will be explained using the example of downsizing as a management strategy as the topic of an argument.

1. **Start by stating the problem you are researching** Let us say we are interested in the issue of downsizing. We want to know why many of the companies that downsize do not appear to reap the benefits in terms of improved financial performance.

2. **Abduction** Abduction means kidnapping. In this stage you raid your store of knowledge and reading to hunt for a possible cause of the problem. You just happen to have read a few journal articles that suggest that the people, the survivors, who remain in the organisation after their friends and colleagues have been made redundant, suffer from guilt and depression. They lose motivation and commitment. This might explain why companies perform less well after downsizing. You 'kidnap' the idea as a possible explanation.

3. **Deduction** Deduction is defined, in this context, as the process of inferring particulars from a general statement. Well, if we think the survivor syndrome (as the sense of depression following downsizing is called) is an explanation, we should be able to deduce some observable consequences for the organisation. We might, for example, deduce that absenteeism and sickness rates would go up, productivity would go down, staff turnover would go up and people would report, in both exit interviews and staff satisfaction surveys, that their morale had diminished.

4. **Induction** Having deduced some practical consequences, we can now go out and do the research to see whether they can be observed. If we find that our deductions are correct, then induction comes into play. Induction is the process of drawing general conclusions from specific and detailed findings. If we have discovered increased absenteeism and sickness rates and so on, then we can infer that our initial speculation was correct.

   If our findings do not support our general theory, then we have to return to the second stage and choose another speculative cause of the problem and begin again.

I suggest that this sequence – problem definition, abduction, deduction and induction – could provide a framework within which you could construct the core arguments of your thesis.

Exercise 6.4

Constructing an argument

Choose a problem or issue that you are trying to explain in your research and use the framework outlined above to try and construct an argument.

Constructing dialectical arguments

In Chapter 5 the dialectic was suggested as a means of interpreting research material. Here I want to make a more general case by arguing that the dialectic can be used to shape your thesis. The dialectic provides an alternative form of argument that can be useful in a MBA or Master's dissertation. This is not as exotic as it sounds. Gareth Morgan (1997) recommends it as a useful metaphor for understanding organisations in his book *Images of Organisations* and Pascale (1990: 142–143) used it to analyse Ford's (then) strategic success, in his best seller *Managing on the Edge*. Pascale used the form of the dialectic developed by Hegel, the German philosopher (1770–1831), rather than the Marxist version favoured by Morgan. In this section we will be using a much simplified version of the Hegelian dialectic. Its usefulness is suggested by an over-heard remark by a student.

> Well I don't agonise over papers. What I say is always pretty much the same. First I wonder, 'What's the main thing in this book?' and then I wonder, 'What's its opposite?' When I write my paper, I claim that these two things, though they seem different, couldn't exist without each other; even that they are really two aspects of the same thing … Near the end of your paper you have to say that your two things, whatever they are, are 'locked in an unstable but mutually constitutive relationship'. Profs just love that.
>
> (Eisaman Maus 2001)

This remark neatly summarises the dialectical method of arguing, which consists of the following triad:

- **Thesis** A formal idea, empty of content. An idea that is separate from the messy practicality of experience.
- **The antithesis** The practical realities that undermine the formal idea in a practical application.
- **The synthesis** This moves understanding of the idea up a notch so that the contradictions become unimportant at a higher and more sophisticated level of understanding.

The synthesis does not declare either the thesis or the antithesis the victor. Rather, it develops a new level of thinking in which the old opposition becomes irrelevant. The dialectical process goes through many such sequences. As soon as a synthesis is reached, new contradictions will arise and it becomes a thesis, a starting point for a new dialectic.

Hegel's most famous application of this triad is known as the dialectic of the master and the slave. In a very simplified form it goes as follows:

- **Formal idea** The master is superior to the slave.
- **The antithesis** The formal idea is contradicted by the following factors:
  - The master is dependent on the slave because he needs the services the slave provides.
  - If the slave were not there, the master could not express his superiority.
  - The master sees himself reflected in the slave. In other words, the master looks on to the inferior, and this diminishes him, but the slave looks at the master and is provided with ambition.
- **The synthesis** The master and slave come to see themselves as mutually dependent equals and develop cooperation.

I am currently doing some work on attempts by western agencies to encourage organisations in the countries of the former Soviet Union to adapt to their new economic and political environment. In particular, I am studying the relationships between the western 'experts' brought in to lead the change, the change agents they select and train in the host country and the local managers in the local organisations that they are encouraging to change. It deals with some of the issues discussed on pp. 115–121. I developed the dialectic structure shown in Figure 6.1 to present an argument about how the relationships between these three groups develop. The dialectic also acts as a conceptual framework for my research.

You can see that the middle dialectic in Figure 6.1 is based on the master and slave dialectic. One feature of this needs a little further explanation. The western experts and the local change agents had different ideas of friendship. The experts' view was that the obligations of friendship little exceeded the requirement for mutual amusement and support. The local change agents had a more eastern concept of friendship and hospitality, which placed greater demands upon friends. This required friends to spare no effort to support each other. Consequently the western experts expected little of their friends amongst the local change agents but the

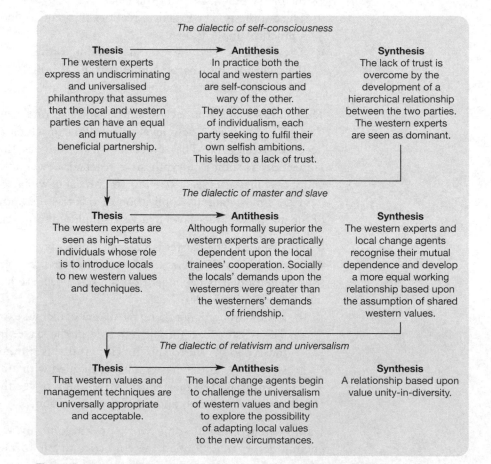

Figure 6.1 The dialectic of western experts and local change agents

change agents expected their western friends to do all in their power to help them with foreign trips and obtaining jobs in the west. In consequence, the formally subordinate were in practice dominant because they were making the greatest demands. This social contradiction was reinforced by the western experts' dependence on the change agents' local knowledge that, again, made the formally superior practically dependent.

If you have found any discrepancies between formal intention and actual practice in your research material, then the dialectic may provide a tool for analysing them.

Supporting your arguments

There are a number of ways in which you can support your argument when you write it up in the dissertation:

- authority – other writers have supported the position you take;
- evidence – selected examples drawn from your research material; and
- persuasive writing style.

Each of these will be considered in turn.

Arguing from authority

An important way of arguing your point is to claim authority for it. You show that your argument is correct by reporting that one or more undoubted experts in the field has written that it is so. There are a number of issues that arise from this form of argument. First of all you need to make sure that the author you are citing is indeed an accepted authority in the field. This becomes a particular problem when, as is common in the social sciences, there are disputes between competing authorities. You also need to be aware that experts, because of their fame, are sometimes prone to pronouncing on areas outside their area of expertise. Other people are accepted as authorities because they are in positions of power rather than because they are expert. Another problem is that a student may well have misunderstood what the noted authority wrote and therefore is claiming authority for an idea that was never proposed. Exercise 6.5 looks at some of the problems caused by arguing from authorities. It reveals that some researchers use literature in the way that drunkards use a lamp-post, for support rather than illumination.

Arguing from evidence – *Alistair Mutch*

Using references is one way of supplying evidence to support your arguments. You will also use evidence that you have gathered directly. Evidence used appropriately can be very powerful. However, there are some pitfalls to be aware of.

Exercise 6.5

Bad habits

What is wrong with each of the following examples of argument by authority and academic citation? The references are fictitious.

Chinese whispers

> The principles of ethnographic technique espoused by Malinowski were ... (Anderson and Burns 1989).

Showing off

> The works of Habermas (1991, 1997) and Roy Bhaskar (1983, 1993) support my main contention ...

The founding fathers

> ... this returns to the ideas of Weber as a core thinker in sociology.

Padding

> ... was influenced by organisational structure (Simon *et al.* 1954; Bear 1972 and 1979; Becher and Kogan 1992; Berquist 1993; Galbraith *et al.* 1993); and institutional culture with five elements ...

Neophilism

> The key writers on motivation and commitment of people at work are Bloggs (2002), Smith (2003) and Jones (2004).

Canonicity

> Let us begin with the idea of a decision (Caputo 1993; Chia 1994; Derrida 1978).

Suggested answer

Chinese whispers

If Malinowski is the key authority it is better to cite him directly rather than through a third party. The problem is that the intermediary may have misrepresented the *echt* (authentic) author. However, this is not a truly wicked crime and in the case of obscure or difficult authors it can be acceptable to quote someone who provides an accessible account of the maestro's work.

Showing off

This is a development of Chinese whispers. The works of Habermas and Bhaskar are large and very difficult and it is likely that most MBA students will not have had the time or inclination to study them. The suspicion is that the writer is merely showing off by claiming to have read works they have not. If the writer has read them, they could indicate this by giving page references to the places where Habermas and Bhaskar make the points the writer claims they do.

The founding fathers

Some authors, such as Weber, are so universally admired that dissertation writers believe that it is necessary to cite them. It isn't.

> ### Exercise 6.5 *continued*
>
> **Padding**
> The writer is so insecure in their argument they have to call on large battalions to support them. This becomes very tedious and it raises doubts about whether the writer has actually read all the works being cited. It would be better to provide arguments rather than lists in support of the proposition.
>
> **Neophilism**
> Citations can never be more than three years old, and any old work should never be cited. This of course is nonsense.
>
> **Canonicity**
> This assumes that something is a universally agreed position or starting point when it may not be.

Theory is underdetermined by data: this point might best be illustrated by an example. Galileo's theory about the movement of the planets made predictions about planetary positions that could not be observed using the telescopes of the time. It was only when such telescopes were developed (prompted by the need to test the theory) that the essential correctness of Galileo's predictions was confirmed. In other words, the theory preceded the data. For your work, the message is that just presenting data by themselves is inadequate.

The 'facts' do not 'speak for themselves': not only does the approach we use determine which 'facts' we will use (and indeed, which we may have created by our observations) but any 'fact' needs interpretation. Remember that during the process of research you will become very close to your material. What seems obvious to you may be very unclear to your reader. You can not stop the readers from making their own interpretations, but you can at least be clear about your own. This means explaining why you are using particular bits of evidence, rather than assuming that the readers will work this out for themselves. What it also means is that you will have to think carefully about the following:

- classification strategies that make sense of your evidence – which should be derived from your conceptual framework;
- ways of presenting the data (tables, charts, diagrams) that fit the data being presented and make the point in a clear fashion.

Do not 'pile it high': the end result will often not contain all the material that you have collected. This can be very frustrating, but you have to be selective. It is important that you do not make the reader do the work of selection. Putting large chunks of interview transcripts into your text, for example, may help the word count but not the reader's patience. *You* have to do the preliminary interpretation and selection, not the reader. Do not be tempted to take the course of putting all this material in an appendix, 'just in case'. Your main text should contain the key points, the appendix essential supporting material. Thus, say you had carried out a survey in which only three questions out of 20 had produced interesting results. You might discuss these three questions in depth and summarise the rest of the results in an appendix. You would not put all the returned questionnaires in the appendix. What is more common is to put interview transcripts in an appendix, but this is not necessary. If we want to see them, we will ask for them.

Weight of evidence: an occasionally successful rhetorical strategy is the piling on of example after example until the reader caves in under the weight. Some historians employ this strategy very successfully, but it has great dangers. It needs to be used sparingly and in the context of a clearly developed theoretical framework. Without this it is in danger of becoming a tedious list. Remember that what is fascinating to you may hold little charm for a wider audience. The meander down a byway that fascinates you but nobody else is one of the most frustrating perils that can snare the researcher.

Persuasive style

In universities in the Middle Ages, learning how to make persuasive arguments, taught under the heading of rhetoric, was a major part of students' curriculum. Rhetoric is re-emerging as a serious topic. Whether you are aware of it or not you will use some of the skills of rhetoric when you are writing your dissertation.

The classical teachers of rhetoric identified five stages in the preparation of an argument:

1. Invention – choosing the materials and arguments to be used.
2. Arrangement – putting the arguments and materials into a proper order.
3. Style – choosing an appropriate style for the audience.
4. Memory – learning the arguments and material is necessary for a spoken presentation but not for a piece of written work.
5. Delivery – making the presentation or writing the dissertation in a persuasive manner. There are many courses available to help you learn these skills.

Exercise 6.6

Establishing an audit trail

- What are the main findings or conclusions of your dissertation?
- What support do you have for each finding/conclusion?
  - authorities
  - evidence.
- How reliable and valid is the evidence?

The previous sections have dealt with the invention and arrangement stages. In this section, style and delivery will be considered. The ancient teachers of rhetoric identified many devices or figures for encouraging an audience to accept the arguments being presented. Technical names were given to many of the persuasive devices. Some are familiar today, such as metaphor and rhetorical question, but others such as epanorthosis have sunk, probably rightfully, into obscurity. It is not necessary for you to know the technical terms but you should be aware that there is an art to constructing convincing arguments. Some of a puritanical temper argue that rhetorical devices should be ignored because they are no more than tricks designed to lure the innocent into accepting ideas and arguments that cannot stand on their own. They tend to contrast rhetoric with reality. It is probably more realistic to accept that rhetorical skill is an inevitable part of all speech and communication, as may be illustrated in Exercise 6.7.

The text in Exercise 6.7 uses rhetorical devices and skill without the back-up of sound argument and evidence. You should aim to use both. The moral of Exercise 6.7 is not that rhetoric is to be despised but that it should be used in support of a good thesis.

Exercise 6.7

Rhetorical devices

The following was a call for papers for a business education conference. Read the passage and then consider these questions:

1. What is the main thrust of the argument?
2. By what steps does the argument proceed and what rhetorical tricks are used in each?
3. Can you find examples of the following rhetorical figures?
   - Metaphor – comparison by referring to one thing as another: 'Life's a beach'.
   - Oxymoron – placing two ordinarily opposing terms next to each other: 'jumbo shrimp'.
   - Rhetorical question (erotema) – a question asked for any reason other than obtaining the answer. 'Why me, God?'
   - Antithesis – juxtaposing contrasting words or ideas: 'It can't be wrong if it feels so right.'
   - Epitrope – turning a thing over to the audience in such a way as to suggest a proof without actually giving one: 'Go ahead, make my day.'
   - Sarcasm – a taunting remark.

Burton's (2000) web site provides an intriguing guide to the exotic world of rhetorical figures of speech.

The call for papers
In the world of today, change is said to be the only constant. Knowledge travels fast, through a variety of distribution channels, many of which were unknown only a few years ago. Therefore knowledge can be a highly perishable commodity. An important objective of the dissemination of knowledge will always be to ensure that it arrives fresh after the shortest possible route. Academic research within the areas of business administration and economics has often been criticised by the business community, which claims that much of it is mainly directed at the establishment of researchers themselves, who reply to and discuss it within the establishment instead of distributing it to the

Exercise 6.7 *continued*

business community. Students may often wonder whether they are studying yesterday's knowledge, instead of being continuously updated on current and relevant research. The proliferation of learning opportunities (for example, technology information) today makes learning for tomorrow even more complicated. In our global society success or failure in business frequently depends on which party has the most current knowledge of the issues and facts involved.

As universities and corporations attempt to prepare management to be alert to future changes improved, and even brand new, teaching methodologies are required. The main focus of the sixth ERGOT conference will be on the distribution and selection of new knowledge. How can business educators deliver new knowledge to students and the business community more rapidly than before? How should we define the core business curriculum when new knowledge becomes old knowledge?

Suggested answers – Alistair Mutch

1. The main argument
The argument is that changes in the world mean changes in both the nature of knowledge and the way in which this should be taught. All three components of this argument:

- the nature of changes in the world,
- that forms of knowledge are changing,
- that changes in teaching are required,

are extremely contentious and there is no necessary connection between them. However, the thrust of this argument is that the links are self-evident. This is achieved through a number of 'dodgy arguments'.

2. The steps
A note of caution: this was a call for papers and not a published paper or an assessed report. Some of the strictures below might seem a little harsh. However, the central issues about the status of the arguments, you might think, apply to any piece of argument.

1. *In the world of today, change is said to be the only constant.*
   We might point out three things about this sentence:

   (a) Is it true? Hasn't the world always been changing? (You might want to look at Henry Mintzberg's (1994) scathing comments about this in *The Rise and Fall of Strategic Planning*, where he notes that, for example, managers in the Great Depression had to cope with a far more turbulent world.)
   (b) Who says? The word 'said' is being used to give a spurious authority to this statement. In an essay you would expect an idea of who has done the saying, so that the reader could judge the respect to be accorded to this assertion. Here we cannot tell, but in passing over it quickly we may get some of the aura of a reference.
   (c) It is a cliché. We might want to follow George Orwell's (1962: 156) advice (although it is not easy!) to 'never use a metaphor, simile or other figure of speech which you are used to seeing in print'.

2. *Knowledge travels fast, through a variety of distribution channels, many of which were unknown only a few years ago.*
   The effect here is cumulative, with the *change* of the previous sentence emphasised by *fast* and *only a few years ago*. The impact of an argument may rest in this rather vague, cumulative impression.

3. *Therefore knowledge can be a highly perishable commodity.*
   There is no support for the *therefore*, other than as a rhetorical device to convince you that there must be a connection. Even if the two sentences were accepted, they say nothing about the *perishable* nature of knowledge. It could change and travel fast, but still not perish.

Exercise 6.7 *continued*

4. *An important objective of the dissemination of knowledge will always be to ensure that it arrives fresh after the shortest possible route.*
   Our acceptance of this assertion depends on the *therefore* of the previous sentence and our subsequent acceptance of the perishable nature of knowledge.

5. *Academic research within the areas of business administration and economics has often been criticised by the business community, which claims that much of it is mainly directed at the establishment of researchers themselves, who reply to and discuss it within the establishment instead of distributing it to the business community.*
   This may or may not be true, but here it is being used to add authority to the argument. We may not be convinced by the previous argument, runs the sub-text, but here is an influential group, so we had better be convinced.

6. *Students may often wonder whether they are studying yesterday's knowledge, instead of being continuously updated on current and relevant research.*
   The crucial contrast here is between *yesterday's* (bad) and *current and relevant* (good), which implies the couplet of 'old' and 'irrelevant'. The use of relevant is designed to touch an emotional nerve – we all want to be relevant, don't we?

7. *The proliferation of learning opportunities (for example, technology information) today makes learning for tomorrow even more complicated.*
   Bringing in the powerful symbolism of technology reinforces the relevance argument, as does the emphasis on *today* and *tomorrow*.

8. *In our global society success or failure in business frequently depends on which party has the most current knowledge of the issues and facts involved.*
   The final sentence of the paragraph uses a few more loaded words to emphasise the point – *global*, *business* and *current*.

9. *As universities and corporations attempt to prepare management to be alert to future changes improved, and even brand new, teaching methodologies are required.*
   We reach a new paragraph bludgeoned into submission! Who could object to this contemporary, up-to-date account? This might prevent us seeing that some very broad assumptions are being made about the equivalence of universities and corporations. We might think that *methodologies* rather than *methods* or even *ways of teaching* lend some scientific authority to this brave new world.

10. *The main focus of the sixth ERGOT conference will be on the distribution and selection of new knowledge. How can business educators deliver new knowledge to students and the business community more rapidly than before? How should we define the core business curriculum when new knowledge becomes old knowledge?*
    You might think that there are deeper questions here concerned with what the real purpose of business education is. However, we see the familiar buzzwords of *new* and *rapidly*, confirming the whole emphasis of the piece on the speed of change. The use of words is geared to giving an overall impression of speed and change – try counting the occurrence of words that support this.

Finally: I have been making an argument here. I have used some rhetorical devices of my own, especially bringing in authority figures, such as Orwell. I think this passage is badly thought-through and uses weak arguments (not necessarily consciously) to make its points. We are led through a chain of sentences that seem to have a logical coherence but that do not. I think the choice of words is made to reinforce a particular point. I think this is sloppily done – but feel free to construct a counter-argument!

3. Rhetorical figures – Colin Fisher

There seem to be many rhetorical figure employed in this piece, some of which I cannot put a name to. But here are some that I could identify:

Exercise 6.7 *continued*

Metaphors
Knowledge as a perishable commodity that has freshness. Knowledge seen as fruit and veg.
Teaching methodologies as a brand in 'brand new' and therefore a product.

Oxymoron
'change is the only constant'.

Antithesis
'when old knowledge becomes new knowledge'.

Rhetorical question
'How can business educators deliver new knowledge to students and the business community more rapidly than before?' Less an enquiry than a call to action.

Sarcasm
'yesterday's knowledge', especially with its echoes of the political campaign slogan 'yesterday's men', just about counts as a bitter taunt.

Epitrope
The last two sentences are implicitly handing the task over to the delegates at the conference.

It is most important when writing your dissertation to have a clear image of the readers and to write it in a style that they will find attractive and persuasive. The most important readers of your dissertation are the academics who will mark it. It should be written for them. You may, however, if you also want to use the dissertation to convince managers in your organisation to take action based on your findings, have to write another version that is designed for their consumption. This will need to be much shorter than the dissertation and be written in a report format. Exercise 6.8 looks at different styles of academic writing and should help you decide which style to adopt in your dissertation.

Exercise 6.8

Focusing on your readers

There follows three extracts from fictitious articles on a business and management topic. They are each in very different styles. The emphasis of this task is on the style of the writing and not on the content. In the following passages, therefore, the arguments are not intended seriously and may indeed be nonsense. The citations are invented. In terms of their content treat the extracts as caricatures. Your task is to:

- identify the similarities and differences in how they are written;
- decide what sort of reader each is best suited to;
- decide which is the closest to the style you think you should adopt when writing your dissertation.

Exercise 6.8 *continued*

Extract 1 From *The Dialectics of Neo-institutional Processes and the Forms of Rationality*

The rationalised myth, according to neo-institutional theory (Weiskopf and Chin 1976, Bullock and Lamb 1985, Sweetens et al. 1989 and Huckleberry and Finn 2002) provides the leitmotivs against which organisations seek isomorphism, although recent writers (Hazelcroft and Tonningen 1999) have argued about whether institutional or rational forces have primacy in the shaping of organisations and their cultures. When western change agents seek, through metropolitan led and funded change programmes, to change the rationalised myths that were dominant in Soviet organisations, competing dimensions of rationality are exposed within the rationalised myths. To understand these agons it is necessary to return to Webber's perspectives on different forms of rationality, as interpreted by Kautilya (1994), that provide a conceptual framework to analyse the responses of organisations in post-soviet countries to the globalising pressures of the western rationlised myth of free markets and rational choice. Webber (1929 and 1932) distinguished deontological rationality, which is concerned with actions based on certain values, from utilitarian rationality, which is based on a means-ends calculation (Bloch and Simon 1996). It will be argued that within post-soviet organisations the conflict between the substantive value rationality of the Soviet order and the formal rationality of the globalising agenda creates, as Webber predicted, a gap into which instrumental, rationality moves. Organisational actors adopt the globalising myth because it moves them towards the goal of economic success but their commitment is mechanical and superficial as their substantive rationality leads them to prioritise the cultural sphere over the economic…

Extract 2 From *To Boldly Go: Counter-institutional strategies in transforming post-Soviet Economies*

Case studies of turn-arounds in successful western companies can provide lessons for those involved with major change programmes in post-soviet countries that are designed to encourage a culture of entrpreneurialism and a commitment to market led growth. Close study of how three internationally admired companies have moved from basket cases to world class financial performers have identified five **Counter-institutional** strategies that act as drivers of cultural change in post-Soviet organisations.

Anatomy of a counter-institutional strategy

1. supply and mould revolutionaries
2. develop new internal brands that challenge the old ones
3. create new safe zones
4. adapt existing vales to new ends
5. create western minders for host country change leaders.

Savvy incumbents of change agent roles in post-soviet organisations reduce the collateral cost of culture change by leveraging the existing contra-cultural undercurrents that exist within any culture. Worldron Inc transformed itself to respond to global competitive pressures when its charismatic CEO finessed the inventiveness of its young Turks in the derivatives trading division and brought about a new commitment to improving financial returns.

Strong leadership from the top is an important driver in all the case studies.

Extract 3 From *Cross-cultural dynamics in western change projects in countries of the former Soviet Union*

Institutionalism and modernisation projects

Smith and Smith (2001: 29) used the concept of institutionalism to theorise about the change processes in modernisation projects in countries of the former Soviet Union. The values, practices and structures of a society form its institutions. Institutionalism is the theory that organisations conform to these institutions. This process is not automatic. It is caused by the choices and actions of people within the organisations. Choice makes it possible for organisations to conform to institutions other than those of the society organisations are located within.

Exercise 6.8 *continued*

Modernisation projects are designed to substitute global (or western?) institutions for local Soviet institutions as the templates against which organisations should model themselves.

Others argue that managerial rationality is more important than institutional pressures in influencing the forms of organisations (Hazelcroft and Tonningen 1999: 235–256). An organisation is designed rationally if its form is as efficient and effective as possible. Local institutions would not figure in managerial rationality. This debate will be considered later in the paper. At this stage the concern is how modernisation projects can be understood in terms of institutionalism.

In case studies Smiles (1996), Dubrovsky (2001) and Aliev (2002) identified five difficulties experienced during modernisation projects. These will be discussed in turn.

1. Western experts employed on modernisation projects are too ignorant of the local culture and language to engage the sympathies of the local managers they are working with. Modernisation projects cannot, argued Aliev (2002: 203–204), involve the re-institutionalisation of indigenous organisations alone. The western experts of the project teams also need to respond to the values and practices of local institutions. A synthesis that creates a mutual process of learning is needed. Local managers respond more positively to western values if the western experts are not dismissive of the local culture.

Suggested answer
Similarities and differences
Use of references
Extract 1 has a very heavy use of references including several multiple references. Extract 2 has none at all. Extract 3 has a smaller number of references with fewer multiple citations. The third extract often gives page numbers so that specific arguments in a book can be easily located.

Use of academic jargon
The first extract uses much academic jargon but gives few definitions or accounts of the concepts. The author assumes the reader to be familiar with the ideas and with the debate in the literature. The second extract is clear of academic jargon. The third extract does use technical terms but mostly gives a brief explanation of them at or near their first use.

Use of management jargon
The second abstract uses managerial jargon extensively. The jargon is taken to be straightforward; but words such as 'drivers', 'leveraging' and 'world-class can become mere habit. When this happens they may imply assumptions that ought to be questioned. The extract also uses colloquial terms (savvy) in an attempt to empathise with the presumed reader. Such approaches can badly misfire. The other two extracts are free of managerial jargon.

Theory, research and anecdote
The first extract is entirely theoretical, although typically in this type of paper there will be some empirical material in the middle before a return to theory at the end of the paper. Both of the other papers have theoretical concerns but in the second extract theory is seen as a guide to action and in the third extract there seems to be a more balanced integration of the case study material and the theoretical issues. Although the second extract refers to its empirical material as case studies it looks more like anecdotes. The case studies mentioned in the third extract look more like rigourous and systematic accounts.

Critical tone
The first extract is critical in the sense described in Chapter 2 as radical critique. It is challenging the purpose and moral status of the modernisation projects. The second extract is more enthusiastic than critical. There are no

Exercise 6.8 *continued*

doubts or nuanced discussions about the ideas being put forward. People are being invited to 'buy into' them and put them into practice. The third extract does identify doubts and arguments about some of the key concepts that are used.

Sub-headings and visual tricks

The first extract favours large solid blocks of text. The second extracts assumes that readers will be terrified of this and breaks up the texts with figures, illustrations, bullet points and extracts of key points printed as aphorisms In boxes. The third extract also uses sub-headings and numbered lists but does not avoid solid paragraphs. The items in the lists consist not of one or few words but of sentences.

Ease of reading

The Flesch reading ease scale rates a text on a 100-point scale. The higher the score, the easier the text is to read. The recommended target for standard texts (which may exclude academic texts) is between 60 and 70.

Extract 1
Flesch Reading Ease Scale   0
Average number of sentences per paragraph   7
Average number of words per sentence   35.1

Extract 2
Flesch Reading Ease Scale   22.3
Average number of sentences per paragraph   1.5
Average number of words per sentence   25.8

Extract 3
Flesch Reading Ease Scale   20.8
Average number of sentences per paragraph   4.7
Average number of words per sentence   15.3

As a general rule, keep your sentences short and your paragraphs long. The third extract is the easiest to read but even in this case the sentences are still rather long. The number of sentences per paragraph is acceptable although at the lower limits of acceptability.

The readers

The first extract is written for a small number of highly specialised academics who understand their subject's jargon and are familiar, and indeed have probably been involved with, the debate. The second extract is for managers who would be scared or suspicious of anything they thought academic. The thIrd extract is probably accessible to the academic and the practitioner, although it would be too academic for managers with academiphobia. It is aimed, to use a very old-fashioned phrase, at the interested and educated lay reader.

Which style would be best for your dissertation?

I would recommend the style of the third extract. Academics will mark your dissertation and although they will have a familiarity with your broad field of study they may not be specialists in the your research topic. It is best to treat them as interested lay readers. Also, if you adopt the technique of explaining and discussing your terms, it helps the markers assess whether you understand them. Many markers would find the style of the second abstract to be unscholarly and full of assumptions that ought to be challenged. The style of the first abstract is almost as hard for a full-time academic to read as it is for you. I doubt you would be tempted to write like this, but in any case don't.

● ● ● ● Style guide

Dissertation, report and paper specifications

There are a number of practical issues concerned with writing up a paper or a dissertation. This section details the house style that Master's students are expected to follow in the business school I work in. You will need to conform to the requirements of the institution you are studying at.

Paper or report specification

A paper or report can be informally bound, that is to say spiral bound or with a glued and taped spine and soft covers. Binding in a report cover bought from a stationer would be fine.

The front cover should include:

Title	OBTAINING VALUE FOR MONEY IN SKEGMOUTH DEVELOPMENT CORPORATION
Full name	POLLY TITIAN Conference paper submitted in part fulfilment of the requirements of The Nottingham Trent University for the degree of [appropriate degree title]
Institution	THE NOTTINGHAM TRENT UNIVERSITY
Date	SEPTEMBER 2004

There should not normally be a need for tables of contents and suchlike for a document of this length, but do include,

- an abstract or executive summary (about 150 words);
- references;
- appendices if appropriate and necessary.

Dissertation specification

The dissertation shall be bound in hard black covers with gold lettering.
The front cover should include:

Title	ECONOMIC MISMANAGEMENT
Full name	POLLY TITIAN
Institution	THE NOTTINGHAM TRENT UNIVERSITY
Date	SEPTEMBER 2004

The spine of the document should include:

Initials and surname	P. TITIAN
Course	M.Sc.
Year	2004

Contents of the bound dissertation

The following should be bound in with the dissertation:

- title page;
- acknowledgements (only if you insist, but try to avoid mawkishness or bad jokes);
- an abstract (also known as an executive summary) of approximately 300 words;
- table of contents;
- list of tables and figures (these are discretionary);
- main text;
- references;
- appendices (these are discretionary).

Submission

Normally two bound copies of the dissertation are required for assessment purposes, one of which will be retained by the university. Check with your institution's requirements.

Style hints

Typing

The dissertation should be printed on white A4 paper with 1.5 spacing using a font size no larger than 12. We have no preference for font, but choose something classy. There is, believe it or not, a British standard, BS4821 (1990), for academic dissertations. However this has now been withdrawn.

Layout

The dissertation should be printed with a left margin of not less than 40 mm, the other margins should not be less than 15 mm. Normally the default settings on your word processor will be fine. The pages should be numbered consecutively.

Title page

The title page of the documents shall give the following information:

- the title of the document;
- the author's name;
- dissertation submitted in part fulfilment of the requirements of The Nottingham Trent University for the degree of [appropriate degree title];
- month and year of submission.

Headings

The use of headings and sub-headings, in addition to chapter headings, is encouraged. Decide your own sequence of typographical features for defining the various levels of headings. For example:

MAIN SECTION

Blah blah blah blah. Blah blah blah. Blah blah blah blah, blah blah blah; blah blah blah. Blah blahblah blah, blah blah blah, blah blah.

Sub section

Blah blah blah blah. Blah blah blah. Blah blah blah blah, blah blah blah; blah blah blah. Blah blahblah blah, blah blah blah, blah blah.

Sub-sub section

Blah blah blah blah. Blah blah blah. Blah blah blah blah, blah blah blah; blah blah blah. Blah blahblah blah, blah blah blah, blah blah.

Sub-sub-sub section

Blah blah blah blah. Blah blah blah. Blah blah blah blah, blah blah blah; blah blah blah. Blah blahblah blah, blah blah blah, blah blah.

Paragraphs

The dissertation or paper should be written in paragraphs. Each paragraph should normally be longer than one sentence and will often take up about a third of a page. If the average number of sentences per paragraph in your writing approaches one, you should do something to remedy the situation. If you are using Microsoft Word you can set the spelling and grammar check to show readability statistics, including the average number of sentences per paragraph. To set this option click on **Tools…Options…Spelling and Grammar** tab and finally check the **Show readability statistics** option. These will appear when you have finished the spell and grammar check.

Paragraphs often have a linking word such as 'next' or 'furthermore' near their start. These linkers, to use Perry's (2000) term, lead the reader from an established idea to a new theme or idea. Each paragraph should begin with a theme sentence that explains the new theme or idea. The rest of the paragraph is dedicated to developing and describing the theme or idea. Each paragraph should deal with only one main idea.

Numbering

Do number the sections if it makes you content. However, I have a personal antipathy to the decimal numbering systems that give each paragraph a number. A reference to 5.6.4.8.ii looks to me as if it belongs to a statute rather than to a dissertation. My suggestion, if you must use numbering, is to use no more than one or two decimal places. If you insist on using a decimal numbering system to the nth degree, the end result will be that every sentence has a number.

Bullet points

Bullet points are acceptable but are no substitute for chunky paragraphs full of argument. So use bullet points for summaries and genuine lists and not as a way of avoiding debate. The following would not be acceptable:

- People are an organisation's most important asset.
- Empowering people means energising an organisation.
- Empowered organisations are more effective.
- Empowered people have freely chosen to do what the organisation requires them to do.

Each of these statements is contentious and ought to be argued through.

Quotes

If they are brief include them in the main text. If they are more than one line long, indent them as follows:

> Blah blah blah blah. Blah blah blah. Blah blah blah blah, blah blah blah; blah blah blah. Blah blahblah blah, blah blah blah, blah blah.

> Blah blah blah blah. Blah blah blah. Blah blah blah blah, blah blah blah; blah blah blah. Blah blahblah blah, blah blah blah, blah blah.

Indented quotations should be in single spacing.

Footnotes

Do not use these for providing citations. Use them very sparingly for comments or information that, whilst not part of the main flow of argument[1], have sufficient merit or amusement value to raise a wry smile on the reader's face.

Tenses

Perry (2000) recommends that the introductory chapters and the conceptual framework chapter should be written in the present tense. The literature review and the student's own research should be written in the past tense. Conclusions should be in the present tense.

---

[1] It seems unlikely but someone has written a history of the footnote (Grafton 1998). He argues that the unwashed read the text but the learned read the footnote.

The personal pronoun

I have no objection to people writing in the first person singular. The more your research is in the ethnographic or action research style, the more appropriate it would be. However, the author recognises that in more traditional research cultures its use would be regarded as unprofessional. C. M. Fisher argues that an excessive use of 'I' is a symptom of egomania.

Appendices

Appendices are very useful. They are not counted against the dissertation word limits. They are places to put subsidiary information (such as the summary of results from a questionnaire), which it is good scholarship to make available to the reader but which is not necessary to the flow of the argument. Appendices that are thicker than the text are a sign of heap making and are best avoided. As Nennius wrote in his ninth century *History of the Britons*, 'Coacevarvi omni quod inveni'.

Foreign languages

The documents should be in English. If you use quotes in other languages, please provide a translation. Just in case your Latin is rusty the quotation in the previous paragraph says 'I made a heap of all that I found'. This may have worked in the Dark Ages but it is no longer a good academic strategy.

Tables, diagrams and boxes

Tables and diagrams should be included in an appropriate place in the text. They should be numbered consecutively with separate sequences for tables, figures and boxes. They should only be placed in the appendices if they are so bulky that they would disrupt the reader's flow of understanding. The use of boxes to contain illustrative material within the text is fine.

Clichés

Clichés, as in Exhibit 6.1, which can be seen on many office pin boards, are best avoided. Especially when, as in the case of this ancient Roman he never actually said it; see: http://www.research. att.com/~reeds/petronius.html.

Exhibit 6.1

As Petronius Arbiter did not say:

We trained hard ... but it seemed that every time we were beginning to form up into teams we would be reorganised. I was to learn later in life that we tend to meet any new situation by reorganising; and a wonderful method it can be for creating the illusion of progress while producing confusion, inefficiency and demoralisation.

Vocabulary

Only use words you understand. This probably excludes the use of bizno-bollocks speak, unless used ironically or within quotation marks. Also be careful with academic jargon. Terms such as 'deconstruction', are frequently used in ways that reveal the writer's ignorance of their meaning. Neologisms, however, would be allowed according to this rule. If you have invented the word it can be assumed you know what it means; but let the reader in on the secret. One good piece of advice, which I frequently ignore, is to allow yourself only one fancy piece of vocabulary per document, and that only in the last paragraph.

Grammar

There are many 'how to write good English' manuals available in libraries and bookshops and on the World Wide Web. I recommend you use them. Unquestioning reliance on Word's grammatical checker is not a good idea. Here are some of the more common mistakes[2] to watch out for:

- Verbs has to agree with their subjects.
- Prepositions are not words to end sentences with.
- And don't start a sentence with a preposition (well, not a paragraph anyway).
- It is wrong to ever split an infinitive.
- Avoid clichés like the plague.
- Also, always avoid annoying alliteration.
- Be more or less specific.
- Parenthetical remarks (however relevant) are (usually) unnecessary.
- No sentence fragments.
- Contractions aren't necessary and shouldn't be used.
- Don't use no double negatives.
- Eschew ampersands, abbreviations, etc.
- Eliminate commas, that are not necessary.
- Never use a big word when a diminutive one would suffice.
- Kill all exclamation marks!
- Use words correctly irregardless of how others use them.
- Use the apostrophe in it's proper place and omit when its not needed.
- Puns are for children, not groan readers.
- Proofread carefully to see if you any words out.

---

[2] There are many versions of this list on the World Wide Web, which helps obscure its origins. William Safire (2002) wrote and/or collected some of them in *Fumblerules*, first published in 1990. An earlier claim to have invented the form and some of the rules is that of George Trigg (1979). A useful starting place for exploring these rules through the web is: http://www.yaelf.com/aueFAG/miffmblrlsdntsndbl.shtml. Otherwise just type in a distinctive phrase from one of the rules into a search engine to begin to experience the number of versions of the rules available on the Web.

Martin Cutts (1999: Ch. 12) argues that several of these crimes should no longer be regarded as serious.

Citation and referencing

On a point of the purest pedantry I want to distinguish between a list of references and a bibliography. You must put in your documents, under the title of references, a list of all the works cited in the document. This is not the same thing as a bibliography, which is simply a list of books that you may or may not have cited. Bibliographies therefore are generally unnecessary.

There are three main systems of citation and referencing: the footnote system, the Harvard system and the Vancouver system.

The business school or other institution that you are studying at will have a policy on which system of citation and referencing to use. It is important not to mix up the systems. The use of ibid. (short for *ibidem*, the Latin for 'in the same source') and op. cit. (short for *opera citato*, the Latin for 'in the work already mentioned') belong to the footnote system and should not be used in conjunction with the Harvard system, which is the most common one in use in business and management studies and the one I will go on to describe. Business schools may require you to follow their own specifications. I have used Fisher and Hanstock (2002) as a guide. There are software products available that make the chore of preparing the references a lot easier. Information is available on the products at: http://aztec.lib.utk.edu/~mell/endnote/.

The Harvard system cites work in a text by mentioning the author(s) and the year of publication. Only these details are needed. An alphabetical list of the works referred to is then given at the close of the text, which includes full details of the work and its publication. The great advantage is that, unlike with the footnote system, the full bibliographic details do not have to be typed out every time a work is cited.

References in the text

Here are some tips about illustrations of citing works in a text.

- If the author's name is included in the sentence, then all you have to do is provide the year of publication in parentheses (brackets), e.g. 'many have argued that Smith (2003) has misunderstood the issues'. Many students feel they must include the author's initials (Smith, C. M. 1975), but this is unnecessary and should not be done.
- If the author is not mentioned in the text, then include it with the year of publication in the parentheses, e.g. 'It has been argued that correct citation is a mark of scholarship (Smith 1999).'
- If there are two authors give both names (Smith and Jones 2003); if there are more than two give the first name followed by *et al.* (Smith *et al.* 2001). You must give all the authors' names in the list of references.

- If you are referencing two or more works by the same author that were published in the same year, use letters of the alphabet to distinguish them, e.g. (Smith 2002a, Smith 2002b).
- If the author is an organisation or an institution give as much information as necessary to identify it, e.g. (Chartered Institute of Management Accountancy 2002). If the organisation is better known by the abbreviation of its full name, then this can either be added in parentheses or used instead of the full title.
- The reference in the text should include page references if you are giving a source of a quotation, a particular piece of information or an argument. This is so that the reader can easily check back to the original material. There is some latitude about the format of this, e.g. (Smith: 29), (Smith 2003 p. 29). Where you refer to several pages the whole numbers should be spelt out (Smith 2003: 245–289).

The list of references

The function of the list of references is to allow the reader to track down and read the material you use in the dissertation. The reference should therefore include all the information needed to achieve this purpose. Note that to make the list of references easy to read, the second and subsequent lines of the reference should be indented.

Normally this includes, for books:

Author(s) Surname(s), Initials or forenames, date of publication, Title, edition, Place of publication, Publisher, pagination when only a part of a work is cited.

And in the case of journal articles:

Author(s) Surname(s), Initials or forenames, date of publication, Article title, Journal title, Volume number, Part or issue number (if available), start and finish page numbers of the article.

With this information, the reader should be able to go unswervingly to the source.

Here are some examples of layout and format for references. There are allowable variations. Titles of books and journals can be <u>underlined</u> or **emboldened** rather than *italicised*. There are other variations you will come across:

- Sometimes the date of publication is given in parentheses.
- Sometimes details of journals are spelt out – Vol. 34, No. 6, pp. 235–245, sometimes they are abbreviated – 34(6), 235–245.
- Sometimes the authors' initials are given; sometimes their forenames are given. Avoid mixing the two.

- Sometimes the titles of works are typed in 'title case' in which all the words (except minor ones) are capitalised. Alternatively the sentence case is used, in which only the words at the beginning of sentences are capitalised. The important thing is, having chosen a style, to be consistent.
- And several other variations that you can discover for yourself.

Books

Badaracco, J. L. Jr (1997) *Defining Moments: When Managers Must Choose Between Right and Right*, Boston, MA: Harvard Business School Press.

Baldwin, S., Godfrey, C. and Propper, C. (eds) (1990) *Quality of Life: Perspectives and Policies*, London: Routledge.

British Airways (2000) *British Airways Social and Environmental Report 2000*, London: British Airways.

Eastwood, A. and Maynard, A. (1990) 'Treating aids: is it ethical to be efficient?', in S. Baldwin, C. Godfrey and C. Propper (eds) *Quality of Life: Perspectives and Policies*, London: Routledge.

Journal articles

Carroll, A. B. (1990) 'Principles of business ethics: their role in decision making and an initial consensus', *Management Decision*, Vol. 28, No. 8, 20–24.

Guerrera, F. (2001) 'Huntingdon seeks nominee structure to protect shareholders', *Financial Times*, 12 May, 25.

Official publications

The proper way of doing this is as follows:

Great Britain. Department for Education and Employment (1997) Setting *Targets to Raise Standards: A Survey of Good Practice*. London: Department of Education and Employment.

But it is not unusual, and appears to be acceptable, for the initial 'Great Britain' to be omitted. If you are citing works from the European Union or countries other than your home country, then you should use European Union or the name of the body or government as the author of the work.

Conference papers

Kärreman, D. and Alvesson, M. (1999) 'Ethical closure in organisational settings the case of media organisations', 15th EGOS Colloquium, *Organisations in a Challenging World: Theories, Practices and Societies*, The University of Warwick, 4–6 July.

Fisher, C. M. (2000) 'The ethics of inactivity: human resource managers and quietism', *Proceedings of the Third Conference on Ethics and Human Resource Management*, Imperial College School of Management, London, 10th April.

World Wide Web and other electronic resources
There is less standardisation in citing electronic resources. The following examples show what information should be provided. It is often difficult to discover the author of a web page, in which case it should be referenced by title.

Transparency International (2001) *The 2001 Corruption Perceptions Index*, Berlin: Transparency International. Available online at: http://www.gwdg.de/~uwvw/2001Data.html [accessed 20 September 2001].

Journal articles downloaded from the Internet can be referenced as follows:

Fisher, C. M. (2001) 'Managers' perceptions of ethical codes: dialectics and dynamics', *Business Ethics: A European Review*, Vol. 10, No. 2: 145–156. Available from Business Source Premier [online] (n.d). Ipswich, MA: EBSCO.

Hammersley, M. and Gomm, R. (1997) 'Bias in social research', *Sociological Research Online* [online] Vol. 2, No. 1. Available at: http://www.socresonline/2/1/2.html [accessed 13 June 1997].

A problem can arise if you view the article in an html format rather than in pdf. The original pagination is lost and it can be difficult to cite page numbers for quotations. If you have a pdf file, then you have a facsimile of the original article, as if you had photocopied it from the journal. In this case I think it is acceptable to reference it as if from the original. This saves you the trouble of tracking down the bibliographic details of the database and including them in the citation as in the Fisher reference above.

You can reference all kinds of other electronic resources such as TV or radio programmmes:

Father Ted (1995) Episode 1, Good Luck Father Ted. Channel 4 TV, 21 April.

Binding

At the end of the programme the dissertation will have to be properly bound according to the institution's guidelines:

- The binding shall be of fixed type so that leaves cannot be removed or added; the front and rear boards should have sufficient rigidity to support the weight of the work when standing upright.
- In at least 24-point type the outside front board in black shall bear the title of the work, the name and initials of the candidate, the qualification, and the year of submission.
- The same information (excluding the title of the work) shall be shown on the title of the work, reading downwards. All lettering shall be in gold.

Summary

- Have a clear chapter structure for the dissertation.
- Make sure there is a clear line of logical argument, or a strong theme, that links all parts of the dissertation together.
- Have logical arguments as well as arguments from authority.
- Write the dissertation in clear, plain English.
- Use rhetorical skill to enhance your style.
- Keep to the house rules on presentation and citation.

Suggested reading

Fairbairn and Winch (1996) are good on constructing arguments and writing a dissertation. Chapter 13 of Saunders *et al.* (2002) is good on writing up. For the tricks of creating a narrative flow in your dissertation see Raimond (1993). Martin Cutts (1999) is a good, quick guide to grammar and writing style. *Troublesome Words* (Bryson 1997) helps with all the words that confuse people and is also good on punctuation and grammar. Perry's (2000) notes for presenting a thesis are useful even though they were written for PhD rather than for Master's students. If you are interested in the layout and design of a report see Orna and Stevens (1999).

Bryson, B. (1997) *Troublesome Words*, London: Penguin.

Fairbairn, G. J. and Winch C. (1996) *Reading, Writing and Reasoning: A Guide for Students*, Buckingham: Open University Press.

Orna, E. with Stevens, G. (1999) *Managing Information for Research*, Buckingham: Open University Press.

Raimond, P. (1993) *Management Projects: Design, Research and Presentation*, London: Chapman Hall.

Saunders, M., Lewis, P. and Thornhill, A. (2002), *Research Methods for Business Students*, 3rd edn, Harlow: FT Prentice Hall.

References

(NB if a work mentioned in the examples and illustrations in this chapter is not included in this list of references it is because it is fictitious.)

Burton, G. O. (2000) *Silva Rhetoricae* Available online at: http://humanities.byu.edu/rhetoric/silva.htm [accessed 24 November 2000].

British Standard Institution (1990) Recommendations for the Presentation of Theses and Dissertations (BS 4821) Bracknell: British Standards Publishing.

Cutts, M. (1999) *The Quick Reference Plain English Guide*, Oxford: Oxford University Press.

Fisher, D. and Hanstock, T. (2002) *Citing References: A Guide for Users*, 4th rev. edn, Nottingham: Library and Information Services, The Nottingham Trent University.

Eisaman Maus, K. (2001) 'Why it's fun to be smart', *Times Literary Supplement* 25 May, No. 5121: 24.

Grafton, A. (1998) *The Footnote*, London: Faber & Faber.

Mintzberg, H. (1994) *The Rise and Fall of Strategic Planning*, Hemel Hempstead: Prentice Hall International.

Morgan, G. (1997) *Images of Organisations*, London: Sage.

Mounce, H. O. (1997) *The Two Pragmatisms: From Peirce to Rorty*, London: Routledge.

Orwell, G. (1962) *Inside the Whale and Other Essays*, Harmondsworth : Penguin.

Pascale, R. (1990) *Managing on the Edge: How Successful Companies Use Conflict to Stay Ahead*, London: Penguin.

Perry, C. (2000) *A Structured Approach to Presenting a Thesis: Notes for Students and their Supervisors.* Available online at: http://www.literaticlub.co.uk/Writing/theses.html [accessed 12 July 2001].

Safire, W. (2002) *Fumblerules: A Lighthearted Guide to Grammar and Good Usage*, New York: Barnes & Noble.

Trigg, G.L. (1979) 'Grammar', *Physics Review Letters*, Vol. 42, No. 12, 747–748.

Index